1st 'Lemon' Edi

RAPTURE RUPTURE!
THE BIG LIE BEHIND
'LEFT BEHIND' EXPOSED

Nathanael Lewis

Nathanael Lewis

McKnight
& Bishop
Ltd

ISBN 978-1-905691-28-9

A CIP catalogue record for this book is available from the British Library

First published in 2014 by McKnight & Bishop Inspire, an imprint of:

McKnight & Bishop Ltd.
28 Grifffiths Court, Bowburn, Co. Durham, DH6 5FD
http://www.mcknightbishop.com
info@mcknightbishop .com

This books has been typeset in Garamond and TRAJAN PRO
Printed and bound in Great Britain by Lightning Source Inc, Milton Keynes
The paper used in this book has been made from wood independently certified as having come from sustainable forests.

CONTENTS

ABOUT THE AUTHOR

By day Nathanael Lewis is chained to desk and PC as a mild-mannered office-worker, by night..... he's in about the same condition at home, doing lots of reading and research. He has an Honours Master of Theology Degree from St Andrews University, the oldest university in Scotland, with a world-class theology faculty. He also writes poetry, composes music - when he has the time - and plays improvisational piano. He is co-author of 'The Targeting of Minority Others in Pakistan' - a seminal work on the human rights situation of minorities in Pakistan, having written the section on Christians, which makes up about a third of the book. His work on the Pakistani Christian situation has been cited by official government reports from both the UK and Canada. For more on this, see:

http://www.britishpakistanichristians.co.uk/blog/the-targeting-of-minority-others-in-pakistan-pakistan

ABOUT THE PUBLISHER

McKnight & Bishop are always on the lookout for great new authors and ideas for exciting new books. If you write or if you have an idea for a book, email us: **info@mcknighbishop.com**

Some things we love are: undiscovered authors, open-source software, crowd-funding, Amazon/Kindle, social networking, faith, laughter and new ideas.

Visit us at: **www.mcknightbishop.com**

INTRODUCTION

The material in this small(ish) book is part of research for a planned full length work refuting the pre-Tribulation Rapture theory that has gained such prominence in much of the Evangelical / Fundamentalist world. It presupposes some knowledge of the debate, and so I often give only the barest of explanations of terms, etc. I suppose I'd better briefly introduce myself and state my qualifications for taking on such a fervently and widely held belief. I am a theologian who studied theology at Scotland's oldest University, St Andrews, and am an evangelical, who was brought up going to churches that often held 'Pre-Tribulation' positions. Thus I know full well the force that such arguments can seem to have, but my theological training enables me to see fundamental flaws in the biblical interpretation and rhetoric that flows from many writers and preachers on this subject. I can't put everything into one small book, but since one of the most prominent spokesmen for the 'pre-Trib' position regularly touts as 'unrefuted' a small table of points 'proving' that the Rapture (the vanishing of the church when Jesus comes to take them to be with him) happens before a final 7 year 'Tribulation' period in human history and must be a separate event from the visible return of Jesus at the end of that same period, I have decided it would be useful to publish a pretty thorough refutation as a stand-alone project.

Tim LaHaye is a doyen of the current generation of 'Pre-Trib' advocates, co-author of the best-selling, multi-volume 'Left Behind' series of novels about the end times (now also a series of movies), and numerous other books, chapters and articles promoting the Pre-Trib interpretation of the Bible and the end times. While studying some of these works, I came across a table of 15 points that he repeatedly refers back to and of which he claims that no opponent of the pre-trib position has even tried to refute, that he knows of. He clearly thinks that they are irrefutable 'proof' of the fundamental pre-Trib position that the Rapture of the church to be with Jesus is a totally separate event from Jesus' visible return to rule and take up the kingdom. (There may be different versions of this table, and I have seen expanded versions with more points by other pre-tribulation teachers on the internet, so for the sake of clarity I should make it clear I am using the chart as found on p55 of 'The Popular Handbook on the Rapture: Experts speak out on End-Times prophecy', edited by Tim LaHaye, Thomas Ice and Ed Hindson, published by Harvest House in 2011).

One thing that should be said at the outset is that many of Lahaye's 'proofs' have such seeming force because they assume a Dispensationalist position and because he is largely talking to an audience that is either Dispensationalist or is thoroughly seeded with Dispensationalist ideas, rhetoric and approaches to end times events. Dispense with this (relatively recent) Dispensationalist interpretation (not something

I have space to do here) and a lot of his arguments lose their force. In addition, his 'proofs' offer a microcosm of some standard rhetorical and interpretational flaws that are rife in the Pre-Trib movement he fronts. For instance, there are several cases of what I call 'Gratuitous Assertion' where assertions are made without any, or completely inadequate, Scripture back-up. All of us do this when arguing a case to some extent, but when it becomes ubiquitous in this debate, it is usually evidence of someone relying on the 'dispensationalist reservoir' of beliefs and themes and misinterpretations to 'prove' their case. Frequently, these involve stating that the bible says something it never says, or assuming that because the bible doesn't say x, y, and z at a particular point, then even the possibility of x, y and z happening in that particular passage or event must be completely ruled out.

A brief summary of the popular pre-trib position is in order here (there are of course variations that different people hold to, but this is pretty much the standard position). To start off with, virtually all believers in a 'pre-trib' rapture are dispensationalists. This means that they believe that God acts in different ways, or has different focuses during different periods of history, and these change from one to another at a very specific given point in time, usually very suddenly. One day you are in one 'dispensation', and the next you are in another. The dispensationalist view has changed through history, and several variations exist, but pretty much all have a dispensation involving the Law of Moses and focusing on Israel, and a distinct and separate church age, sometimes known as a 'dispensation of grace'.

This is pretty much invariably tied in with a particular interpretation of a prophecy in the Old Testament book of Daniel, chapter 9. Here, God tells Daniel in a vision about the future of Israel and the Jerusalem temple dating from the time a decree was made to rebuild the Temple destroyed by the Babylonians, with a very specific chronology, made up of 'weeks' or 'sevens' (of years). There are 70 'weeks', and after 69 'weeks', the 'anointed one' – i.e. the Messiah – will be 'cut off' (killed). It then says that the Temple will be destroyed by the people of the 'ruler who is to come', interpreted as the antichrist. Then a number of events happen in the 70th week involving that 'ruler who is to come', who makes a covenant or treaty for seven years with 'many', usually taken to mean the nation of Israel. However, halfway through this 'week' or 'seven' this ruler puts an end to the sacrificial system in Jerusalem and desecrates the temple until he is destroyed. The anointed one who is killed is, of course, Jesus, whose death occurred at the right time to fulfil this prophecy. However, between the 69th and final 'seven' there appears to be a gap in which a number of events occur, including the destruction of the Temple and Jerusalem (this happened in AD70, with a further destruction in AD135). Wars will continue until the final 'seven' which has not occurred yet. This passage, combined with a dispensationalist belief system, is key to understanding the 'pre-trib' position. The gap between the last two 'weeks' or 'sevens' is interpreted as the 'church age'. Since Israel as a nation rejected their promised Messiah, the 'clock' to do with the promises of God to Israel was paused, but will start again in the final 'seven' at the end of age. (Very) broadly speaking, I accept this interpretation, but not the insertion of a 'church age'.

However, what dispensationalists believe is that the 'church age' is brought to an end just before the final 'seven' by the rapture, in which Jesus invisibly returns to take all Christians, dead or alive, to be with him in heaven. Those living just vanish as they are changed into their resurrection bodies and rise to meet Jesus who hovers in the atmosphere. They escape the 'Great Tribulation', the final seven years of history, in which God pours out his anger on a world that has rejected the gospel. The ending of the 'church age' and the disappearance of Christians triggers the restart of the prophetic 'clock' from Daniel 9, and God's focus is once again on Israel, as all the prophecies about Israel and the end of the age come to pass before Jesus returns visibly from heaven with the church and the armies of heaven to rescue Israel from the nations of the world who have attacked her at the battle of Armageddon. During the final hellish 7 years on earth, dispensationalists believe, the Christians are in heaven where a number of things happen. They believe that each Christian is judged at 'the judgement seat of Christ' and receive their eternal reward for the deeds they have done in this life. In addition, Jesus and the church marry, and the 'Wedding supper of the lamb' referred to in Revelation 19 takes place, before Jesus and the church return to earth for the final battle and to set up the rule of the Messiah in a thousand year glorious 'millennium'. After that, God totally transforms the universe into a new heavens and earth, and all souls are to be found in heaven or hell forever.

Thus for these dispensationalists, the rapture of the church (described in 1 Thessalonians 4 and 1 Corinthians 15), although part of the end of days sequence, is a separate event to the return of Jesus to rule on earth. It is in support of this belief system that LaHaye offers his 15 points that 'prove' the two are different events. We will come back to deal with them after a fairly short but very important diversion to examine Jewish rabbinic methods of quoting and alluding to scripture.

Why is this important? Well, both Jesus and Paul were rabbis, and taught and thought as Rabbis. Because Rabbis normally had an audience who typically had low literacy levels, but knew great screeds of the Old Testament off by heart, their method of signposting scriptures was not like ours in our literate and book or text rich, but often bible knowledge poor, society. We cite exact chapter and verse, but back in those days, this reference device was still to be invented. What they did was to either quote enough of the passage, or occasionally paraphrase it using sufficient distinctive words or concepts, for their well-trained listeners to identify the passage involved. They would expect their hearers to not only know the passage, but also to bring to mind the context of that passage as well. In Israel, this expectation of knowledge applied to all Jews, not just dedicated rabbinic disciples (the latter would be expected to memorize lots of rabbinic teaching and legal interpretations, as well as the scriptures). It could get quite sophisticated. For instance, you could quote two phrases from two separate passages back to back, and listeners would be expected not only to remember the particular 'verses' as we would say, but the context of both passages, and an understanding of exactly why the teacher had linked the two - usually because of some common theme in the surrounding context. Alternatively, if a concept or phrase was particularly unique, the tiniest of snippets would serve the listeners evidence of what was being talked about. Jesus once managed to essentially cite a whole series of passages and a concept just by the particular form of one verb he used - and at least one section of his audience - admittedly one made up of expert teachers of the law - got it (and weren't at all happy). This happened in Mark 2.1-12, where in v5, Jesus uses the passive form of the verb to 'forgive'. He didn't say, 'I forgive', but rather 'Your sins are forgiven'. The teachers of the law present were immediately outraged, and protested this. 'Only God can forgive sins! Who does this man think he is?' They recognized that Jesus had made a pronouncement that only authorized priests acting in the name of God and making sacrificial atonement could legitimately pronounce. There are a number of passages in the Old Testament where God is asked to forgive using the active tense, but the only places where sins were pronounced forgiven in the passive tense where those involving forgiveness after the priestly sacrifice (a number of times in Leviticus chapters 4 and 5, also in 6.7, 19.22 and Numbers 15). For Jesus to make such a pronouncement was to implicitly make an outrageous claim about himself and his authority, and his audience instantly got it - all because of one word using one particular tense of that word!

Because Jews believed every word of the Old Testament was inspired by God, attention could focus on individual words and their meaning, and fundamental debates could turn on very small points, as we saw in the Mark 2 story. To take another example from the life of Jesus, when he debates the Sadducees of his day over the resurrection (Matthew 22.23-33, Mark 12.18-27, Luke 20.27-40) Jesus defeats the Sadducees (who didn't believe in the resurrection of the dead) by noting the tense God uses to Moses when speaking of the long dead Israelite forefathers Abraham, Isaac and Jacob. God said to Moses 'I *am* the God of Abraham, Isaac, and Jacob', not 'I *was* the God of Abraham, Isaac and Jacob'. Jesus used a similar subtle linguistic nuance very soon after this incident when he turned the tables by asking the Pharisees a question about the nature of the Messiah using Psalm 110.1.

All this leads me, however, to one caveat here. Out of this attention to the tiniest detail there arose some different - and to us, rather stranger - methods of interpreting Scripture that were in use in Jewish religious thought at that time, where passages and phrases could be taken in a way that ignored, or at least on the surface seemed to ignore, their context. There are a few places where the New Testament writers used the Old Testament scriptures in such a fashion, noticeably in works directed primarily to Jewish readers or those who understood Jewish teaching nuances. Hebrews 1 and Paul talking about Abraham's 'seed' in his letter to the Galatians spring to mind here, but perhaps the most famous examples occur in the first two chapters of Matthew's gospel, particularly 'the Virgin shall conceive' and the 'Out of Israel I called my son' passages, along with the assertion that the prophets prophesied that 'He will be called a Nazarene'. (In fact, sometimes these methods were used to allude not only to Scripture but to the teaching of other sacred Jewish literature of the time – the small letter of Jude in the New Testament does this a lot, for instance). They could also take the fact that two very different passages use the same word to indicate the two passages should be used to interpret each other, leading to some – to us – very strange interpretations. I mention this, not because it will be important to our argument, but because if I didn't mention that there were some exceptions to the 'take passages in context' approach, someone would doubtless try and undermine what I am about to say by pointing to those exceptions.

Despite the existence of these alternative approaches, the foundational, the basic 'bread and butter' approach was to cite passages with a view to their context, even if they also had an attention to tiny detail that we might miss or think unjustified. What is important for our purposes here is that for Paul, as a rabbi trained under Gamaliel, who has one of, if not *the* leading rabbi and Jewish teacher of his day, this approach to scripture would have been about as natural to him as breathing, and when he became a disciple of Jesus, naturally he would apply the same method to the teaching of Jesus, since Jesus was the promised Messiah of Israel, and the 'prophet like Moses' that the original Moses had predicted in Deuteronomy, and thus the new Law-giver. Now the only two passages that unequivocally describe 'the rapture' – and when I say unequivocally, I mean that explicitly talk of living believers being transformed directly to their resurrection bodies at the coming of Jesus – are both in Paul's letters – namely 1 Corinthians 15 and 1 Thessalonians 4. What is more, these were both written to predominantly non-Jewish churches, who we can assume would be familiar with the common sense basic approach of scripture interpretation, but probably not the more specialist advanced methods, and to whom we can assume Paul would use basic, and not advanced, interpretative approaches. The 1 Corinthians 15.50-58 passage is part of a long and detailed argument about the nature of the resurrection, and deals with the resurrection of dead believers (a.k.a. 'the rapture') quite briefly, but the 1 Thessalonians 4.13-18 passage is rather more detailed, and contains a collection of specific events and actors in the rapture event – the descent of Jesus from heaven, a loud command, an archangel, the sounding of the trumpet, and the gathering of Christians to be with Jesus in the air. Not only that, but Paul is explicit that the events he describes are 'according to the word of the Lord' a phrase indicating he was alluding directly to the teaching of Jesus, not drawing something from his own understanding. (At this point, if you notice, as I did, that Paul follows his 'word of the Lord' with a phrase involving the order of the resurrection of the dead and the living, before going on to these other elements of the rapture, and wonder where the former idea comes from in Jesus' teaching, have a look at Appendix 1 for several possible solutions to this question.) And those specific elements I listed only appear all together in one other place in the entirety of the Old and New Testament, in the teaching of Jesus about his return and the times leading up to it, something that will be _very_ significant in the 'pre-trib rapture' debate, as we shall see as we turn back to deal with Tim Lahaye's allegedly 'irrefutable' proofs of a pre-tribulation rapture.

Lahaye pairs off opposing statements in a table, with one column said to describe the rapture, the other the second coming of Jesus. I start with two 'proofs' that very much go together, so I take them together, rather than in LaHaye's order.

PROOF 1

In the Rapture, Christ comes in the air _for_ his own (1 Thessalonians 4.14-17) but at the Second Coming Christ comes to earth _with_ his own (Revelation 19.11-16).

PROOF 5

In the Rapture, the church is taken to heaven (1 Thessalonians 4.16-17), but at the Second Coming Christ sets up his kingdom on earth (Revelation chapters 19 and 20)

In the passage in 1 Thessalonians 4.14-7 Paul writes to a church he has just founded, made up entirely of new Christians. Verse 13 indicates Paul's purpose in writing about the events of the 'rapture'. He wanted the new believers to understand and be reassured about what happened to Christians who died before Jesus returned:

> 'Brothers and sisters, we do not want you to be uninformed about those who sleep in death, so that you do not grieve like the rest of mankind, who have no hope'

Paul is not offering a detailed explanation or schema for what happens at the end of time, but is writing to reassure his readers that those they have lost to death will not be excluded from the coming of Jesus, nor are they lost to the living forever. For our purposes, the key points start in v16:

> 'For the Lord himself will come down from heaven, with a loud command, with the voice of the archangel and with the trumpet call of God, and the dead in Christ will rise first.'

The passage says that 'the Lord' - meaning Jesus - will come down from heaven. V17 continues:

> 'After that, we who are still alive and are left will be caught up together with them in the clouds to meet the Lord in the air. And so we will be with the Lord forever.'

Notice first, that despite 'proof' 5's confident assertion that the church is taken to heaven, the passage in 1 Thessalonians *does not say that at all!* It says that Jesus comes from heaven, and it says that we, the church, meet Jesus in the air. It never says he *returns* to heaven. That is total eisegesis (reading something into the text that just isn't there) on the part of LaHaye and pre-tribulationists. Paul just says that we will be with Jesus forever from that point on. The being with Jesus, wherever He is, is the key point.

When Jesus came to Jerusalem from Bethany, he was met by crowds who welcomed him as the promised Messiah. He did not then return to Bethany with them, but went into Jerusalem, from where the crowds had come. This was typical of how conquering kings or victorious heroes would be welcomed to a city. This is the imagery that Paul was thinking of - the Greek word he used for 'meet' was used for exactly that kind of scenario. The specific word is used in the New Testament to describe when the Christians of Rome travelled out to meet Paul himself and bring him back to the city in Acts 28.15. Additionally Jesus used it, significantly, in his parable about his second coming commonly known as 'The Wise and Foolish bridesmaids (or virgins)' in Matthew 25.6. There Jesus describes himself as the bridegroom, and the bridesmaids are called to go out and meet him, and then in v10, they do not go back with him to his house, but rather take him back with them to the banqueting venue.

Notice also that Paul says that we meet with Jesus and the resurrected Christians 'in the clouds'. That incidental point is important. It's not there to prophecy the weather on the day of the rapture! Clouds are often associated with the presence and glory of God in the Old Testament. Also, one of the most fundamental promises about the coming of the Messiah in the Old Testament is in Daniel 7 where 'one like a son of man' will come 'with the clouds of heaven' and to whom eternal rule over all nations would be given, and who would receive worship from all the world.

Paul's readers would also know about the clouds of God's presence that covered Jesus at his transfiguration (Matthew 17). Since Paul would have just a few months earlier taught them about what Jesus had said about his second coming, they would also know that Jesus said that at his Second Coming all the earth would see him coming 'with the clouds of heaven' (Matthew 24.30), or, as Luke reported it 'coming in a cloud with power and great glory (Luke 21.27). They would have heard of the trial of Jesus, where in Matthew 26.64 he answered a question as to whether he was the Messiah by saying:

> 'From now on you will see the Son of Man sitting at the right hand of the Mighty One and coming on the clouds of heaven'

(Interestingly, the book of the bible most concerned with the end times, Revelation, opens with the same theme in 1.7 where John says:

> "Look, he is coming with the clouds,"
> and "every eye will see him,
> even those who pierced him";
> and all peoples on earth "will mourn because of him."
> So shall it be! Amen.

Notice that this is clearly a public event for the entire world to see.)

And finally, Paul's readers could think of Jesus ascending to heaven in Acts 1, when he was hidden from the watching disciples' sight by a cloud. In other words he was 'in the air' when they were parted from him on the Mount of Olives. However, angels immediately appeared and told them that Jesus would 'come back in the same way you have seen him go into heaven'. Whether Paul's readers were yet aware of the following, we don't know, but Paul certainly knew that the prophet Zechariah predicted in chapter 14 that the feet of God would touch down on the Mount of Olives in the final battle for Jerusalem and Israel. Go figure!

But there is more. Go back to 1 Thessalonians 4.16-7 a moment. There is Jesus returning from heaven, there is a 'loud command', the 'voice of an archangel' and 'the trumpet of God'. Then all believers, living and dead are gathered to be with Jesus. Now head back to Matthew 24.30. There is Jesus, coming back from heaven. But read v31, and you will find angels being sent out 'with a loud trumpet call' to gather 'the elect' from the entire world.

To what do you think Paul was referring when he used all of these terms to describe the rapture - the events described in Zechariah 14 and in the teaching of Jesus in Matthew 24 about his Second Coming, or a mysterious event that appears nowhere in their teaching? Go read Matthew 24 (and the equivalent passages in Mark 13 and Luke 21) and try and find any hint of a 'rapture' or 'gathering' of Christians at any point in Jesus teaching on the end times except when he returns for all the world to see. Jesus specifically gave the time frame for this event in Matthew 24.29 (and I am here using specifically the Darby translation precisely because Darby is revered as perhaps *the* foundational teacher of the pre-trib rapture position):

*'But immediately after the **tribulation** of those days.....'*

Who would have thought! (And by the way, in Latin, the language from which we get much of our technical terms, this passage literally reads 'Post tribulationem'. The post-tribulation rapture is literally and explicitly in these words of Jesus - in red letters, so to speak.)

But turning to Revelation 19-20 where Jesus is said by LaHaye to come 'with his own', meaning the church, does the text justify the weight he puts on it? For this we need to look at some key words in Revelation. Those returning with Jesus are described as 'the army of Heaven' who as well as riding on white horses are also 'dressed in fine linen, white and clean' (Revelation 19.14). Revelation is a highly symbolic book, full of allusions both visual and verbal, in a typically Jewish style of writing.

If we look at references in Revelation to 'linen' and to 'white' garments, there are variations in usage. It is true that sometimes Christians or the church are referred to. For instance, in Chapter 3, when Jesus is giving messages to individual churches, in one case he refers to a few Christians who were 'dressed in white' and did not participate in the corruption found in their church. He promised that those who are victorious would also be dressed in white. Conversely, he pleaded with a lukewarm and indifferent church to *'buy from me.... white clothes to wear, so you can cover your shameful nakedness...'* (3.4-5 and 18). Clearly there are issues of purity and righteous living here. However, the very next reference to individuals 'dressed in white' refers to heavenly beings - the '24 elders' who surround God's throne (4.4). In chapter 6 we are still in heaven. In the vision, John sees the souls of those martyred for their faith in Christ beneath the heavenly altar. These are given white robes while told to wait until all those destined for martyrdom meet their destiny (v9-11).

By chapter 7, the focus of the vision has switched back to earth. A large number of Jews are sealed with a divine seal before judgements are unleashed on the earth. Immediately after this, John sees a vast multitude from all the nations of the earth, dressed in white robes, and 'standing before the throne'. An angel tells him that these are those who have 'come out of the great tribulation' and who have 'washed their robes white in the blood of the lamb'. It is not totally clear whether, like the souls in chapter 6, they have been martyred, or whether they have survived faithfully through the tribulation, although I suspect the former (see the latter part of my refutation of Proof 3 below). It is also not entirely clear whether they are in heaven or on earth. The sealing of the Jews suggests that they are on earth, yet they are described as being 'before the throne'. However, being 'before the Lord' is a term used in Jewish sacred literature to describe an attitude or lifestyle of worship. Whether these worshippers are actually in heaven before the throne, or are worshipping on earth, their worship clearly impacts and inspires the heavenly beings to worship.

If they were dead and in heaven, then clearly there is no problem with them returning with Jesus in chapter 19. If they are living, and remain so, then there might be a problem if Revelation 19 is referring to them.

However, the phrase 'linen' also crops up in Revelation. If we exclude those uses of the word which clearly refer to literal 'linen' in earthly trade and commerce, then we find a reference in Revelation 15.6, where seven angels appear dressed in 'clean, shining linen'. Then, in Chapter 19.6-8, just before Jesus and the heavenly armies descend to earth, we find linen again. A great multitude shouts praises to God, because:

> 'the wedding of the Lamb has come,
> and his bride has made herself ready.
> Fine linen, bright and clean,
> was given her to wear.'

The writer then goes on to explain that:

> 'Fine linen stands for the righteous acts of God's holy people.'

(Notice by the way, that contrary to the assumptions of pre-tribulationists, the passage does not say that the church is in heaven. Nor does it state or in any way infer that the wedding of the Lamb has already taken place in heaven. If anything, the fact that the church has just at this time made herself ready and is a 'holy people' truly doing 'righteous acts' suggests she is on earth. After all, if she had already been transformed to be like Jesus and been before the 'judgement seat of Christ' as they allege, then the bride would have been made ready seven years before, at or immediately following the alleged 'pre-tribulation' rapture'.)

So when a few verses later, the army of heaven returns with Jesus, the language used combines characteristics of both the saints and of the angels when it talks of the army being *'dressed in fine linen, white and clean'.*

In the view of pre-tribbers like LaHaye, this passage remains 'indisputable' proof that the church is in heaven during the tribulation and returns with Jesus, but as we have already seen, the evidence earlier in Revelation is problematic. Certainly the souls of those saints who are martyred for their faith in Christ are in heaven and return with Jesus, but anything more than that is going beyond what the text of Revelation would immediately support. And it is true that there is no mention in Revelation 19 of the church rising to meet Jesus in the air. Rather it has heaven opening to reveal Jesus and the armies of heaven with him descending to earth. But here we run into the problem of the symbolic nature and the particular focus of Revelation. After all, just like Paul's readers in Thessalonica, the readers of Revelation would know what Jesus had said about the moment of his return in Matthew 24 when he sends out angel to gather his people from all across the world. John would not need to have written about this in detail, but could *assume* this knowledge amongst his readers. In addition, so much of the language in Revelation is symbolic and allusional. Whatever your particular interpretation of Revelation, it is quite clear that it is meant to reveal behind the scenes happenings to events on the earth in the last days, where the visible reality on earth is a reflection of events in heaven, designed to lead up to the revealing of who Jesus is and who his people are in a totally unambiguous way to the entire world. All through both the New and Old Testaments, God's day of judgement not only entails an emphatic punishment of the wicked, but a justification and vindication of those righteous people they have oppressed. This principle reaches its climax in Revelation 19 at the end of the age. Thus the significance of the heavens standing open to reveal Jesus is not so much a 'literal' event (although it is undoubtedly that – in Matthew 24 Jesus talks of 'the sign of the Son of Man in heaven' before he talks of his actual return) as the moment when the true nature of Jesus and his bride are revealed to a world that has rejected the preaching of the church about Jesus. The oppressed become the victors. Heaven is revealed to earth, and the secret kingdom of God, previously advanced hidden in human hearts, is made manifest. As the author, John, said in one of his letters *'when He is made known, we shall be like Him, for we shall we shall see Him as He is'.* (1 John 3.2). The true reality is unveiled. Interestingly, in Revelation, it talks about the resurrection of at least some of the believing dead in Chapter 20 – 'the first resurrection'. However, despite the chapter divisions in our bibles, there is no indication in the text that this event is separated in time from the events of chapter 19 and the visible return of Jesus.

I suggest that the apparent 'contradictions' here are rather like the 'contradictions' between Matthew and Luke about Jesus' birth. Matthew starts in Bethlehem, has an angel speak to Joseph, has the holy family flee to Egypt after the visit of wise men, and then has the family go to Nazareth. In Luke, the focus is on Mary, and the story starts in Nazareth, goes on to the birth and shepherds in Bethlehem and has no visit to Egypt - the family just reappear in Nazareth. But there is actually no outright contradiction - each writer has a different focus and chooses to highlight different events. The two accounts of Jesus first coming can be woven together without contradiction. In the case of these two passages about Jesus second coming, we have already established that 1 Thessalonians does not indicate in any way that the rapture involves the church going to heaven. It is quite clear from the language that Paul uses that he is referring to Jesus' visible return as taught in Matthew 24. As for Revelation 19, it does reveal the armies of heaven coming with Jesus but is not explicit as to the nature of those making up the armies. For instance, it is quite possible to fit in dead saints being revealed and gaining their resurrection bodies at the moment the heavens opens and the trumpet mentioned in both Jesus and Paul's teaching sounds, immediately joined by the living rising to join them in the air and return. Just because Revelation 19 does not speak of this detail does not mean it cannot be happening. In other words, far from proving the separate nature and chronology of the rapture and Jesus visible return, these passages point in the opposite direction, particularly the way Paul clearly points in 1 Thessalonians 4 to Jesus' teaching in Matthew 24 and parallels about his visible return to earth.

PROOF 2

At the Rapture, all the Christians are translated or raptured (1 Thessalonians 4, 1 Corinthians 15), but at the Second Coming no-one is raptured.

We have pretty much already covered this in 'proofs' 1 and 5 above, but there a couple more things to notice there. I think it is telling that he cites no Scripture to back up his claim that no-one is raptured at the Second Coming. He is relying on audiences who are already indoctrinated in the 'pre-trib' pattern of thinking, and demonstrating something of how much the position he holds means imposing a framework on the bible. If he is thinking of passages like Revelation 19 to back up his claim about no rapture at the second coming, then, as we have seen, the fact that there is no mention of a rapture event as described in Paul's writings is hardly decisive. Here, as in so many other places in his 'proofs', we need to remember that absence of evidence is not necessarily evidence of absence. After all, we can assume that John at least, and almost certainly his readers, were already familiar with the same teaching of Jesus on the end times that Paul refers back to in 1 Thessalonians 4, where all the believers are gathered to be with Jesus when his 'sign' appears in the heavens – 'after the tribulation'. So this 'proof' turns out to be singularly lame.

Since we're talking about how 1 Thessalonians 4 refers back to Jesus' teaching on the end times in Matthew 24 and parallels, there is something else to say, that I might as well say here. According to the Pre-trib position, the rapture happens before the tribulation. We have seen how Paul's language in 1 Thessalonians 4 about the events of the rapture matches the post-trib rapture in Matthew 24, but is there another clue within 1 Thessalonians 4 that Paul is thinking in what we would call 'post-trib' terms? I think there is, in v15 and v17, which read

> *According to the Lord's word, we tell you that <u>we who are still alive, who are left until the coming of the Lord,</u> will certainly not precede those who have fallen asleep.*

After that Paul describes the rapture event, stating the dead are raised first, and then v17 reads

> *After that, <u>we who are still alive</u> and are left will be caught up together with them in the clouds to meet the Lord in the air. And so we will be with the Lord forever.*

In Appendix 1, I discuss the question of how Jesus' teaching in Matthew 24 could be understood as teaching that the dead are raised first, but here I want to focus on something else. Paul said that according to Jesus' teaching, we who are still alive, who are left until the coming of the Lord will also join with Jesus. Now, given that the focus of the passage is on the issue of what will happen to those believers who die, this could simply mean that by 'we who are still alive, who are left' it is just contrasting those who are living with those who are dead, but I suggest that in view of the strong links back to Matthew 24, it means more than that – Paul is reminding his hearers that just before the coming of the Lord, there will be great persecution of Christians in which many will be martyred. He writes this to a church that is already undergoing severe persecution, and needs encouragement. He not only reassures them about the fate of those who have already died, from any cause, but also encourages them that if they – and by extension we – die faithful in persecution, the same applies to us, and alludes to Jesus' strong implication that not many Christians will be left alive when he returns, and also that 'the one who stands firm to the end will be saved.' (Matthew 24.13). Thus, although his primary focus is on reassuring them that those who have died are not lost to them, but will be reunited with them as they rise to meet Jesus at the second coming, Paul is also implicitly encouraging them to stand strong in persecution when he ends with v18:

Therefore encourage one another with these words.

The encouragement is not just in the face of grief, but in the face of persecution or the prospect of persecution that will take courage to face. He provokes courage partly be alluding to Jesus' teaching on the need to stay strong and courageous in the face of end-times persecution, and tells us that we need to encourage and strengthen one another in the same manner – looking to the hope that is to come, even in the face of hopeless circumstances.

PROOF 3

At the Rapture, Christians are taken to the Fathers House (John 14.1-3) but at the Second Coming the Resurrected saints do not see the Father's House.

Just to let you know, this turned out to be a very looong refutation, not because this is particularly difficult to refute, but because in properly interpreting the passages (both the one stated in the proof, and the unstated ones behind this 'proof), my thoughts rather carried me away, but I trust you will find what follows enlightening and informative. I found it quite exciting to write.

Anyway, once again we see some circular reasoning here. There is no scripture to back up his claim about the 'Resurrected saints'. To anyone not familiar with the details of the typical 'pre-trib' position espoused by LaHaye and his cohorts, this 'proof' will seem especially confusing. After all, isn't a major component of the Rapture that all the dead saints get resurrected? Indeed that observation in itself should set up warning flags that this 'proof' is anything but conclusive. Yet again, LaHaye is relying on an audience indoctrinated into 'pre-Trib' understandings of Scripture. The understanding LaHaye is both relying on in his own and in his audience's thinking and at the same time trying to 'prove' here is that after the church is raptured out of the way, many people, both Jew and non-Jew, will turn to faith in Jesus during the Tribulation. These are generally known to pre-tribbers as the 'Tribulation saints', a huge number of whom they believe will be martyred by the forces of the anti-Christ. Usually they use a combination of the fact that saints on earth appear in Revelation 4-18 (something we have already touched upon in refuting 'proofs' 1 and 5 above) and their belief that the church has already been raptured to heaven before the Tribulation. They believe that these murdered 'Tribulation saints' are those referred to in the 'First Resurrection' mentioned in Revelation 20 (even though it is actually the second resurrection if you hold a pre-trib position, given that the Rapture involves the resurrection of 'church age' saints).

That said, does this proof carry any water? First we need to examine John 14.1-3, which is part of a long talk given by Jesus to his disciples at the Last Supper, the night before he was crucified. The passage reads:

> *'Do not let your hearts be troubled. You believe in God; believe also in me. My Father's house has many rooms; if that were not so, would I have told you that I am going there to prepare a place for you? And if I go and prepare a place for you, I will come back and take you to be with me that you also may be where I am.'*

Tim LaHaye and many other pre-tribulationists see this passage as one of three 'foundational passages' for belief in a pre-trib rapture. The other two are 1 Thessalonians 4 and 1 Corinthians 15, which are obvious candidates, given that they describe an event where living believers are transformed into resurrected bodies, even if we may (as I do) seriously challenge the assertion that they 'prove' a specifically pre-tribulation rapture. But John 14.1-3 contains no such clear reference, so why do they see it as so fundamental to their case? For that, you need to understand how they make a number of assumptions about this passage, each one of which is highly questionable.

The first assumption – and this might startle you – is the assumption that Jesus is talking about his return at the Second Coming (and here I include any possible pre-trib rapture as part of that Second Coming). The fact is, as they so often do, those advocating a pre-trib rapture have taken this verse out of context. The very next verse would raise warning flags that this may not be about the Second Coming at all. Jesus goes on to say:

> *You know the way to the place where I am going.*

Why is there any need to know the way to where Jesus is going if all that is going to happen is that Jesus will return to take his own 'home' to be with him? It just doesn't make sense.

Let's look at the wider context. Firstly, the chapter divisions were never in the original text. They and verse numbers are a later tool invented for convenience, but psychologically they also have a negative side effect: they let us ignore the context, the patterns of thinking the bible writers expressed. And this sits very well with the way dispensationalists and 'pre-tribbers' atomize the bible, taking a verse from one book, a passage from another, a phrase or word here or there, out of context, and build them into a belief system that frequently violates the original intent and message of the Scriptures about the last days. I am not particularly blaming them - all of us in Western Christianity tend to do this. It is probably a reflection of the same trends that have made us such an individualistic society. But.... I have noticed that so often it is the dispensationalists who take this aberrant approach to the nth degree. (Well, there are the hyper-dispensationalists who go even further, but we won't get onto that favourite bug-bear of mine..... they are another story again).

In John 14, Jesus starts 'Do *not let your hearts be troubled....*'. To understand why he might have started that way, we need to look at chapter 13. From v18 on, Jesus has been warning his disciples that one of them will betray him, that one of those intimate with him (one who has 'shared my bread') will turn against him. Then in v33, after Judas has left to betray him, he tells them that he will be with them only a little longer. He says that the disciples will look for him, but '*just as I told the Jews, so I tell you now: Where I am going, you cannot come*'. Here he is referring to a dispute he had with the Pharisees in John 8.12 onwards. The writer of the gospel notes in v20 that '*no-one seized him, because his hour had not yet come*' after Jesus has said in the Temple - near where the offerings were put, no less - that if his opponents knew him, they would know the Father also. This comment is important. It means that John, a complex and subtle theologian, is framing the debate in terms of the sacrificial temple, and what follows needs to be understood in that light. Jesus goes on to say in v21: '*I am going away, and you will look for me, and you will die in your sin. Where I go, you cannot come*'. The Jews asked if Jesus was going to kill himself, and if that was why Jesus had said they couldn't come where he was going. Jesus replies by saying that his opponents will die in their sins if they do not believe that '*I am He*'. When his listeners don't understand, Jesus says '*When you have lifted up (or 'exalted') the Son of Man, then you will know that I am he and that I do nothing on my own but speak just what the Father has taught me. The one who sent me is with me; he has not left me alone, for I always do what pleases him*'. Two things to note here. Firstly, when Jesus says 'I am He', the Greek is literally 'I am'. Now Greek often leaves out as understood words we would put in, so 'I am He' is a perfectly acceptable translation, but the literal translation 'I am' makes clear that Jesus is equating himself with God, since 'I am' in the Old Testament is a Divine Title. Secondly, in paradoxical fashion, as is typical with Jesus - and especially in John's gospel - Jesus describes his coming death in incredibly positive terms - as being 'lifted up' or 'exalted', and he also ties it in with his claim to Divinity. When the Jewish leaders have had Jesus killed, then they will know that He is 'I Am', and does nothing except speak what God has taught him. Not only that, but God the Father is always with him and does not leave him alone.

All this is important to note, because in John 13, Jesus refers back to this incident, and he would expect his disciples to remember the context - the temple background and the fact that he talked, in however allusive terms, about his sacrificial martyrdom. Importantly for us, he also talked about how God was always with him, and never left him alone, because these are themes that crop up later on in Chapter 14 onwards. But to start off with, the key point is that the disciples can't go where Jesus is going, because he is going to die - not just any death - but the ultimate, sacrificial death. Peter doesn't get this, and he asks in 13.36 'Where are you going?' Jesus says *'Where I am going, you cannot follow me, but you will follow later.'* We find out when he will later follow right at the end of John's gospel, where in chapter 21 Jesus makes allusion to Peter's future death as a crucified martyr. Peter asks why he can't follow Jesus now, and declares his willingness to lay down his life for Jesus. However much bravado there is, he is aware, if not from Jesus teaching, then certainly from the political situation and the opposition to Jesus, that following Jesus is likely to mean death. Jesus hits back, predicting that Peter will disown him three times that night. In other words, all that Jesus had just said gave ample reason for their hearts to be troubled right at that point. What Jesus is doing in John 14.1-3, this strongly suggests, is telling them that the purpose of his death (his going away) is to 'prepare a place' for his disciples, and once he has done so, he will come back to take them to be 'with' him, so they 'also may be where I am'. Now if Jesus is referring to heaven, why does he not simply say so? After all, in the first six chapters of John, Jesus repeatedly refers to heaven, often specifically the fact that he has come down from heaven (see, for instance, 1.51, numerous times in John 3.12-31, as well as in 6.31,58).

This means that the assumption, never examined, of pre-tribbers, that when Jesus refers to the many rooms in 'My Father's House', he is speaking of heaven, is highly suspect, if not outright wrong. That suspicion about the pre-trib interpretation of this passage is strengthened if you look at the context following the quote. We've already noted Jesus' comments about his disciples knowing where he is going in v4. When the disciples ask how it is they can know the way because they don't know where Jesus is going, Jesus replies *'I am the way... No one comes to the Father except through me. If you really know me, you will know, my Father as well.'* He goes on to ask them *'Don't you believe that I am in the Father and the Father is in me?'* Jesus then says that he will ask the Father who will give them another advocate to help them and be with them forever - the Spirit of truth, saying *'I will not leave you as orphans; I will come to you'*. This will happen when the world does not see Jesus anymore, but his disciples do. *'On that day, you will realize that I am in my Father, and you are in me, and I am in you.... The one who loves me will be loved by my Father, and I too will love them and show myself to them'*. This is the context of what Jesus was saying. He will go away (in death), and there will be a time when the world won't see him, but the disciples will - because they have been sent the Spirit.

These themes go on all through the rest of chapter 14 to 17. The disciples are given peace because Jesus will send the Holy Spirit (14.25-7).

Keep looking at those themes. For instance, John 14.1-3 talks about Jesus coming back to '*take you to be with me so you may be where I am.*' Similar themes about unity with Jesus crop up in chapter 15 when Jesus uses the analogy of the vine and says '*Remain in me, as I also remain in you*'. When Jesus talks in 14.3 about coming back to take his disciples to be where he is, he tells us what he means just a few verses down where he says that the Spirit '*lives with you and will be in you*' and goes on to explain '*I will not leave you as orphans; I will come to you*'. When this whole large section reaches a climax in Jesus' prayer in Chapter 17 these themes of the unity of the Father with Jesus and Jesus and the Father with his disciples remain dominant. When he looks ahead to the church throughout the ages (v20-5) he prays:

> "*I pray also for those who will believe in me through their message, that all of them may be one, Father, just as you are in me and I am in you. May they also be in us so that the world may believe that you have sent me. I have given them the glory that you gave me, that they may be one as we are one – I in them and you in me—so that they may be brought to complete unity. Then the world will know that you sent me and have loved them even as you have loved me.*

> "*Father, I want those you have given me to be with me where I am, and to see my glory, the glory you have given me because you loved me before the creation of the world.*

> "*Righteous Father, though the world does not know you, I know you, and they know that you have sent me. I have made you known to them, and will continue to make you known in order that the love you have for me may be in them and that I myself may be in them.*"

Notice that in all these passages, the emphasis is on being in Jesus, and being with him, and among other things this is achieved by the sight and knowledge given by the Holy Spirit, and by loving and obeying Jesus. In other words, all through these passages, 'being with' God or Jesus is not about *spatial location* but rather is a matter of *spiritual connection*. Thus both the wider and the closer contexts of John 14.1-3 indicate that we should interpret the language in that passage about being with Jesus in the same way - that it is about spiritual connection to do with the death and resurrection of Jesus and his ascension along with the consequent pouring out of the 'Spirit of Truth' on his disciples. It is by that same Spirit that Jesus comes back to take the disciples to be 'where he is' in John 14.3. Jesus wants them - and us - to be with him and seeing his glory, the God given glory bestowed on him because God has loved him from the before the creation of the world (17.24). We are to be taken right into the middle of the love relationship between the Father and the Son, and to see the glory of Jesus the Son as displayed in the supreme divine love he embodied in his death on the cross for our sins. In John's gospel, from Chapter 12.23 on, both Jesus being glorified and the Father being glorified are intimately connected with Jesus' death. In John 12 Jesus explicitly links his death and glorification:

> *"The hour has come for the Son of Man to be glorified. Very truly I tell you, unless a kernel of wheat falls to the ground and dies, it remains only a single seed. But if it dies, it produces many seeds.....*
>
> *"Now my soul is troubled, and what shall I say? 'Father, save me from this hour'? No, it was for this very reason I came to this hour. Father, glorify your name!"*
>
> *Then a voice came from heaven, "I have glorified it, and will glorify it again."....*
>
> *Jesus said, "..... And I, when I am lifted up from the earth, will draw all people to myself." He said this to show the kind of death he was going to die.*

Since we have established that John 14.1-3 makes no explicit reference to heaven, and almost certainly no implicit or allusive reference to heaven, in the way that LaHaye et al would have us believe, the question then arises, to what was Jesus referring when he talked about his 'Father's House' that had many rooms? Well, Father's House only appears in one other place in John's gospel, and that is in John 2, where Jesus uses it to refer to the Temple in Jerusalem. (Jesus used to refer to the Temple with that term from a very young age. In Luke 2.49, at the age of about twelve, he refers to it in that way to Mary and Joseph). Jesus also uses the phrase when he drives out traders and commerce from the Temple precincts. When he was challenged by onlookers as to his authority to do such a thing, Jesus said *'Destroy this temple, and I will raise it again in three days'*, something that confused his interrogators, since the Temple – still being rebuilt – had thus far taken 46 years. But as the author of the gospel comments *'But the temple he had spoken of was his body'*.

Now two very different examples and contexts do not prove that each use of the phrase must mean basically the same thing, but it is the logical starting point. LaHaye and his pre-trib fellow travellers tend to recognize this natural assumption here, and rush to argue that two slightly different forms of the word Greek word for 'house' are used in the two passages, and say that the use of these two different forms in the Septuagint (the predominant Greek translation of the Old Testament of the time, usually abbreviated LXX) indicates that the masculine form in John 2 is only ever used of the Temple, whereas the feminine term used in John 14 never is. Now I don't have the time or the expertise in the subtleties of Greek grammar to debate the details of that issue here, but I do want to point out that there is some very interesting Temple language in John 14.1-3 that - as far as I am aware - all pre-Tribbers miss.

But we also need to have a quick look at what exactly the function of a Temple was in the minds of the ancients (and to save space, I am going to have to make a number of 'gratuitous assertions' of my own here, but believe me, I can back them up!). Scholars generally agree that the core function of a Temple was as a 'navel' or contact point between God (or gods) and their people. It was the place par excellence where the realm of God and men intertwined and communicated and were joined together. Now the thing is that John, a brilliant theologian, repeatedly makes allusion to all sorts of Temple / Tabernacle themes in his gospel. (The Tabernacle was the original tent version of the Temple in Israel before Solomon built a stone Temple.) As an aside here, I personally believe that, contrary to common belief, the 'John' who is the author of this gospel and the other New Testament documents written by 'John', was not the John who was one of the Twelve disciples, but another disciple called John who was actually a priest at the Temple, but that is another issue. As we have seen, John is a complex writer. In this gospel, not only is Jesus' body the Temple, but Jesus is also the sacrificial offering (*Behold the Lamb of God who takes away the sins of the world* in John 1) and yet Jesus is also somehow the priest who makes the offering of a sacrifice to God - the offering in this case being himself. It's not for nothing that Jesus' prayer the night before his death in John 17 is often referred to as his 'High Priestly prayer'.

Now the Jewish Temple had a sacrificial system which functioned - among other things - to make atonement for the sins of the people. Most evangelical Christians believe that the way this works is that the blood of the sacrifice covers over and cleanses the sin in the individual, and there is indeed some truth to this. The thing is, though, that without repentance, the sacrifices availed nothing. The prophets repeatedly said that repentance was more importance than sacrifices. More, a number of scholars argue that the blood was not so much to cover the sin in the individual as to cover the impurity or defilement that their sin caused in the Temple, a defilement that violated the holiness of this most Holy Place and offended God, causing a breach in the communion between heaven and earth, God and humans. I cover this, because I think - and I am far from alone in this - that it illustrates something later on in John's gospel that is relevant, namely why it is that the just resurrected Jesus tells Mary Magdalene not to touch or hold on to him because he has not yet ascended to the Father. He tells her to tell the disciples that he is ascending to '*my Father and your Father, to my God and your God*' (20.17-8) (which indicates a form of atonement - literally at-one-ment - his ascending to the Father is the means by which the disciples and Jesus become one, having the same Father and God). However, later on he is fine for the disciples to touch him. Mary could not touch Jesus because he was in the process of ascending with the offering of his blood to purify the heavenly altar and temple, and in that holy task as the High Priest, Jesus could not be touched or contaminated by the unholy. Once this was done, physical touch with his disciples (like when Jesus invited Thomas to explore his wound-scars) was not a problem.

But anyway, back to the specifically Temple / Tabernacle language in John 14.1-3 - it is simply the word 'a place' which appears twice. Jesus is going away to prepare 'a place' for his disciples. In Deuteronomy, Moses repeatedly refers in chapters 12, 14, 16 and 26 to '*the place the LORD will choose as a dwelling for his Name*' or similar. This place was the place (or places - different locations at different times) where the Tabernacle of the Lord would be and to which the people would come to enter into the presence of God - where heaven and earth intersected, and where people would eat their festival sacrifices in an act denoting fellowship with God. God's 'Name' denoted his character, his nature. Right from the start of John's gospel, 'name' is important. In chapter 1, those who believe in the name of the true light of the world are given the right to become children of God (v12) and soon after John uses Tabernacle language, in the famous verse 14: '*The Word became flesh and made his dwelling (or Tabernacled) among us. We have seen his glory....*'. In Chapter 2, right after Jesus talked of his own body as the Temple of God, '*many people saw the signs he was performing and believed in his name*' (v23), and significantly this happened during Passover, a time when Deuteronomy commanded all Israelites go to the place where God's Name dwells (Deuteronomy 16.6). The importance of God's name or Jesus' name crops up in John 3.18 as well, but the key passages start in chapter 12, right where Jesus talks of his death. Jesus prays in v28:

> "*Father, glorify your name!*" *Then a voice came from heaven,* "*I have glorified it, and will glorify it again.*"

The importance of Jesus' name crops up again and again in Chapters 14-16, mainly about how the disciples are now to start asking for things in prayer in the name of Jesus. And finally, in the high priestly prayer in John 17, in verses 11-12, there is a highly significant use of 'the Name'. The Father will protect Jesus disciples by '*the power of Your name, the name you gave me, so that they may be one as we are one.*'

While I was with them, I protected them and kept them safe by that name you gave me.'

So this 'Name' that God placed on the tabernacle was now given to Jesus, and it is linked in to Jesus' unity with both his Father and his disciples. In other words, Jesus himself is the meeting point of heaven and earth, God and man - just the function that the Temple or Tabernacle had.

In John's gospel Jesus is not only the Temple / Tabernacle where sacrifices were offered, but he is also implicitly the High Priest who offers the sacrifice, and explicitly the sacrifice itself ('*Behold the Lamb of God who takes away the sins of the world*' John 1.29, 36).

Now, all the incarnations of the Jewish Temple consisted of more than just the Holiest place, the Holy Place and the Outer Courts, but also had many little rooms around the complex and the temple where serving priests prepared food and sacrifices and the like. Even the Tabernacle, when it was at Shiloh between the conquest of Canaan and King David, had a complex of rooms round about it, as per the findings that archaeologists at Shiloh were announcing just at the time I wrote this section. So when Jesus talks about the Father's House having many rooms, it fits perfectly with the Temple imagery. Jesus is the temple, and it is through his work on the cross and in resurrection that he provides many rooms for believers as serving priests to dwell and be joined in union with God and heaven, and the passage has no link to the second coming of Jesus (in fact, arguably the only times John's gospel refers to the end time events is when it talks of the general resurrection and judgement (5.28-9) and a brief allusion to Jesus return in the discussion between Peter and Jesus about the gospel authors fate (21.22-3)).

But let us grant, for the moment, the assumption that somehow Jesus is speaking about his second coming in John 14.1-3. Would the passage then have to mean what LaHaye and his ilk say? Would it prove a pre-trib rapture position? The answer must be no. We have already seen in our discussion of 1 Thessalonians 4 and its reference to Matthew 24 that going to be with Jesus at the end of the age does not entail going to heaven, but meeting with Jesus as he returns to earth. Not only that, but the book of Revelation, also authored by John, ends with the depiction of the new heavens and earth, where the central feature is the New Jerusalem descending from heaven to earth, described as '*the bride, the wife of the lamb*' (21.9). It shines with the very glory of God (v11), and in v3 clear Temple language is used - '*God's dwelling place is now among the people, and he will dwell with them. They will be his people, and God himself will be with them and be their God*'. Significantly, there is no Temple in the city, because God and the Lamb are its temple. There is no need for sun or moon, because *'the glory of God gives it light, and the Lamb is its lamp'* (v22-23). If we remember that in v11 the city itself shines with the glory of God, we are meant, I think, to realize that the Lamb in effect is the city, in which all the saved worshippers reside (many rooms!). Jesus / the city / the bride are all one, intertwined, and constitute an enduring connection between God and man, heaven and earth.

Now, I know we have gone on quite a rabbit trail of a detour, but there is a reason – apart from it just all flowed out when I was thinking about this issue. The reason is that one of LaHaye's favourite aphorisms is that 'a text without a context is a pretext' (or a 'proof text') and that we need to know the literal and historical background to understand a passage properly. I have dealt with the historical and biblical background and context and shown the rich Temple language involved in the passage, and situated it in the wider structure and argument of John's gospel – all to do with the coming death of Jesus, the purpose of his death and the coming of the Holy Spirit. Compare that with how LaHaye and company lift the passage totally out of context and make it refer to something – the Second Coming – that appears nowhere in the context or the flow of Jesus' thought. In other words, taking this verse out of context is the only way LaHaye and friends can justify making it the 'fundamental proof text' of the pre-trib rapture they claim it to be.

I should add one brief point here. Many pre-tribbers assert this passage must refer to a pre-tribulation rapture due to the wedding customs of Jesus times. They assert that the bride was taken into the groom's father's house for seven nights and that this corresponds to the rapture and seven years in heaven (God's house) in the pre-trib scenario. A groom would prepare a room / home, often in his father's house, for his bride before coming to take her 'home'. Wedding imagery is rife in Jesus' and New Testament teaching about his return. As we have already seen, it is far more likely that temple imagery is in view here. However, it is theoretically possible that John, being a complex and subtle theological writer, also intended echoes of wedding themes here. After all, the first 'sign' of Jesus that reveals his glory is at a wedding (John 2). And the themes of oneness and unity between Jesus and his followers in the imagery of the vine and branches in John 15, and in the prayer of Jesus in John 17 are easily compatible with the core concept of wedding and marriage. Even if there is a slight secondary allusion to marriage imagery here, though, as we have seen, both the immediate and longer context following this passage militate against any reference to Jesus' second coming. It is all about unity *now* with Jesus by the power of the Holy Spirit whom Jesus will send. And as we shall see in the next half of this section, the wedding language in Revelation 19-22 does not at all fit a pre-tribulation scenario. However, since the pattern of Jewish weddings turns up repeatedly in pre-tribulation justifications for their teachings, I include some more considerations specific to that topic in Appendix 2.

Let's go back to cover one other issue concerning 'the resurrected Saints'. As we saw, LaHaye gives no scriptural reference to back up his claim about 'Resurrected Saints'. However, we know the kind of arguments he and his camp will use, and one that you will see or hear being rammed home time and time again is the allegedly conclusive 'proof' provided by the fact that in the book of Revelation, the 'church' only appears in the first three chapters and the last three or four chapters. They claim that this means that chapters 4-18, which lack mention of the church, must be describing a time when the church per se does not exist – in other words, the period between the church's 'rapture' and the return of Jesus. To back this up, they claim that the first few verses of chapter 4 symbolically describe the rapture. These verses are where John is called up to heaven in his vision. These pre-trib teachers say that since John is a member of the church, a Christian, his calling into heaven in these verses should be taken as referring to the church being called to heaven before the tribulation. Also they argue that because there is a voice like a trumpet blast that calls him, this must refer to the rapture which similarly happens with a voice and trumpet blast in 1 Thessalonians 4. Although Revelation 4-18 do contain some references to God's people or 'saints', the pre-tribbers say that those that are not obviously referring to the Jews are 'tribulation saints' separate from the church age. An awful lot of pre-tribbers will also say that the messages to the seven churches in Revelation 2 and 3 are meant to indicate the changing character of the church through sequential time periods over the 2000 and counting years of its history.

Now, for people who take great pride and store in taking the bible 'literally' there seems to be a great deal of very unliteral interpretation going on here. When I read the letters to seven churches in seven Turkish cities in Revelation chapters 2 and 3, I understand.... letters to seven churches in seven Turkish cities in the 1st Century. When these pre-tribbers read it, they see depictions of different ages of the church with intricate analysis of different eras of church history and how they fit the bill. Now, if God had meant for us to have some inkling that these letters have a secret message that prophetically describe broad future church eras or trends, then surely some chronological markers might be in order? For instance bridging between each message to the churches by saying 'And *then* to the church in .... write...'. That would give at least some implication of chronological progression. But no, when you look at chapter 2 and 3 there is absolutely no hint of chronological progression, just.... wait for it.... letters to churches in different cities. There is no chronological linking, just the same structure : '*Write this letter to the angel of the church in...*' But immediately after these chapters, there *is* a chronological phrase when John is called to heaven in 4.1 '*Then* as I looked....'.

Again, when I read 4.1 I see an account of a vision where the one seeing the vision is called to heaven, but pre-tribbers, who claim to be oh-so-careful literalists, see indubitable evidence that the rapture is being referred to here. If this is supposed to be a reference to the rapture, which is a bodily resurrection, then how come in v2, it describes John as being taken to heaven 'in the Spirit', a phrase used in the Old Testament prophets like Ezekiel to refer to being taken somewhere in a vision? (That little gem wasn't my idea. I should have spotted it, but hat tip to a US pastor guy called Steven Anderson on youtube – I'm stealing it Mr Anderson, even if thou dost preach blasphemous calumnies about ye modern bible translations!). And what are we to make of the 'voice like a trumpet blast' link with 1 Thessalonians 4? Well, we've already seen that 1 Thessalonians 4 should be understood as referring to the second coming, not a separate rapture. That said, each bible writer uses words in a different ways – they have different literary styles. If references to a voice like 'a trumpet blast' must refer to the rapture, then what are we to make of Revelation 1.10 where the same phrase is used? Are there two raptures? Yes, if you read Revelation 1.10, John is not called to heaven there, but he does see Jesus - and isn't that the heart of the 'rapture' – the saints see Jesus as he is? Or could it be that pre-tribbers, yet again, are twisting scripture to suit their doctrine? If it looks like an account of a visionary going to heaven, sounds like an account of a visionary going to heaven... then it must, apparently, really be a prophetic foretelling of a rapture event. I don't think so! So much for reading the bible and prophetic works 'literally'!

Finally, let's go the core of this line of interpretation – that because the word 'church' is not mentioned from chapter 4 on, it should be understood that the church as we know it is not participating in the events on earth anywhere after chapter 4 until Jesus returns. Firstly, if the use of the word 'church' was meant to be an indicator of when the church departs and returns to earth, then the fact is that the church doesn't even return with Jesus in chapter 19! The word church / churches only reappears in Revelation 22.16, in the very closing sentences of the work. The verse reads *'I, Jesus, have sent my angel to give you this message for the churches. I am both the source of David and the heir to his throne. I am the bright morning star'*. If you look at this in context, it demonstrates how facile and off-beam the 'no word church = no church' line of interpretation really is. It happens in the closing exhortations. If we go back to chapter 1, we see similar use of the term church. The book of Revelation, although it contains a long prophetic vision, is in actual fact in the form of a letter. The first four verses read :

This is a revelation from Jesus Christ, which God gave him to show his servants the events that must soon take place. He sent an angel to present this revelation to his servant John, who faithfully reported everything he saw. This is his report of the word of God and the testimony of Jesus Christ.

God blesses the one who reads the words of this prophecy to the church, and he blesses all who listen to its message and obey what it says, for the time is near.

This letter is from John to the seven churches in the province of Asia.

Grace and peace to you from the one who is, who always was, and who is still to come; from the sevenfold Spirit before his throne....

Note v3 – it explicitly states that this prophecy is to the church, which is urged to listen and obey. This is rather strange if the bulk of the work is dedicated to describing a time when, according to pre-tribbers, the church is no longer around, a time when any believers in Jesus form a separate category of 'Tribulation saints' that can't properly be called the church. If we go back to 22.16, with an understanding of the literary customs of the time to do with letter writing (remember, pre-tribbers *say* that the literal interpretation should take into account such matters) then we see that here is a conclusion of the letter, using the same terms it started with. In 1.1-2, the revelation is sent from Christ to the church via an angel. In 22.16 Jesus concludes by saying '*I have sent my angel to give you this message to the churches*'. In other words the use of the word church here is an 'inclusio', a well recognized pattern whereby an author would bookend a letter with the basic summary or key message of the letter. (By the way, inclusio's aren't just for the start and end of letters. They can also work on a smaller scale, to indicate the start and end of a particular paragraph or argument). All the other uses of the word 'church' or 'churches' appear in chapters 1-3 where the writer is instructed to write to seven individual local churches, the same context in which 22.16 appears. Now 'church' means 'an assembly' or a 'gathering together'. It comes from an Old Testament concept of an assembly of the people of the Lord / Israel, and later Judaism developed a version initially for those living in communities in exile – 'synagogue' – which has essentially the same meaning as church – a gathering together. This explains why sometimes the New Testament refers to the church as a whole – the entire body of believers – and sometimes to individual congregations. Each author has different patterns of usage, and many other terms to describe the disciples of Jesus as a group or body of people. Originally the church was known as 'the Way', but later the nickname 'Christians' came to be used, as we know from the book of Acts. The terms 'saints' or 'holy people' and the phrase 'brothers' were also used, sometimes in combination with the word 'church'. Even individual authors varied their usage of the term 'church'. For instance, in the letter to the Ephesians, Paul only uses the word 'church' in the sense of the entire body of believers worldwide, but addresses his letter to 'God's holy people in Ephesus', whilst in other letters he greets his audience as 'the church(es) in xxxx' ((e.g. Galatians 1.2, 2 Corinthians 1.1). If we were to apply the same method of interpreting the pattern of usage of 'church' to some of Paul's letters as pre-tribbers do to Revelation, the absurdities become even more apparent. For instance, the word 'church' does not appear at all in the body of Paul's letter to the Romans, only appearing in chapter 16 when Paul conveys various personal greetings and messages. Does this mean that Romans 1-15 is really only for the Tribulation Saints, and perhaps Romans 16 should be taken symbolically as comforting messages of communion for the raptured church, maybe referring to them coming back to earth? Or take Colossians, where the word church is only mentioned in the first and last chapters. Does that mean that here we have the same pattern – the church, the rapture, events on earth for tribulation saints, and then the return of the church with Jesus? 'But you are being silly' might come the reply. Yes I am, but how is this any different in principle to the view that Revelation must mean there is no church on earth during chapters 4-19 because the specific word 'church' is not mentioned?

Try this on for size. When the book of Revelation focuses on the here and now, on letters to individual congregations, it talks of churches. When it goes into vision mode, from chapter 4 on, whenever it describes the church, it describes them as a vast body of individuals, as God's holy people. To quote a certain meerkat, 'Seemples, no? Cchhk!'

Most of the focus of Revelation is on the judgements of God against those who resist his rule and righteousness. However, there are a few places where those who are faithful to God pop up. Let's go through Revelation and have a look at these themes. We'll start with a key theme – white clothes. In chapter 3, Jesus rebukes the church in Sardis, saying that unless they wake up and do right, he will come suddenly:

> *As unexpectedly as a thief. Yet there are some in the church in Sardis who have not soiled their clothes with evil. They will walk with me in white, for they are worthy. All who are victorious will be clothed in white. I will never erase their names from the Book of Life, but I will announce before my Father and his angels that they are mine. (v3-5)*

Notice it is those victorious, those who do not do evil, who are clothed in white. And also note that even if we take the view that this is describing part of the church age, it can't be the very last age of the church according to the schema adopted by those pre-tribbers who read it this way, as Jesus addresses one more church afterwards. Similarly, in rebuking the church in Laodicea for their indifference, Jesus urges them to buy white garments from him (v18).

Revelation 4 and 5 focus largely on heaven. In 4.4, the 24 heavenly elders who surround God's throne are dressed in white also. In chapter 6, martyred saints appear, calling out for justice for their murder. They also are given white robes to wear, and told to '*rest a little longer until the full number of their brothers - their fellow servants of Jesus who were to be martyred - had joined them*' (v11).

I want you to notice a few things. Firstly, why are they clothed in white after their martyrdom? We have in effect, already been told. Jesus had already told the church in Sardis that *all* who are victorious would be clothed in white - those who did not soil themselves with evil. These martyrs had been victorious, they had refused to bow down to evil, and had remained faithful witnesses to Jesus, paying with their lives. In the early church, this counted as a great victory over the enemies of God. Secondly, this is the first mention of martyrs in the vision portion of Revelation. Therefore, it is likely that these are martyrs from all the previous generations. Even by the time of the writing of Revelation, many Christians had been martyred. Now, if there really was a pre-trib rapture that marked the end of the church dispensation, surely this passage would contain some clue that the martyrs to come were different to the martyrs past. However, there is no such distinction. Those yet to be martyred in the great tribulation are simply called 'servants of Jesus' and 'brothers' to those already martyred. 'Brothers' here is not just some religious word, but is significant - meaning men and women *of the same community or group.* You can't get much more continuous than this. They are of a piece. Think about it. According to the pre-tribbers, there is a rapture of the church, including Christians who are dead, and then a completely different set of 'tribulation saints'. But here those martyred go straight to join those earlier martyrs - which is rather strange if the 'strict division' rationale behind the pre-trib position has any validity, wouldn't you say?

In Revelation 7, the angels place seals upon the foreheads of Jewish people who belong to God, so that they can escape the judgements to come. This has echoes not only of the Passover, where the Jews escaped God's judgement, not by being removed physically, but by being spared spiritually, in the midst of judgement on their oppressors, but also of another passage which listeners familiar with the Old Testament would immediately grasp - Ezekiel 9. In that passage, the context again is God's judgement on sinners. God's glory is preparing to depart the Temple because of the sins of Israel. God tells the angels to put a mark on the foreheads of all those who weep and sigh and mourn for the sins being committed in Jerusalem, and to then start killing all those without the mark. Once again, the righteous are not swept out of the way, but remain in place, spared in the midst of judgement. (I emphasize this, because one of the great planks of the pre-trib position, repeated ad naseum by many of its proponents, is that 'Jesus as a loving groom wouldn't let his church go through the tribulation.') Revelation 7 goes on to refer to a crowd beyond numbering from every tribe and nation, all dressed in white, and praising God around the throne. They are described as '*the ones who came out of the great tribulation. They have washed their robes in the blood of the lamb and made them white*' (v14). Now at least some prominent pre-tribbers say that this refers to the church in heaven, while the Tribulation goes on below on earth. They say that 'come out of' really means 'people preserved from'. However, virtually all other scholars believe that 'come out of' means those martyred in the Tribulation. This is supported by a number of factors – firstly, the focus on martyrdom in the book of Revelation, when the visions touch upon God's people. Secondly, these believers are clearly in heaven – because they have 'come out of the tribulation', v15-17 describes their reward as serving in God's temple, with God giving them shelter. Never again will they be hungry or thirsty, or scorched by the sun. Every tear will be wiped from their eyes. If this is a description of the already raptured church, then they already have had their tears wiped away and are living in bliss. It hardly makes sense to say that a body of people are vanished from earth to spare them from the trials of the tribulation, but are then given recompense from the trials they have suffered, but it makes perfect sense that this is a reward of those who have suffered death for the sake of Jesus during the great Tribulation. Not only that, but it fits in well with the pattern of exaltation of those who have been oppressed which we find all through Scripture.

In chapter 12, there is an account of a cosmic battle between Satan and his angels and the heavenly angels, and Satan, 'the accuser' is thrown out of heaven and cast down to earth. A loud voice proclaims in v10-11 :

> ... *the accuser of our brothers*
> *has been thrown down to earth—*
> *the one who accuses them*
> *before our God day and night.*
> *And they have defeated him by the blood of the Lamb*
> *and by their testimony.*
> *And they did not love their lives so much*
> *that they were afraid to die.*

Firstly, Satan accuses brothers, which as we have seen is an identity marker that links those already martyred with those martyred in the Tribulation. Here, these same brothers whom Satan accuses defeat him in part because they were prepared to die. Now, if these brothers are the church in heaven, as the pre-trib position suggests, they have either already died, or never died at all but were transformed directly to resurrection bodies! Pre-tribbers, of course, will say that these are their 'Tribulation Saints'. But if we go on a little further, to v17, we find that Satan, symbolically described as a dragon, declares war against '*all who keep God's commandments and maintain their testimony for Jesus*'. Tribulation saints, the pre-tribbers will doubtless say again. However, if we go to Revelation 19.10 and 22.9 we find virtually the same phrases. In 19.10, John is rebuked by an angel he is about to worship, saying '*I am a servant of God, just like you and your brothers who testify about their faith in Jesus*'. 22.9 is virtually the same scenario, except that the angel says he is God's servant, '*just like you and your brothers the prophets, as well as all who obey what is written in this book.*' Now, if pre-tribbers were to be consistent, then since they say that John being called up to heaven shows he represents the church (being raptured), then when angels talk to John about him and his brothers, he must still represent the church. And since the same book of Scripture also refers in passages like chapter 12 to 'brothers' persecuted in the tribulation, using virtually the same terms of description, doesn't that rather suggest that here we simply have the church of Jesus Christ as we know it today in the Tribulation?

Revelation 13.7 briefly mentions 'God's holy people' in the context of a satanically empowered political power, symbolized as 'the beast', which was allowed not just to make war on 'God's holy people' or 'saints', but actually to conquer them. John expected his audience to be familiar enough with the Old Testament to pick up exactly what he was alluding to here – the book of Daniel, particularly chapter 7, where there is a similar beast, who was similarly boastful against God and God's people, and was permitted to wage war on them and defeat them, until God '*came and judged in favour of his holy people*' (v21-2, but see v 8-10 and 19-27 in general). This theme of God's people being persecuted at the end of the age and having to endure defeat and purifying trials also occurs in Daniel 11.33-6 and 12.10. Similarly Revelation goes on in 13.10 and 14.1 say that persecution '*means that God's holy people must endure persecution patiently and remain faithful*' and '*God's holy people must endure persecution patiently, obeying his commands and maintaining their faith in Jesus*'. There are a couple of references to 'God's holy people' in 17.6 and 18.24 concerning a symbolic great prostitute / Babylon who is '*drunk with the blood of God's holy people who were witnesses for Jesus.*' But the real kicker for pre-tribbers comes in 19.8. You see, for them, Revelation 19 describes '*the wedding feast of the Lamb*' which they believe to be the raptured church in heaven, the '*bride who made herself ready*' (v7) and who then descends with Jesus at his return. V8 says

> *She has been given the finest of pure white linen to wear."*
> *For the fine linen represents the good deeds of God's holy people*

There it is again – exactly the same phrase - 'God's holy people' - used without anything to distinguish it from the usages earlier where, according to the pre-trib view, Revelation refers to 'Tribulation Saints' rather than the church. What's more, just like those saints in the Tribulation, the church is wearing pure white. The conclusion is inescapable for those who will truly pay attention to the literary imagery. The persecuted saints earlier on are the same group as the church here. And for completeness' sake, we should note that Revelation ends at 22.21 with *'May the grace of the Lord Jesus be with God's holy people'*. And this comes after the word 'church' reappears in v16. In other words, if we trace the themes through Revelation, then the idea of a separate group of 'Tribulation saints' to be resurrected separately to the church is utterly unwarranted, a figment of pre-Tribbers imagination.

Now, I know this has been more like elephant trails than rabbit trails - long ones, but I thought it was important to show how a more proper exegesis - really looking at the context, literary and historical - completely undermines the Pre-Trib assertions on these points. And one, final, final (no - really!) point on this 'proof', although it could equally apply elsewhere: notice the repeated exhortations to the saints - which we have established means the church, not some special separate group - to patiently endure suffering, and focus on martyrdom. Compare that to the repeated emphasis of many pre-Tribbers (and LaHaye is a prime culprit here) that Jesus will rapture the church because he loves them too much to let them go through the Tribulation (which to them is also known as 'the Wrath'), and that their view of the rapture is an encouragement, whereas any other view is fear-mongering. Aside from the insult to those brothers and sisters being martyred and suffering right now - funny how the comfortable Western church escapes suffering in this scenario - we have already seen how in Revelation there are a number of clear allusions to Old Testament events and passages where the righteous are not *taken out of the way* of judgement, but are spared *in the midst* of God's judgement. The pre-trib view also does not sit at all well with Jesus' depiction of the persecution of his disciples in the last days in Luke 21.12-19 and parallel passages in Matthew 24 and Mark 12. Just like in Revelation, Jesus warns that only those who stand firm to the end will save their souls. But the key point is that Jesus' view of well-being in these circumstances is paradoxical in the extreme. V16-18 read *'Even those closest to you—your parents, brothers, relatives, and friends—will betray you. They will even kill some of you. And everyone will hate you because you on account of my name. But not a hair of your head will perish!'* The will kill some of you, yet not a hair of your head will perish? Hardly the words of someone planning on putting on a 'rapture rescue mission' to spare the church suffering, is it?

On a wider note, we as disciples are called to be followers of Jesus, and both Jesus and the apostles repeatedly say that following him in suffering is a part of that process (Jesus - *'Take up your cross and follow me'*. Paul for example says in Colossians 1.24 *'I am glad when I suffer for you in my body, for I am participating in the sufferings of Christ that continue for his body, the church'* or Romans 8.17 *'And since we are his children, we are his heirs. In fact, together with Christ we are heirs of God's glory. But if we are to share his glory, we must also share his suffering'.* Then there is 1 Peter 4.1 *'So then, since Christ suffered physical pain, you must arm yourselves with the same attitude he had, and be ready to suffer, too. For if you have suffered physically for Christ, you have finished with sin'.* Finally note that Barnabas, a nickname meaning 'Encourager', and Paul at one point strengthen the new believers in Acts 14.22. How do they do this?

> *'They encouraged them to continue in the faith, reminding them that we must suffer many hardships to enter the Kingdom of God').*

I could go on with similar general quotes, but specifically suffering in obedience, a theme found in Revelation at several points, also pops up to do with the perfecting process and glory. It applied to Jesus (Hebrews 2.10 *'God, for whom and through whom everything was made, chose to bring many children into glory. And it was only right that he should make Jesus, through his suffering, a perfect leader, fit to bring them into their salvation')* and if you remember, those passages in Daniel 11 and 12 about the suffering of God's holy people (aka 'saints') explicitly say that the purpose is to perfect and purify. In Revelation, it is only after much suffering and the number of martyrs being completed that the church is described as having 'made herself ready' (19.7). *Then* the time of the wedding feast of the lamb comes, because the bride is ready - because she is like him, she has been perfected through suffering, just as Jesus was. Only now can she also share in his glory. Amen.

PROOF 4

At the rapture, there is no judgement on earth, but at the Second Coming Christ judges the inhabitants of the earth (Matthew 25.31-46).

PROOF 11

At the rapture, there is no mention of Satan, but at the Second Coming, Satan is bound in the abyss for 1000 years (Revelation 19.20-20.3)

PROOF 12

At the rapture, there is the judgement seat of Christ (1 Corinthians 4.5, 2 Corinthians 5.9-10, but at the Second Coming, there is no time or place for the judgement seat of Christ.

Although these aren't quite as closely intertwined as 'proofs' 1 and 5, they are still somewhat related, so I will take them together. Firstly, the claim that in a pre-trib rapture there is no judgement on earth has a major internal inconsistency. If you read the vivid accounts of the rapture in the pre-trib publications, both fiction and 'non-fiction', they will describe the alleged terrible after effects – families ripped apart by loved ones disappearing, planes and cars and essential systems crashing as many of their pilots / drivers /operators vanish in a split second. In the bible a disaster of such cataclysmic proportions would surely be called a judgement, especially if it is the consequence of the righteous being removed.

Leaving that point aside, here we have, yet again, several assertions without any Scripture to back them up, and unsurprisingly, we once again find circular reasoning, where the tenets of a pre-trib rapture are assumed and then the logical outcomes of that assumption are used to 'prove' those very same inbuilt assumptions. Let's look more at the 'no judgement on earth at the rapture' thing. No scripture support is given, but the argument is basically that 1 Corinthians 15 and 1 Thessalonians 4 have no mention of earthly judgement of any kind, therefore there is none during the rapture event described there. But absence of evidence does not mean evidence of absence, particularly in the case of these passages. They are in letters directed to specific churches to address specific issues germane to their situation. They are in no way attempting to set out an even remotely comprehensive account of events in the end times in the way that Revelation does (after a fashion). In 1 Thessalonians 4, Paul deals with the issue of what happens to believers when they die? Will there be any chance of seeing them again? Paul reassures his readers by telling them that Jesus will bring the dead souls of believers with him and at that moment the resurrection of the dead occurs, and the souls are re-united with their resurrection bodies, and straight after, those believers alive are transformed and all these resurrection bodies meet Jesus as he returns to earth. Why would Paul want to talk about the fate of unbelievers, when his sole purpose here is to reassure grieving Christians about their recently deceased brothers and sisters (remember Paul had only recently founded the church he was writing to, and in the meantime at least one believer must have died)? Thus the fact that no judgement is mentioned in the passage has absolutely no evidential weight in the way that LaHaye et all try and force on to it. Nor is the fact that Satan is not mentioned relevant in any way.

Similarly in 1 Corinthians 15, Paul is dealing with the false belief of some Christians in the Corinthian church that there is no future resurrection. Paul deals with this via a number of arguments, pointing out that Jesus is the 'first fruits' of the resurrection and that all those who belong to him will be resurrected when he returns (v23). *Then the end will come, when he will turn the Kingdom over to God the Father, having destroyed every ruler and authority and power'* (v24). Now the resurrection of the dead Christians is here immediately followed by Jesus' turning the Kingdom of God over to God, having destroyed every ruler and authority and power. This would be rather nonsensical if the pre-trib position were true, since in that belief-system after the resurrection of Christians, then the powers and rulers – whether we take these to be spiritual demonic beings or evil earthly rulers – are wreaking havoc on earth for seven years. Now, it is true that you could argue that there is room for a gap here, and that Paul is talking about what happens seven years later, but by far the most natural reading is that the 'end' immediately follows the resurrection. After all, if Paul wanted to indicate or allow a time gap, he could have said 'Sometime after this the end will come', rather than 'Then the end will come'. Later on Paul describes the events of this resurrection in terms of a 'rapture' that includes the transformation of living Christians (v51 on). The point for us is that once again, the absence of any reference to judgement is not evidence that there is no judgement, but rather reflects the fact that Paul's concern here was to refute disbelief in the resurrection among some Corinthian Christians. There was no need to him to refer to the fate or experience of non-believers at all. Oh, and by the way, if we take the rulers and authorities that Jesus destroys in v24 as spiritual powers of darkness, then in actual fact Satan *is* in effect mentioned in a passage that deals with the resurrection and rapture.

Let's turn to judgement. Let's look at that passage in Matthew 25 about Jesus judging the nations of the earth. Let's look at .... context! It is preceded by two parables that all appear to concern the behaviour of *believers* in relation to his second coming. All of them feature judgement for deeds done or not done, preparations made or not made. Then Jesus describes judgement at his second coming. Now the fact that the preceding parables concern solely believers does not *prove* that believers must be included in those judged at Jesus visible return to reign described immediately after, but it does *very* strongly suggest it. In the view of most pre-Tribbers I have seen, the judgement described in the 2nd half of Matthew 25 does *not* include the church / Christians, precisely because they believe the church has been judged in heaven during the Tribulation, a belief we will consider a little later on. However, is there anything in this text that would support that notion? Quite the opposite. Jesus describes himself as having all the nations gathered before him, at which point he will separate the people out into the righteous and the evil. The criteria is deeds of charity or otherwise towards the 'least of my brothers', variously interpreted as the Jews, Christians, the poor, or combinations of these groups (personally I suspect all three are in view). Those who are righteous are told *'Come, you who are blessed by my Father, inherit the Kingdom prepared for you from the creation of the world'* (v 34) whereas the wicked undergo eternal judgement. Who inherits the Kingdom? Well, the New Testament tells us who. In James 2.5 God has promised the kingdom to those who love him - that would be the church, wouldn't it? And in several letters, Paul warns his (Christian) readers that those who do not live right will not inherit the kingdom of God (1 Corinthians 6.9-10, Galatians 5.21 and Ephesians 5.5). But most interestingly of all, Paul introduces his discussion about the rapture in 1 Corinthians 15 with v50, which says that our mortal physical bodies cannot inherit the Kingdom of God. In Matthew 25.31, if the pre-trib scenario is true, these are survivors of the Tribulation who remain in their earthly bodies, and yet there is no sign of there being a need for a resurrection transformation of their mortal bodies before they inherit the kingdom of God. Of course, pre-tribbers might argue that this is just like my earlier arguments about why no judgement of unbelievers is mentioned in Paul's rapture passages - it's not germane to the writer's purpose. Jesus is not detailing the end time events precisely, but is focussed on the coming judgement and nothing else, pre-tribbers might say. So here's a challenge for you. Go to Matthew 25.31 on and see if there is any hint that believers aren't included in this judgement. There isn't any. It just speaks of all the peoples or nations being brought to judgement, and individuals judged. And that's without taking into account the earlier parables aimed exclusively at Jesus' disciples (and the fact that this teaching was made only to his disciples).

Let's finish this section with proof 12. Here LaHaye starts off by saying that at the rapture, there is 'the judgement seat of Christ', by which he means a judgement of believers for their deeds done in life. He cites two passages, 1 Corinthians 4.5 and 2 Corinthians 5.9-10. In the former, Paul is talking about making judgements about our fellow believers, or even ourselves, and then he says:

> *My conscience is clear, but that doesn't prove I'm right. It is the Lord himself who will examine me and decide.*
>
> *So don't make judgements about anyone ahead of time—before the Lord returns. For he will bring our darkest secrets to light and will reveal our private motives. Then God will give to each one whatever praise is due.*

Paul's focus is on the *fact* of judgement, and not at all on the *timing* or *location*. We can infer that the judgement happens when 'the Lord returns', as anytime before that is 'ahead of time' for making judgements. Now, of course, a pre-tribber would say that this return of the Lord is the rapture, but can you see anything in the text that indicates a judgement seat in heaven? I can't. The Lord is said to 'return'. If he is in heaven, there is only one place he can 'return' to, namely the earth. The only way you can make this apply to the rapture is by a complete 'gratuitous assertion'. You have to assume the complete panoply of pre-trib assertions to make this 'proof' work. Similarly, in 2 Corinthians 5, Paul is discussing living for God, whether in our earthly bodies or out of them (i.e. dead, without a body, waiting for a resurrection body), when he says:

> *So whether we are here in this body or away from this body, our goal is to please him. For we must all stand before Christ to be judged. We will each receive whatever we deserve for the good or evil we have done in this earthly body.*

Again, is there any indication that could lead us to conclude that this judgement will happen in heaven some seven years before Jesus returns? No. To reach such a conclusion you have to *assume* a pre-trib position, with its belief in the rapture of the church and judgement in heaven while judgement is poured out against unbelievers on earth. There isn't even a hint of a time indication, although we can assume that Paul is talking about the end of the age. Pre-tribbers like LaHaye often label this as 'the Judgement Seat of Christ' to contrast it to what they call 'the Great White Throne Judgement' (see the next 'proof'). It sets up a division in both their own and their hearers' minds, giving the idea of a discrete event which they can then use to 'prove' their 'clear' distinctions between the rapture and the Second Coming.

LaHaye asserts without any Scriptural reference at all, that there is 'no time or place for the Judgement seat of Christ' at the second coming, by which he means judgement specifically of Christians. Firstly, given that the passages he quotes for the 'Judgement seat of Christ' make no claims as to place, how can LaHaye assert categorically that there is no 'place' for the Judgement seat of Christ at his visible return to earth? We have already seen that the implicit claim that believers aren't among the subjects of judgement at the end of the age described in Matthew 25 is almost certainly false. I suggest that the believers are judged at the same time as everyone else (something we will come back to later). And even if we grant the assumption, so closely tied up in the pre-trib position, that there is, in fact, a separate judgement for believers, surely the eternal and omniscient God can render good judgement on all believers in a nano-second of time? Thus even in a post-trib position such as I hold, believers could be raptured, judged in a split second of time when they join Jesus, and then return with Him in triumph, all as part of the same continuous sequence of events. This just goes to show that LaHaye's bald assertions here prove nothing, even when we generously grant a number of pre-trib assumptions into the equation.

I want you to look at all these passages about judgement, whether of all the people, or of believers - in Matthew 25, Revelation 20, and the two passages in letters from Paul to the Corinthians that we quoted just a few paragraphs ago. In each case, the criteria of judgement are deeds done or the secret motives of the heart. Two out of the four (the Corinthian passages) focus on believers, naturally, as the audience was the church, but neither do these actually exclude non-believers from the judgement referred to. The other two, Matthew 25 and Revelation 20 talk about people being judged by their deeds, but also about eternal salvation or damnation. In Revelation 20, it mentions the book of Life, usually understood to mean recording those who belong to Jesus or are destined for eternal life, but as one amongst many books which have recorded the deeds of all, those in the book of Life and those not. In short, when you look at the New Testament passages on the Final judgement, it looks like the same event of judgement is the scene for the judgement of all, believers and non-believers alike. The burden of proof is on those who claim otherwise (especially since - as far as I can see - this position has been the one taught throughout church history up until relatively recently). And quoting a couple of verses out of context and pretending they have any link to a rapture or judgement in heaven, like LaHaye does with the two Corinthian quotes, just isn't going to cut it.... such desperate interpretations do not even remotely resemble a responsible *'rightly dividing the word of God'*.

PROOF 15

At the rapture the Tribulation begins (Matt 24.9-32, 2 Thess 2.3-12), but at the Second Coming the 1000 year kingdom of Christ begins (Great White Throne) (Rev 19.11-15, 20.4-6).

I'm skipping around a bit, and I include this one here, as it also touches on judgement, which was the main theme in the last set. The first thing that immediately jumped out at me as suggesting considerable confusion in LaHaye's mind is that bit in brackets 'Great White Throne'. If you read Revelation 20, v4-6 does seem to report a judgement at the start of the 1000 year reign of Christ on earth, but it is not the 'Great White Throne' judgement. This happens *after* the 1000 year reign in Revelation 20.11-15. It is the very final judgement of all the remaining dead, just at the point where God then brings in the new heavens and earth (21.1). The 20.4-6 'judgement' is explicitly said to only refer to those who were martyred during the great tribulation. For such a basic factual error to occur in a set of supposedly 'irrefutable' proofs based on 'literal' interpretation of the bible - well, quite frankly, it does not particularly inspire one's confidence!

There are several other points to note here; one is that if you look closely at 20.4-6 then labelling it a judgement seems overstating the case. Certainly there are people seated on thrones who are given authority to judge. But who are these people? The passage goes on to describe seeing those who were faithful unto death during the tribulation, and that these martyrs are raised from the dead, and made into priests of God and Christ, who will reign with Christ for 1000 years. Reigning - thrones, it's pretty obvious. Note that they were given authority to judge, but it never actually mentions judgement. Now, to a pre-tribber like LaHaye, this passage is made to fit his scenario by claiming that these are resurrected 'Tribulation saints', but this, once again is a form of circular reasoning. The only way you can make this a special non-church group of followers of Jesus is if you assume the pre-trib scheme of interpretation anyway. Take away that forced interpretation, and the natural way to read it is to take it as referring to Christians, members of the church body, who have refused to deny Christ during the reign of the anti-Christ. Secondly, there is nothing to say that Revelation includes everything in chronological order. Originally there were no chapter divisions. It is more natural, I suggest, to read Revelation 19.1 to 20.6 as referring to a whole series of events that occurred all at one time - in one day, in fact. Thus a resurrection of believers in Jesus at this time fits neatly into a post-trib interpretation, even though it might not appear to match the order of events described by Paul. But notice that Revelation author's concern here is not so much the sequence of events as a description of how the rule of Christ in the Millennium was to be ordered and delegated. John saw at that point in his vision the souls of dead saints resurrected to reign, just as the apostle Paul talked, with a slightly different emphasis, of the resurrected and transformed church going to be with Jesus forever at the moment returns (and where is Jesus? As ever, he is now and will ever be until the end of the age, reigning on the throne, dispensing righteous judgement, just as these saints are seated on thrones and given authority to judge).

In Revelation, however, only those martyred for their faith under the antichrist are referred to in this first resurrection, whereas in the rapture as told by Paul in 1 Corinthians 15 and 1 Thessalonians 4, it is the whole church - all the dead along with the living - that receives resurrection bodies. Surely this is a contradiction? People like LaHaye would argue that this is evidence for something like their separate 'Tribulation saints'. However, the problem with that assertion is that if the pre-trib rapture view is correct this is not the first resurrection, as it is labelled in Revelation 20, but the second one - the rapture being the first, since Paul clearly refers to a bodily resurrection in both his passages dealing with the rapture. I suggest that what we have in Revelation 20.4-6 is an example of what is called a synecdoche, where part of something is used to stand for the whole. The focus in Revelation 4 onwards, when it has touched on the church, has been the fact that it will be faced with tremendous opposition under the anti-Christ, and that many will be martyred. I don't think there is a single passage in Revelation 4-18 where the saints of God are mentioned apart from oppression, bloodshed and martyrdom. The author is, I suggest, continuing this theme by referring to the resurrected martyrs only, but has in view the entire body of believers in Jesus. I suspect that there is a clue supporting this view just a few verses earlier. This is where, just before Jesus and the armies of heaven are revealed as they return to earth, John starts to fall down to worship an angel, the angel forbids him, saying *'I am a servant of God, just like you and your brothers who testify about their faith in Jesus'* (19.10). Those referred to in the first resurrection in 20.4-6 are similarly described as those who were beheaded *'for their testimony about Jesus'* with the additional information that they had refused to take the mark of the beast or worship the image of this false God. This faith-attitude is what would be expected of any true Christian through the ages. The author's visions are about the church in the end times, so this is what he focuses on, but this first resurrection was of all the believers. Notice it doesn't quite say that *just* those martyred under the anti-Christ are referred to here, it just doesn't mention anyone else. It also says those in the first resurrection do not need to fear the second death, something that also suggests to me that it refers to all those who belong to Christ. Revelation 20.4-6 does however refer to 'all of the rest of the dead' being resurrected after the 1000 year reign of Christ. (Having just about finished the book, I found out that there is a probable translation issue in Revelation 20.4-6, and that the arguments I have used in the paragraphs above and below are partially unnecessary, although still potentially useful. The Greek text and the verb tenses mean the passage is most literally translated as reporting what John saw, but also adding explanatory notes which show that he was referring to all saints, and specifically mentioning the Tribulation martyrs as a subset within the group. A good translation to capture this sense of the Greek would run something as follows - something I have lifted from the article on Revelation 20 in the useful sources at the back of the book:

> **And I saw thrones, and they sat upon them,**
> *(and judgement had been given unto them AND the souls that were beheaded for the witness of Jesus, and for the word of God, and which had not worshipped the beast, neither his image, neither had received his mark upon their foreheads, or in their hands);*
>
> **and they were living and reigning with Christ a thousand years.**
> *(But the rest of the dead lived not again until the thousand years were finished);*

The bold bits represent what John saw in his vision, the rest his explanation with the proper tenses indicating past tenses and the fact that there martyrs are a subset of the whole.)

Another reason I suspect that a resurrection of all the saints is being taught here is because of one of the earliest church documents, one that may be older than some of the New Testament, commonly known as the Didache (Teaching). Its full title translates roughly as 'The Teaching of our Lord through the Twelve apostles to the Nations (i.e. Gentiles)' and it is something like a basic church manual, containing instructions for church life and teaching for new converts on proper moral Christian living, and I have no doubt that it summarizes accurately the views of the twelve apostles. In the very last chapter it deals with the end of the age. Firstly - and very germane to the whole debate - it instructs believers on what to expect under the reign of the anti-Christ and urges them (and us) to remain faithful to the end and so be saved, even amidst the suffering. Tellingly, it then describes clearly the rapture right after the reign of the anti-Christ and clearly ties it in with the visible coming of Jesus. The whole Didache ends with: *'And then the signs of truth shall be revealed. First, the sign of a spreading rift in heaven; then a sign of the sound of a trumpet; and third, the resurrection of the dead, but not all of the dead. But as it was said, "the Lord shall come and all His Holy Ones with Him."Then the world shall see the Lord coming in the clouds of heaven'.* Thus it appears that for the apostles, the rapture resurrection is only of the righteous, and happens at the time that Jesus appears and returns to reign, which coincides pretty closely to what find in Revelation 19-20.6, especially if we accept the view that the description of those resurrected includes all of God's saints.

So what of this second resurrection, and the 'Great White Throne judgement'? It comes immediately after an account of one last rebellion against Christ, inspired by Satan who was released from his 1000 year imprisonment, with a great many killed. Then 'all the dead' appear before God's throne of judgement. They are judged for their deeds, but those whose names are not written in the book of Life are thrown into the lake of fire for eternity, which is also described as the 'second death'. Those who were resurrected in the first resurrection have no reason to fear the second death, we were told in 20.4-6. If my view is correct, then that is because they are 'saved', believers who trust in Christ. (I believe that they are not the only ones to escape the lake of fire in Revelation 20. Everyone at the final judgement is judged on deeds, and the passage never says that only those who believe in Christ escape the lake of fire. This category also includes, I suggest, those who have remained faithful to God before the time of Christ, and also those counted worthy who had never heard the gospel, but responded to the divine light they had, and lived according to it).

Let's now turn to the Rapture part of this 'proof'. As evidence for the rapture being the start of the Tribulation, LaHaye cites two passages, Matthew 24.9-32, and 2 Thessalonians 2.3-12. On Matthew 24, my first question would be – why does LaHaye only start at v9? I don't know for sure, but I suspect I know why. This is the point where Jesus predicts persecution as a sign of his coming. That's fair enough, you might say, if LaHaye is talking about the rapture preceding the tribulation. However, if people were to look at that thing that LaHaye (correctly) claims is so important – context – then it would rather undermine his position. The disciples drew Jesus' attention to the stupendous building blocks of the Temple, and Jesus assured them that the whole building would be completely demolished. They privately ask him about both this, and (since they would doubtless – primed by the prophecies in Daniel about the abomination desolating the temple, have associated the destruction of God's holy Temple with the time of apocalyptic disaster before the coming of the promised Messiah) about the signs of Jesus' return and the end of the age. Jesus starts (v4-8) by warning of false prophets and Messiahs, saying that there would be wars and threats of wars, earthquakes and famines, which he described as just the first 'birth pangs'. These are things that LaHaye knows all his target audience - the church in the west - will be very aware of as happening now. For LaHaye's pre-trib schema to work, there has to be a radical break between what we experience now and the tribulation which won't affect the church. Now, Jesus answers his disciples by teaching about things which are ongoing now, and moves straight into v9 with not a gap. There is no sign of some radical break in Jesus teaching here. He just goes on talking to 'you' – his disciples, and by extension us – those who are also disciples and who obey the teaching of the apostles - about what will happen to us. There is not even the slightest hint that there is a break where suddenly it will not be the disciples and those who are spiritually descended from them as it were, but another group entirely who will face the suffering and persecution he refers to. If the rapture is such a big deal in the end times for the church as LaHaye assets, why does Jesus not even hint, however obscurely, at such a division or event? LaHaye, I suggest, is in fact - if not necessarily in intention - relying on an audience so used to accepting snippets of scripture taken out of context, that they will simply accept that v9 starts an account of what happens after a 'secret rapture' of the church. It really is ultra-secret - so secret that Jesus never even hints at it!

Another thing that really bugs me about this kind of dicing and splicing of scripture here is the way it undermines the suffering of non-Western Christians. Unfortunately, the Western church as a whole tends to be somewhat unaware of the level of persecution Christians undergo outside the Western World right at this moment. As a trustee of a charity that exists to help such Christians in one nation where they are badly persecuted, I am very aware of the suffering of my brothers and sisters. I suggest that a major reason LaHaye can get away with chopping off this passage to start at v9 is the lack of true awareness of the suffering of the church in much of his intended audience. For many of our brothers and sisters, not only is the part before v9 part of their daily experience, but so is that of v9 and the immediately following verses. Those suffering brothers and sisters would, I suggest, be far more likely to spot this artificial division for the fraudulent interpretation that it is.

And so, if you read your way through Matthew 24, you will find Jesus repeatedly referring to his disciples or his church's role or attitude in these matters, never that of any special group of 'Tribulation' saints. And, as we saw in refuting 'proof 1', Jesus in this chapter is absolutely crystal clear and explicit about when the events of the 'rapture' occur - the world-wide gathering of believers, the blast of the trumpet occur at the time of his visible appearing when he is descending to earth (in other words, these gathered-together believers meet him in the air). And he introduces this section of his teaching with one, utterly decisive statement that should put the pre-trib position to bed for anyone who takes the words of Jesus seriously: '*After the tribulation (or anguish) of those days....*' (v29). Given that Jesus is answering a question about the end of the world, and given that the only other time he mentions the word 'tribulation/anguish (Greek word *thlipsis*) is in v21 where he says that the tribulation of those days will be the greatest there ever has or ever will be, so great that if God did not cut them short for the sake of his 'chosen ones' or 'the elect' not a single person would survive, we have to conclude that this must be *the* 'Great Tribulation' that pre-tribbers claim the church avoids. Now who are these 'elect' - or, as other translations have it 'chosen ones' - for whom the tribulation will be shortened? The passage immediately tells us. After v22, where these 'elect' are first mentioned, Jesus goes on to say:

> *Then if anyone tells* **you***, 'Look, here is the Messiah,' or 'There he is,' don't believe it. For false messiahs and false prophets will rise up and perform great signs and wonders so as to deceive, if possible, even God's* **elect***. See, I have warned* **you** *about this ahead of time.*

> *"So if someone tells* **you***, 'Look, the Messiah is out in the desert,' don't bother to go and look. Or, 'Look, he is hiding here,' don't believe it!* (v23-6).

I have emphasized a few words to demonstrate something. Jesus warns of false prophets whose great signs and wonders will deceive, if possible, even the 'elect', and then says 'Look, I've now warned you ahead of time'. There is no hint that this warning was to be stored up for some separate group in the future. It is his disciples, his church, whom he warns of these things. Why warn them of these things if they are not going to be around because they have been raptured? They would have no need to heed such warnings, for they would be safe in heaven. Jesus, just before his death, thought it vitally important to warn his disciples about what would occur to them and those they spiritually 'fathered' in the tribulation of the last days. He goes on in the next verse to contrast all these false and secret comings of the Messiah (*'Look, he is hiding here'*) with the nature of the true coming of the Messiah, which will be as visible and public as the lightening flashing across the sky (or the sun's spreading dawn across the sky, the language is ambiguous and could refer to either natural phenomenon). But according to the pre-tribbers, the actual 'return' of Jesus in the rapture is in itself an invisible event to the world, not something public (although they believe the effects will be visible). There is a reason why one fairly commonly used term for this kind of pre-trib position is 'the *secret* rapture' or 'secret coming'. Hmmmm!

It is also these 'elect ones' who are also 'you' – i.e. the disciples and their spiritual descendants – who are the ones that Jesus gathers together in the rapture at the end of the tribulation in v30-1. This puts paid to the ridiculous counter-argument I have seen by at least some pre-tribbers, which is that the 'elect' here that go through the tribulation and are 'raptured' at its end are the Jews, the nation of Israel, with all those Jews outside the land of Israel supernaturally brought in to the promised land from out of the nations where some will still be scattered. Because they have been so brainwashed by the dispensationalist / pre-trib ideology, they insist that the Jews only must be in view here, since they 'know' that it is the Jews and Israel, not the church who will go through the Tribulation. Thus they end up believing that a key part of the 'end times' program is that the church is raptured out of the way, even though

Jesus never refers remotely to any event like this before the tribulation but persists in referring to 'you' - the disciples - as the ones who will endure these sufferings. They are so blinded by the pre-trib ideology that they imagine a rapture of the church in the text where there is none, but ignore the rapture of the followers of Jesus at the very point where Jesus clearly and explicitly teaches it. They have to explain it away, so elevating the human tradition of the evangelical elders that it nullifies the very words of the Messiah, the son of the living God, just as the Pharisees so exalted the 'traditions of the elders' that the very law of God was nullified and made void in practice. This is a staggering and glaring example of blatant eisegesis, reading something that is just not there *into* the text. Those holding these kinds of views tend to say that as the initial question Jesus is answering had to do with the Jewish temple, and all his disciples were Jews, his teaching must be taken as referring to the Jews. But there are some things that tell against this. Firstly, if Jesus wanted a message to go out to all the Jews, there were crowds of Israelites and Jews from every nation in the city at that time (Passover, a time when as many Jews as possible made it to Jerusalem). He could have made this teaching public, but instead, he gave it to his disciples in private. A possible counter argument here would be that Jesus gave the teaching in private because he was answering a question that the disciples asked in private (v3). That would be fair enough, except that if Jesus were referring to Jews in general, and Jews only, he would talk about persecution because of the Torah, or the covenant, or circumcision or the like, but instead he taught that they would be persecuted 'because of my name' - in other words, because they were Jesus' disciples, Christians (v9). If a teacher who named himself Messiah, and even the Son of God, who saw his mission as the renewal of Israel and the fulfilment of prophecy, or the raising up of a faithful movement - a remnant of Israel who were to be his followers, what other name would he call them other than 'the elect' or the 'chosen ones'? Other sects in Jewish life of the time that focussed on a renewal of worship and life, like the Essenes, would also refer to their adherents in similar terms. And if Jesus had in mind here some other separate group of followers from his disciples and their spiritual progeny, he was quite capable of making that clear. In John 10.16, when speaking of himself as the good shepherd to his Jewish disciples, Jesus says that '*I have other sheep, too, that are not in this sheepfold. I must bring them also.*' A simple analogy like that would have served admirably if Jesus had some species of 'tribulation saints' as distinct from the church of his disciples in mind here. Now, it is true that Jesus does talk quite a bit about specifically Jerusalem and Judah based issues and events, particularly to do with the Temple in v15 and following. But this is hardly decisive proof that Jesus was talking only of Jews to the exclusion of any other of his followers here. For a start his disciples were Jewish and asked a question specifically about the Temple and about the end times. Secondly, even if they had asked only about the end times in general, we would expect any Jewish rabbi to speak in terms of what it would mean for Israel and in terms of the Old Testament prophecies, which is what Jesus did when he spoke of the 'abomination of the desolation' mentioned in Daniel. And surely the very fact that so many Gentile Christians today, particularly in the Dispensationalist and pre-trib evangelical world of LaHaye and company, also debate endlessly and in detail on such Jewish issues as the restoration of the Temple and so forth shows the full futility of trying to claim that Jesus talking about such things meant that he only had Jews, not Christians in mind? We know that the disciples and apostles carried this teaching about the end times to their new Gentile converts. Indeed, we should expect it even if we had no actual evidence, because that was the job of a disciple – to accurately convey his teacher's teaching and wisdom to further generations of followers. But we do have evidence. For instance, in the chapter on the last days found in that document from the twelve apostles teaching that we mentioned earlier, the 'Didache', it clearly points to this teaching of Jesus. Interestingly, given the fact that it was titled the 'Teaching of our Lord... *to the Gentiles'* it doesn't mention the specifically Jewish / Judean parts about the Temple and Sabbath, but it does neatly summarize all the other parts of Jesus' teaching in Matthew 24 – remaining firm in the faith to the end, the rise of false teachers and love turning to hate, the increase of wickedness and betrayal, the rise of the deceiver who claims with signs and wonders to be the Son of God, the tribulations, and then the rapture occurring with a sign in the heavens, a trumpet blast and the gathering of the saints with the resurrection of the believing dead, all at Jesus' actual visible return. I say again, all these things, including the post-trib rapture of the church, were taught by the apostles *to the gentiles.* Clearly, they did not understand Jesus' teaching here as referring only to Jews or some special last day breed. Not just the Twelve, but also Paul in the New Testament, applied the rapture to the gentiles. As we have seen, using standard methods of Jewish interpretation, Paul clearly links his 'rapture' teaching to Matthew 24, using the same elements as Jesus did there, and, as we have just seen, the same elements the apostles referred to in the Didache – angels, trumpet blasts, resurrection, the gathering of Jesus' followers to be with him. Paul did this writing to the churches in Thessalonica and in Corinth, both of which were largely *gentile* churches. If there was some such Jew-Gentile distinction to be made as these pre-tribbers claim, Paul was also well able to make the distinction. For instance, in his letter to the Ephesians, another predominantly Gentile church, the first half of his line of argument means that he had to continually distinguish between himself and other Jewish believers, and the Gentile believers he was addressing, which he simply and subtly did by referring to 'us' and 'you' repeatedly where necessary. Now, if the particular pre-trib argument we are discussing were true, then not only do we have Jesus teaching in a very misleading manner, but we also find that both the apostles and Paul are also very confused on the issue of who exactly is being raptured in Matthew 24. As Paul says earlier in his first letter to the Corinthians (14.33) *'For God is not a God of confusion......'* (yes, I know I'm taking it somewhat out of context, but hey, what's life without a little inconsistency!). Now, if the typical pre-trib understanding of Matthew 24 and who is being raptured at the end of the tribulation there is correct, then Jesus is one confused dude, as are the twelve apostles and the apostle Paul. And since Matthew 24 and Paul's letters are part of God's word then gee, God must be a very confused God too! But if God is not the author of confusion, then I know who my money's on as the confused ones here......

OK, so moving on to the other passage that LaHaye cites here to support the notion that the rapture marks the start of the tribulation, 2 Thessalonians 2.3-12. After having written to the Thessalonian church in his first letter, Paul now writes again, and in 2 Thessalonians 2.1-12 he starts by saying he is clarifying some things about the coming of Jesus. Once again, the question is why does LaHaye start his citation at v3, when Paul actually starts his discussion of the return of Jesus at v1? Again, I suspect it is because these verses have content that totally undermine his pre-trib position. Remember, he is trying to claim that this passage is 'proof' that the rapture happens before the 7-year Tribulation and rule of the anti-Christ starts. Firstly, the wider context - Paul refers back to what he had taught the church when he had founded it. We don't know what that specific teaching was, but we can have a pretty good idea by looking at the teaching of Jesus and of the apostles, which we have discussed above. The points where we don't know what he was referring to occur in v5-8, where Paul talks about something that is holding back the spirit of lawlessness that will give rise to the anti-Christ, but will at some point be removed, allowing the anti-Christ to rise to power. There are all sorts views about what or who it is that is holding the forces of lawlessness at bay in this passage, precisely because it is so unclear to us. I'm not going to even attempt to untangle them. But what is relevant is that LaHaye and many other pre-tribbers believe that it is the church and the Holy Spirit in the church that is referred to here. For them, the church being raptured out of the way allows the rise of the anti-Christ and the Tribulation period.

Even without knowing for sure what Paul was referring to here, can we evaluate the likelihood of LaHaye and company's explanation being the correct one? I suggest we can. Firstly, as we have just seen, if this is what Paul meant, he would be going against the teaching of both Jesus and the other apostles in the early church documents we have. More to the point, the key is in what is clear - in the verses that LaHaye carefully did not include his reference to this passage. Paul starts this section about the end times by saying he is clarifying issues not only about the return of Jesus, but also about '*how we will be gathered to meet him*' (v1). Given that in his previous letter to the Thessalonian church Paul had devoted half a chapter to discussing how both the dead and the living saints will come together and then meet with Jesus, it is pretty obvious that this is what Paul is referring to here in his second letter to them. And as we established, Paul was clearly referring to the events Jesus prophesied in Matthew 24.30-1, which Jesus explicitly placed after the Tribulation. Even if we didn't have such a link via the passage in 1 Thessalonians 4, we could deduce with a fair degree of confidence that Paul was referring to the events of Matthew 24.30-1 because he uses exactly the same Greek word for 'gathering' as is used in both of those gospels that report Jesus' words about this ingathering – Matthew 24.31 and Mark 13.27.

Paul then goes on to urge his readers in v2, not to be disturbed by people who claimed that 'the Day of the Lord' has already begun. This 'Day of the Lord' is a fairly common phrase among the Old Testament prophets, used of a day when God will come in judgement, and understood to pre-eminently refer to the coming of God in final judgement at the end of the age. Paul then goes on in v3-4 to say that this 'Day of the Lord' will not come until the rise of the 'man of lawlessness' – aka the anti-Christ – amidst a great rebellion against God, or a falling away from God (there is some debate about whether this phrase refers to a general rebellion against God, or a mass apostasy or falling away from the Christian faith). He makes it clear by allusion that this figure is the one predicted in the prophet Daniel, who even sits enthroned in the Temple of God. (Daniel 9.27 and 2 Thess. 2.4)

Then Paul goes on to remind his readers that they know what is holding back this final culmination of evil. He reminds them that they know who / what is holding back the tide of darkness. Now if it was they and us, as the church, that Paul was referring to as the one holding back evil, why didn't he say so? If he believed and was teaching that the church would be raptured, and that this event is the 'stepping away' of 'the one holding it back' (v7), why didn't he just say so? All it would take would be the changing the form of one word from 'he / the one' to 'we'. And more broadly, if this passage was meant to contain the message that the church would be raptured before the rise of the anti-Christ, why did Paul go into all detail about his attributes and activities? If the pre-trib rapture was what he had taught these concerned converts, all he needed to do to reassure them that the 'Day of the Lord' hadn't come yet would be to say words to the effect of 'You dopey people, you are still here on earth, aren't you? Of course the Day of the Lord hasn't come yet'. The fact that he doesn't take this simple route rather suggests that whatever Paul is talking about in v5-8, it isn't the pre-trib rapture of the church. And that's without considering the clear language of v1 linking this teaching in with Jesus account of a post-trib rapture that we mentioned earlier.

Once again, LaHaye has cut and snipped scriptures out of context, distorting them and teaching that they say the opposite of what they do actually mean. In this case, although v5-8 is unclear to us, LaHaye and those who take his view would do well to practice what many of them doubtless preach – that when interpreting difficult scriptures, we should use the clear to interpret the unclear, not the other way round. In this case, LaHaye cites only part of the passage, while ignoring the preceding verses that make it clear that Paul is not referring to a rapture of the church before the coming of the anti-Christ.

PROOF 10

The rapture occurs before the 'day of wrath' (Revelation 3.10, 1 Thessalonians 5.8-9), but the second coming occurs immediately after the Tribulation (Matthew 24.29-36).

So we don't really need to deal with the latter point, except to re-emphasize the way LaHaye and pre-tribbers have been so brainwashed that they would use as an 'irrefutable proof' for a rapture before the Tribulation *the very passage of scripture* where Jesus describes the rapture and explicitly places it *after* the Tribulation. The inability to see this very clear point is, I suggest, evidence of <u>extreme</u> deception.

Turning to his scriptural proofs that the rapture occurs before the 'day of wrath', let's start with Revelation 3.10. There is a long tradition of pre-tribbers / dispensationalists badly abusing this verse in exactly the fashion LaHaye does here. Firstly, we've already seen that despite their claims of being the only eschatology that truly takes the relevant bible passages 'literally', when it comes to the letters to the seven churches in Revelation 2 and 3, pre-tribbers have a great tendency to descend into elaborate – and frequently contradictory – allegorical interpretations about how this is really describing different ages of church history. The verse in question reads as follows:

> *'Because you have obeyed my command to persevere, I will protect you from the great time of testing that will come upon the whole world to test those who belong to this world.'*

On the face of it – i.e. a literal interpretation – this is a message from Jesus to a church in Philadelphia in Turkey in the late 1st Century AD, addressing their particular circumstances. (The church in Philadelphia was the only one of the seven churches for which Jesus had no criticism, only praise). But for these pre-tribbers, this is actually secretly a promise of a pre-trib rapture. Because the passage refers to a time of testing that comes upon the whole world to test those who belong to the world, and given that they are conditioned to see global tribulation as meaning 'the Great Tribulation' of the last days when the church has already been rescued-by-rapture, and the world is being judged, their minds jump to the assertion that this is a promise that the whole church will escape the Tribulation of the very last days. Many will claim that the church in Philadelphia is somehow a prophetic picture of the church just before the Tribulation, to which the promise of rapture is given. They generally interpret the next and final church, Laodicea, which Jesus condemns as lukewarm and good for nothing, and does not have any words of praise for, as the false and apostate church that, because it is not the true church, is left behind at the rapture and forms part of the false one world religion that underpins the rule of the anti-Christ (which is how they tend to interpret the Whore of Babylon and one of the beasts in the book of Revelation). Aside from the fact that if the church in Laodicea is representative of a false church that is destined for destruction and judgement, it seems rather pointless that Jesus would urge this doomed group to repent, and says that he corrects those he loves, it is also instructive to note that some other pre-tribbers who also take the seven churches of Revelation to refer allegorically to different periods of church history actually read the Laodicean church as being the church just before the rapture. They link it to the idea that there will be a great apostasy from the faith just prior to Jesus' return, as described both by Jesus, and by Paul in the 2 Thessalonians 2 passage we discussed in the last 'proof'. They say that although this apostasy from the true faith reaches its nadir during the Tribulation, the rapture will be preceded by a rising tide of apostasy from the faith, lukewarmness, lack of love and fervency in the church, and so on. Such confusion is the result of supposed champions of literal readings taking an essentially non-literal and allegorical approach to Scripture.

For a moment, let's just for a moment grant the idea that 'church ages' are being described here. Would that mean that Revelation 3.10 has to refer to the church being raptured to escape the Tribulation of the last days? Far from it. It could just mean that God would protect the church in the midst of this time of testing and tribulation for the ungodly world, just like the Israelites in Egypt were spared most of the plagues against Egypt, even whilst remaining in the midst of that nation that was undergoing extreme judgement from God.

I suggest that if LaHaye and co want to teach on the last days, they should practice what they preach and take Revelation 2-3 literally. It refers to late 1st Century churches, not church ages through history. Some will give an additional argument for understanding this verse as referring to the rapture. They will say that the verse refers to a time of testing coming upon the whole earth, and that this means it must refer to the end times. Firstly, there have actually already been times of testing that have come upon the whole earth. Archaeologists and historians have found evidence of periods of time when some sort of climate change appears to have affected the crops of the whole earth at about the same period of time, with various social upheavals and wars the result. But more to the point, they would again do well to practice what they preach and study the historical and cultural and literary context of this passage. It was standard practice in the Roman world to say something will affect 'the whole world' when they meant just the Roman Empire. As an example, just look at Luke (who was writing his gospel sponsored by or dedicated to a wealthy Roman citizen).

In 2.1 he says that the Roman Emperor decreed a census for 'the whole world'. (Some translations render this - correctly, though not strictly literally - as 'throughout the Roman Empire'). We are not to imagine Roman census takers sailing to Australia to number the aboriginal people, or trudging to India to number that nation, or crossing the channel to enumerate the tribes of Britain. It is quite clear from usage and the context that only the Roman Empire is meant. So too does Revelation 3.10 only refer to a time of testing for the whole Roman Empire. As the Roman Empire has long since passed, as indeed has the church in Philadelphia, there is no way that this is some prophecy to be fulfilled in our future with a rapture of the church.

Interpreting it literally as referring to a 1st Century church does not mean that it only has historical interest to us, and no practical application to the last days. The church in Philadelphia was praised for having little strength, and yet persevering in obedience and not denying Christ, all the while being persecuted by their enemies. God promises to protect this powerless church during a time of testing (implicitly judgement) on the rest of their society. This could quite easily apply as a promise to a persecuted, yet faithful church now, or indeed in a future tribulation.

Let's now turn to 1 Thessalonians 5.8-9, which reads:

> 'But let us who live in the light be clearheaded, protected by the armour of faith and love, and wearing as our helmet the confidence of our salvation.
>
> For God chose to save us through our Lord Jesus Christ, not to pour out his anger on us'.

Now I have no idea why LaHaye has included v8 in his 'proof' as it has no conceivable link to the rapture (I am proceeding as if it is not a typo, but that may be one explanation - v9-10 could have been meant). V9 is the key here. But you might say that v9 also has nothing to link it to the rapture either. I think you'd be right, funnily enough, but let's look closer at this. The reason that LaHaye and the like believe this verse is a 'proof' of the rapture is because it mentions the wrath or anger of God. In the elaborate schema they have dreamed up, mention of 'the wrath' immediately makes them think that the passage means the 7 years of the Tribulation when God's wrath is to be poured out on all the world. If this is so, then being saved versus being subject to wrath must, in this very rigid approach, mean the rapture to remove believers from the earth, pretty much regardless of the context. You will often see pre-Tribbers using exactly the same approach to another isolated verse in 1 Thessalonians - 1.10, which says:

> *'....you are looking forward to the coming of God's Son from heaven–Jesus, whom God raised from the dead. He is the one who has rescued us from the terrors of the coming judgement.'*

In this case they have the added 'support' that this verse explicitly links rescue from future wrath with the return of Jesus from heaven. These verses are yet again examples of having to *assume* a pre-trib position in order to pretend to 'prove' the same position. Firstly, given the teaching of Jesus and the apostles about the timing of the rapture after the tribulation, it is surely far more natural to read the reference to the return of Jesus as being that of his glorious return from heaven in the Second Coming 'proper' as opposed to any separate 'secret' rapture. The rapture is only in the passage if you are already indoctrinated with a pre-trib, dispensationalist position. Such people will insist that because such passages mention the wrath of God, they must refer to the 7 year tribulation and the rapture, but funnily enough, I have never come across someone claiming that other passages in Paul's letters that mention the wrath of God being poured out on the ungodly have to be only restricted to the Tribulation and therefore have to involve a pre-tribulation rapture. For instance, I've yet to see anyone claim that the mentions of eternal life for the righteous, but the anger of God for the wicked in Romans 1 and 2 are anything to do with the rapture, even among all the pre-trib / dispensationalist books, chapters and articles I have read. Romans 1.18 comes immediately after a verse describing how the gospel (not the rapture) makes us right with God, and says:

> *'But God shows his anger from heaven against all sinful, wicked people who suppress the truth by their wickedness'*

The passage then goes on to develop the point by saying that the wrath of God is evidenced in the ensuing consequences in human understanding and society in general, things that no-one claims only occur after the 'rapture'. The passage that mentions wrath in chapter 2.5-11 is, I think, worth quoting in full to show the context:

> *'But because you are stubborn and refuse to turn from your sin, you are storing up terrible punishment for yourself. For a day of anger is coming, when God's righteous judgement will be revealed. He will judge everyone according to what they have done. He will give eternal life to those who keep on doing good, seeking after the glory and honour and immortality that God offers. But he will pour out his anger and wrath on those who live for themselves, who refuse to obey the truth and instead live lives of wickedness. There will be trouble and calamity for everyone who keeps on doing what is evil–for the Jew first and also for the Gentile. But there will*

> *be glory and honour and peace from God for all who do good—for the Jew*
> *first and also for the Gentile. For God does not show favouritism'*

This, like 1 Thessalonians 1.10, must be referring to the final Day of judgement associated with Christ's return. It is clear that this judgement is universal in scope – God will judge *everyone* for what they have done. This is not some separate judgement for a raptured church, even though Paul is writing to a church. He says the judgement (again notice it is based on deeds!) is for everyone. The righteous are rewarded with eternal life, but the wicked face the wrath and anger of God. While there may be room here to consider end-times judgement (from just before Jesus returns) as part of the package, it is clear that the focus is on the eternal consequences and position of people, because it is chiefly focusing on 'the age to come'. God's wrath before he comes may be the precursor of the fate in the age to come of the wicked, but it is not the substance Paul has in view here. Nor is there, unless you have some incredibly powerful 'pre-trib' glasses on, any room for a separate secret rapture. The judgement happens all at the same time, and the righteous are rewarded with eternal life at the same time as the wicked are punished – in other words, there is no room at all to legitimately claim that this refers to the rapture where the church receives eternal life in a separate event. So why do pre-tribbers focus on single verses that they insist must mean something contrary to what Paul teaches here in Romans 2? Apart from the pre-tribbers penchant for taking verses completely out of context, I suggest it is because verses like 1 Thessalonians 1.10 and 5.9 taken in isolation allow them to claim that the events are something that affects only the church.

Let's go back to 1 Thessalonians 1.10 a minute. How does it describe this wrath it mentions? It calls it the 'coming wrath' or 'the wrath to come'. This is parallel to passages which describe 'the age to come', the Messianic age. The 'age to come' was a standard phrase that meant the Messianic age, referring to something that happens in the next age, not this one. There is no need to invoke a pre-trib rapture to explain this verse. Without wearing pre-trib goggles, the real meaning becomes apparent. Jesus has saved those who believe in him from the eternal punishment of God that will come upon the wicked in the next age, and Paul indicates this by his use of the phrase 'coming anger'. In fact, there is another clue in the context. Romans 1, that we mentioned earlier, notes that one reason for God's anger shown in society was because people had turned from worship of the living God to worshipping idols, and are thus 'without excuse'. This was standard in Jewish and Christian thinking and teaching. God is angry at those who persist in worshipping false gods, and they will face eternal punishment if they do not repent. And that is precisely the context we find here. 1 Thessalonians 1.9 talks of how the church in Thessalonica had *'turned away from idols to serve the living and true God'*.

But back to 5.9. The verse before, v8, talks about godly qualities of faith, love and the confident hope of *salvation*. These are things that are of value in any age. They do not pertain exclusively to the last days, but talk of what should be normal Christian experience and lifestyle. The verse after, the one that LaHaye does not quote, is possibly even more telling. Why does he not quote the verse that does mention the return of Jesus? It says:

> 'Christ died for us so that, whether we are dead or alive when he returns, we can live with him forever'.

What is the salvation from wrath that Paul is talking about here? Is it, as Christian doctrine has always held, salvation from eternal damnation, achieved through the death of Christ for us, or is it through a mystical, mythical snatching away of the church to spare them trouble in the last days? If context is king, then it is clearly the former. If Paul wanted to teach the latter, he could have phrased it differently. He could have said that when the Lord returns, we will 'escape the Tribulation' or 'dwell in heaven', but he never says this. In fact, 5v10 alludes back to the central 'rapture passage' a few verses earlier at the end of chapter 4. 5v10 talks of Christ dying for us, so that when he returns both dead and living saints will be able to 'live with him forever', just as the 1 Thessalonians 4 passage (v17) ends up with us being the Lord forever. Chapter 4 also talks of how Jesus died and rose again and how this means that he will bring the dead with him. We've already seen that the classic rapture passage of 1 Thessalonians 4 passage cannot refer to a pre-trib rapture, so how can this even vaguer passage that harks back to chapter 4 constitute 'proof' of such a position?

But there is one more thing to say here. LaHaye's wildly popular series of novels based around a pre-trib theology focus on the 'Tribulation saints'. These 'Tribulation Saints' believe in Jesus and are saved, and are largely preserved from the judgements of God, though not from the enmity of evil men. How are they saved? By believing in the death and resurrection of Jesus, just like we, as the church, do now. Now, if the church has to be 'raptured' out of the way because they have not been 'appointed to wrath' but for salvation, which is what LaHaye is trying to argue for here - taking the usual line here that the wrath is the 7 year tribulation period, then how come these Tribulation saints can be saved in the midst of wrath? Did not Christ die for them, just as he did for the church? According to pre-tribbers, the answer is yes, yet strangely, in spite of this, their compelling theological need for the saved of the church age to be exited prior to the wrath / Tribulation continues. If these Tribulation saints are saved and preserved from God's wrath in the pre-trib schema, why on earth are teachers like LaHaye and company getting so worked up about how terrible it is that post-tribbers believe exactly the same about the church in the tribulation? They go on about how a 'loving God' wouldn't let the 'pre-Tribulation' saints of the church suffer during the Tribulation, yet they have no problem believing that the same loving God lets the 'Tribulation saints' go through the same Tribulation. This strange incoherence shows a fundamental inherent contradiction at the heart of the pre-trib schema (and, as we saw before, doesn't fit at all with how Jesus taught about God's providential care exhibited in the case of martyrdom – *'They will kill some of you, but not a hair on your head will perish'*).

PROOF 13

The rapture is the marriage of the Lamb (Revelation 19.7-10), but at the Second Coming the bride descends with the Lamb as an army (Revelation 19.11-14, Jude 14).

I don't know about you, but I find it immensely strange that LaHaye somehow manages to take one continuous, coherent passage from Revelation 19, split it in two, and tout is as 'proof' that it is really talking about two completely separate events taking place seven years apart! Talk about taking things out of context! I've already shown in several earlier proofs that Revelation 19 and the early part of chapter 20 speak of one day – or at the least, a very short time period. For pre-tribbers, God uses the Tribulation to destroy the apostate church / religion and ungodly systems of this world, as depicted by the destruction of Babylon and the Great Whore in Revelation 17-18. Chapter 19.1 continues *'After this, I heard....'* and goes on to describe the rising paean of praise in heaven that culminates in shouts of acclamation because the time of the marriage feast of the Lamb has come. Now, don't you think that if John (or rather Jesus who gave John the vision) wanted to clearly establish a pre-Trib position where chapter 4.1-2 is the rapture, he would have put an account of the marriage supper of the Lamb there where pre-tribbers believe it was initiated? Wouldn't putting it in a passage which more naturally links it to the return of Jesus be just a tad misleading; duplicitous even? And as I have also shown, the language about a church who has finally made herself ready in chapter 19 militates against a pre-trib position, which would have the church perfected when they are transformed to be like Jesus at the claimed 'rapture' in Revelation 4. If the marriage of the Lamb happened in Revelation 4, it is also strange that Revelation 19 never says it has happened already, but rather that the time has *now* come for the marriage of the Lamb. This fits perfectly in a post-tribulation scenario where this is the moment that the church and Jesus are united in the air, but if God is a pre-tribber, then he must be a very confused, and not to say confusing, pre-tribber to arrange this revelation of the marriage of the Lamb in the way he does.

LaHaye also cites Jude 14 as proof that the Second Coming is a separate event to the rapture. Jude is a very short letter written by one of Jesus (half) brothers to a church or group of churches – almost certainly primarily Jewish – experiencing grave difficulty with some false teachers who were teachers of what is now known as 'hyper-grace' doctrine, a problem that is increasing in some evangelical circles today (and anecdotal evidence suggests it is especially common in some pre-trib circles, interestingly enough). This is the doctrine that says that because God's grace covers our sin, it is OK to live as we please and sin as much as we like, because 'God's grace will take care of it'. After what looks like a sustained and intemperate rant against these false teachers (but which is in fact a highly subtle piece of argument in a traditional Jewish style absolutely packed with allusions not only to many Old Testament passages but also passages from other popular Jewish sacred literature of the time), Jude says in v14-15:

> 'Enoch, who lived in the seventh generation after Adam, prophesied about these people. He said, "Listen! The Lord is coming with countless thousands of his holy ones to execute judgement on the people of the world. He will convict every person of all the ungodly things they have done and for all the insults that ungodly sinners have spoken against him" '

Aside from the fact that this is clearly a reference to the visible return of Jesus, I can't think what this proves at all in terms of the pre-tribulation position. And what is more, when I started to think about this verse in context, I realized that it actually tends more to *disprove* the pre-trib scenario. Have a think about it. V14 starts off by saying that Enoch prophesied about *'these people'*. Who are these people? The false teachers Jude has spent the whole letter describing in lavishly negative terms. These were false teachers *in* the church. The Enoch quote has God and his 'holy ones' coming to execute judgement on the whole earth, yet Jude applies it specifically to false teachers and corruption *within* the church. In the pre-trib scenario, the true church is removed from the scene and judgement comes on those left behind, and then there is the coming of the Lord to fully execute judgement, but here in Jude there is no hint of such a gap. Jude uses 'these people' several times in the earlier verses to describe the false teachers who were plaguing the church, and made it clear that the judgement at the second coming applied to these same people. He says in v12 'When these people eat with *you*...', not 'when they eat with a separate group of saints', or anything else even hinting at the pre-trib scenario involving separate 'Tribulation saints'. To avoid this conclusion you will have to invent a gap between the description of the church troubles up to v13 and the account of the coming of Jesus and his 'saints' to judge those who trouble the church. Although, as we have seen in Revelation 19 and other places, it is not at all beyond LaHaye and other pre-tribbers to invent imaginary gaps or weird breaks to support their false teaching!

PROOF 8

The rapture is for believers only (1 Thessalonians 4.14), but the second coming affects all humanity (Revelation 1.7).

PROOF 14

At the rapture, only His own see Him (1 Thessalonians 4.14-17), but at the Second Coming every eye shall see Him (Revelation 1.7)

These two proofs are just examples of the type of false reasoning we have seen before. And the fact that to get his full fifteen 'irrefutable proofs' LaHaye has to pad things out by using the same two verses to make what is essentially the same point in proofs 8 and 14 illustrates something of the desperation the pre-trib position requires to justify itself.

So let's deal, however briefly, with proofs 8 and 14, which centre on the assumption that since 1 Thessalonians refers only to believers in the events it is describing, the events so described must not involve or apply to non-believers in anyway. If nothing else, this is simply false logic (anyone who dislikes anything that smacks of algebra, pass over the next few lines). Just because a text only describes x, it does not therefore exclude non-x, unless x and non-x are contradictory. And if the text is something that is written to a specific audience or situation that necessitates only a focus on x, then to infer, as LaHaye does here. that non-x is necessarily - or even likely to be - excluded is even more precarious logic. As we have seen before, 1 Thessalonians 4 is directed specifically to Christians who were wondering about the relationship between the second coming of Jesus and the death of their fellow believers. Why on earth should Paul refer to unbelievers here? As we have seen before, Jesus describes the rapture in terms of his coming to the whole world, so Paul writing to believers about an aspect which is specifically for believers is anything but the conclusive 'proof' the way LaHaye tries to assert. If we look at proof 14, LaHaye's reasoning is even dafter.

Revelation 1.7 reads:

> *'Look! He comes with the clouds of heaven.*
> *And everyone will see him—*
> *even those who pierced him.*
> *And all the nations of the world*
> *will mourn for him.*
> *Yes! Amen!'*

The 'everyone' who will see him – well surely 'everyone' must include believers? Unless of course you assume a pre-trib position – but even then, if the church is coming with him, they will see him. If even those who pierced him will see him, then surely his own will see him? But even more to the point here, the issue of 'seeing' is not really an issue in 1 Thessalonians 4.17. Sure, it is implied that believers will see him, but it is the meeting Jesus that is important, not the seeing. So trying to make a verse that doesn't even mention 'seeing' proof that the event described in such a passage must be held separate from events in another passage where everyone sees Jesus is, well, not at all persuasive, quite frankly. Once again, for this to have any kind of persuasive force, even as a defensive argument against opponents to shore up your own pre-trib followers, you and the followers both have to *assume* the pre-trib rapture. I rather suspect that the real force behind such an assertion is the memory of the vividly portrayed scenes in Left Behind style films and books depicting events following the secret rapture, where the believers vanish, with the unbelievers having no idea why (except for those who have been aware of the pre-trib belief-system).

We don't even need to chop logic here. We just have to look at context and verbal links. We have already seen the clear link between Paul's teaching in 1 Thessalonians 4 and Jesus' teaching of a very public rapture at his second coming, after the Tribulation. Even if we did not have this link, look at the language used in 1 Thessalonians 4 about this rapture event. There is no hint of secrecy at all. Paul was writing as a Jew, and those Jews who believed in a bodily resurrection all – as far as I am aware – saw it is a public, visible, apocalyptic event, not a secret one. When an ancient writer used language that includes a 'commanding shout', 'the voice of an archangel' and 'the trumpet call of God', it takes an awful lot of spiritualizing to make it a 'secret' event. The resonances are with Old Testament passages, particularly the one where the children of Israel first encounter God at Mount Sinai and God gives them the 10 commandments and starts to initiate covenant with them, a very public event indeed. There the voice of God is associated with the sound of a rams horn and thunder, the ram's horn being the Old Testament equivalent of a trumpet (Exodus 19.16-20 and 20.18-19). It was so terrifying and awesome that after God proclaimed the 10 commandments in such a fashion, the people begged that God speak only to Moses, afraid that to hear more would mean their death. This is the kind of scene Paul would have in mind when he describes a 'commanding shout'. Definitely not a secret event! This was the voice of God and the trumpet blast he had in mind, and this is confirmed by the way the Sinai encounter is described in the New Testament book of Hebrews – 12.18-20a:

> 'You have not come to a physical mountain, to a place of flaming fire, darkness, gloom, and whirlwind, as the Israelites did at Mount Sinai. For they heard an awesome trumpet blast and a voice so terrible that they

begged God to stop speaking. They staggered back under God's command.....'

There is more. Even if we did not have the passages in Matthew 24, Mark 13 and Luke 21 where Jesus describes the rapture in terms of his physical and visible return after the tribulation, we could infer that the rapture was not a secret believers-only event by something else Jesus said. Remember that one of the things that links the events of 1 Thessalonians 4 with the visible coming of Jesus was the way it describes the coming of Jesus from heaven in terms of clouds, a link to Daniel 7 where the Son of Man comes with the clouds of heaven. Well, there is at least one other time when Jesus alludes very much to the Daniel 7 passage, and that is when he is on trial for his life before the Jewish Sanhedrin and his mortal enemy, the High Priest, Caiaphas, who demands to know if Jesus believes himself to be 'the Messiah, the Son of the living God'. Jesus replies:

> *'You have said it. And in the future you will see the Son of Man seated in the place of power at God's right hand and coming on the clouds of heaven'* (Matthew 26.63-4).

Jesus' coming on the clouds of heaven here will be seen by the archetypal non-believer, one of Jesus' very own enemies. Thus the allusion to clouds of heaven in Paul's rapture passage can hardly be concerned with a secret believers-only event, then!

Let's consider the irony here. The very passages that LaHaye here considers as 'proofs' that the rapture and the Second coming must be different events use precisely the same imagery of Jesus coming from heaven with clouds. I feel like saying 'I rest my case, m'lud'! But there is yet more. Let's go back to Matthew 24 and consider Revelation 1.7 in the light of Jesus' teaching. John, just like Paul, was a Jewish theologian so, just as with Paul, attention to verbal allusions is important. Revelation 1.7 not only describes Jesus as coming with the clouds of heaven, just as in Matthew 24 and 1 Thessalonians 4, but it also describes how all the nations of the world will mourn for him. This mourning by all the nations is also precisely what Jesus describes in Matthew 24.30 when the sign of the Son of Man's coming is seen in the heavens. But remember, this verse is sandwiched between v29 which positions these events as *after* the tribulation, and v31 in which the rapture happens. Once again, we see that the *very passages and phrases* that LaHaye uses as claimed 'proofs' for the pre-Tribulation position flatly and comprehensively contradict and disprove that false teaching.

PROOF 9

The rapture is a time of joy (Titus 2.13, 1 Thessalonians 2.19-20, 4.18) but the Second Coming is a time of mourning (Revelation 1.7).

Once again, we have some rather dubious reasoning. We have already seen in an earlier section how in the Old Testament the same judgement event is seen as a time of woe for those - both within and without God's people - who are rebellious, but a time of joy and vindication for the righteous. Indeed, the same pattern appears in the New Testament - just look at Mary's magnificent 'Magnificat' in Luke 1 where the pattern of God's judgement in history is described in terms of the humbling of the proud opponents of God and the vindication of the humble and oppressed righteous. Even in Revelation 1.7, which LaHaye here claims proves the Second Coming is a time of mourning doesn't prove the distinction he says it does. That applies even if we take the verse in isolation from the context of the book of Revelation. After all, when John excitedly opens the verse with 'Behold, He comes with the clouds of heaven' and closes with 'Yes! Amen!' it is hardly an expression of woe or mourning. For him, this is joyful anticipation. It is only a time of mourning for the nations of the earth who have rejected Jesus and persecuted his church. In other words, even this one verse expresses the double sided nature of God's judgement - joy for His own, the righteous, and mourning for those who oppose both Him and His people (remember Jesus in John's gospel : *'If the world has hated me, it will also hate you'*).

The wider context of Revelation supports this. I don't really need to go into detail, except to point out firstly that when Revelation focuses on those believers who are slain for their faith, it depicts them as looking with eagerness for God's day of Judgement (6.9-10 for example:

> *'When the Lamb broke the fifth seal, I saw under the altar the souls of all who had been martyred for the word of God and for being faithful in their testimony. They shouted to the Lord and said, "O Sovereign Lord, holy and true, how long before you judge the people who belong to this world and avenge our blood for what they have done to us?"').*

We can also perhaps note the repeated emphasis that Jesus is *'the lamb who was slain'* (5.6 and 12, 13.8). In addition, John, when writing this, was in exile on the harsh penal colony island of Patmos, sent there because of his faith in Jesus. Almost straight after 1.7 he says in verse 9:

> *I, John, am your brother and your partner in suffering and in God's Kingdom and in the patient endurance to which Jesus calls us. I was exiled*

*to the island of Patmos for preaching the word of God and for my
testimony about Jesus.*

Many pre-tribbers like LaHaye when trying to deal with post-trib arguments will
frequently accuse post-tribbers of fear-mongering, and attribute to post-trib positions
a loss of hope and joy for those who hold such views. They will accuse people who
teach such doctrines of robbing the church of its 'Blessed Hope', a phrase that they
have torn out of context and illegitimately use as a sort of technical term or title for
the pre-trib rapture. We will come back to that phrase later. The point is, if a hope is
false, then it *needs* to be taken away. When pre-tribbers insist that God is too loving
to let the church go through the last days suffering, a number of responses come to
mind (sometimes along with a very un-Christian desire to bash their head against a
bible and ask whether they actually read it and why on earth they are choosing to
undermine Jesus' stark warnings to his disciples about suffering and martyrdom in
the last days and a whole host of other events, including that it will be the days of
greatest anguish ever where he goes on to say '*See I have warned you ahead of time*' in
Matthew 24.25). Number one is to point out that a repeated theme of Jesus' and the
apostles' teaching was that we are called to be disciples and imitators of a suffering
Saviour, not some kind of indulgent Messiah who wants to mollycoddle or over-
mother a group of comfort-clinging spiritual sofa-monkeys. I personally really don't
want to face up to the fact that I may have to go through suffering or face
martyrdom, but that emphatically does not mean that I have any right to twist
scripture to try and ignore its clear teaching on the subject, as pre-tribbers do. Quite
frankly, I think those that call the pre-trib position a kind of eschatological
prosperity gospel have it exactly right. Soothing voices claim that the saved won't
have to go through the tribulation but will be snatched away to heavenly bliss,
whereas Jesus when he taught his disciples about the suffering of the last days had
quite the opposite emphasis. His perspective was '*But the one who endures to the
end will be saved*' (Matthew 24.13). The verse comes just a couple of verses after a
passage where Jesus warned of false prophets. The Old Testament has repeated
warnings about those who proclaim peace and security falsely. Again, I am going to
take it a little out of context, but when I listen to the repetitive refrain of pre-tribbers
about how any post-trib view is fear-mongering, and how it will all be alright, despite
what Jesus warned us of, I am reminded particularly of Jeremiah 23.16-8:

This is what the Lord of Heaven's Armies says to his people:

"Do not listen to these prophets when they prophesy to you,
filling you with futile hopes.
They are making up everything they say.
They do not speak for the Lord!

They keep saying to those who despise my word,
  'Don't worry! The Lord says you will have peace!'
And to those who stubbornly follow their own desires,
  they say, 'No harm will come your way!'
"Have any of these prophets been in the Lord's presence
  to hear what he is really saying?
Has even one of them cared enough to listen?

I am also reminded of several warnings in Paul's letters, one about people following their own desires, and one about the end times. 2 Timothy 4.3-4 says:

> *For a time is coming when people will no longer listen to sound and wholesome teaching. They will follow their own desires and will look for teachers who will tell them whatever their itching ears want to hear. They will reject the truth and chase after myths*

I very much think there is a strong element of this in the popularity of the pre-trib view amongst so much of the evangelical and fundamentalist church. People don't want to hear about suffering, they want to hear that they will be spared it. But Jesus said differently:

> *Blessed and joyful are you when people mock you and persecute you and lie about you and say all sorts of evil things against you because you are my followers. Be happy about it! Be very glad! For a great reward awaits you in heaven. And remember, the ancient prophets were persecuted in the same way* (Matthew 5.11-12)

The other passage about the end Times is immediately after the 1 Thessalonians 4 rapture passage. In 5.2-3 Paul says:

> *For you know quite well that the day of the Lord's return will come unexpectedly, like a thief in the night. When people are saying, "Everything is peaceful and secure," then disaster will fall on them as suddenly as a pregnant woman's labour pains begin. And there will be no escape.*

People usually take this to mean that unbelievers will be resting in a false security, and that it doesn't apply to believers. Maybe, but I'm not so sure. It is true that in the very next verse Paul says that the Thessalonians won't be taken by surprise by the Day of the Lord coming like a thief, but the interesting thing is that he follows this up by an exhortation for his Christian readers not to live like the people of the world, but to be clear-headed and alert. Have a look and see!

In the pre-trib or dispensationalist position, the Tribulation comes just before the full breaking in and manifestation of God's kingdom on earth. With this I agree wholeheartedly, but here's an interesting quote from Paul, teaching brand new believers and churches in Acts 14.22. It is very instructive, especially in the light of pre-tribbers insistent assertion that any denial of a pre-trib rapture is deadly discouragement to the church. Paul is accompanied by Barnabas (who was given this nickname because of his immense reputation for encouragement – it means 'son of encouragement') and they are going back through towns where they had just recently planted congregations of new believers. Luke says that they *strengthened the believers. They encouraged them to continue in the faith, reminding them that we must suffer many hardships to enter the Kingdom of God'*. That word translated 'hardships' is in fact the Greek word *thlipsis* or 'tribulation'. It is the exact word Jesus used in Matthew 24.29 when he placed the rapture and his return as *'Immediately after the Tribulation of those days.....'*. Now Paul isn't here talking about *the* Tribulation, but it is the principle that counts. As individual believers we have to go through many tribulations to enter the kingdom of God. It is fitting, then, that the body of believers, the church, will have to go through the fullest time of Tribulation before the fullness of the Kingdom comes on earth. As a stand-alone argument, this verse would not work as a pointer to a post-trib position, but it very much fits once you take into account what Jesus warned his disciples, the nascent church, about their role in the Tribulation in Matthew 24.

Now, as I have said, many pre-tribbers make a great song and dance about how denial of the pre-trib rapture robs people of their hope and joyous expectation of Jesus' return. However, in my experience – and others have made similar observations too – when people go through suffering for the name of Jesus, unless they let it turn them bitter and away from Christ, it means that they look with even greater joy for the coming of Jesus. Those who live in comfort and ease – in other words the Western and especially much of the American church – are more likely to treat the subject with indifference or with an intellectual cerebral fascination, as evidenced by the myriad end-time prophecy charts and tables and diagrams, etc. But where people are suffering persecution and injustice for Christ, and have remained steadfast, there you will almost invariably find a living and joyous longing and expectancy for Jesus' return, when there will be no more death, or suffering, and Jesus will wipe away our tears. That is the true joy and hope of which the New Testament speaks. This dynamic is borne out by the teaching of the bible. Contrary to the pre-trib 'only an escape from Tribulation view can be an encouragement' line, Hebrews 10.32-5, for instance encourages and exhorts its hearers not to give up their confidence in God, and to remember the great reward their faith brought by reminding them of the great suffering they had already endured, and the joy that came with it. Hebrews 12.11 talks about the painful nature of discipline, but then uses this as the basis for an exhortation to strength in v12-13 (*'So take a new grip with your tired hands and strengthen your weak knees. Mark out a straight path for your feet so that those who are weak and lame will not fall but become strong'*). And when the prophet Jeremiah complains to God about injustice and suffering and discouragement (12.1-4), God's response is not to encouragingly say in effect, 'it will soon be over and you will be in clover', but rather asks (paraphrasing the poetic original) 'If you can't hack it now, how will you deal with things when it is far worse?' and goes on to warn that in future even his family will turn against him (v5-6). So the pre-trib rapture version of joy and hope as escape from trial and tribulation is a deceptive hope, a phony angel of light luring people into false comfort, ease and complacency, and away from a truly biblical attitude to suffering and the Kingdom of God.

Let's turn now to the verses LaHaye uses as proof for his assertions about the joyous nature of the rapture as a separate event. One is 1 Thessalonians 4.18. This comes immediately after the rapture passage. It simply says *'So encourage each other with these words'*. This is precisely the kind of false notion that we mentioned above. LaHaye and pre-tribbers use this verse to try and claim that anything other than a pre-trib position is less than a comfort, because it would involve going through some (in the case of a mid-trib position) or all (in the case of a post-trib position) of the Tribulation period. Such a notion would not involve comfort, they say, so the fact that Paul concludes this rapture passage with an exhortation to comfort each other about the rapture 'proves' that he must have a pre-trib rapture in mind. As usual, they take the verse out of context. This passage is used often in funerals, and the funeral people, not the pre-tribbers are the ones who use this passage contextually (at least if they are burying a believer in Christ). Remember that the concern Paul was addressing here was the issue of 'What happens to believers who die? Will they forfeit the blessings of being here when Jesus comes again?' The comforting Paul commanded here was chiefly to do with comforting grieving family and friends with the hope of resurrection, not with some esoteric and complex eschatological schema. (And, as we have noted above, Paul then goes on in the next chapter to warn the church that the Day of the Lord will come with sudden disaster.)

Similarly, in the other passage from the same letter, LaHaye ignores context and tears out a living verse from its place to dump it on his edifice of verses taken from their moorings and precariously piled up to support his claims. 1 Thessalonians 2.19-20 reads:

> *'After all, what gives us hope and joy, and what will be our proud reward and crown as we stand before our Lord Jesus when he returns? It is you! Yes, you are our pride and joy.'*

What does that have to do with a pre-trib rapture? Sure, it has the return of Jesus, and joy, but what does that prove? In fact, the context is not some doctrinal assertion about the end-times but an expression of Paul's intense longing to see these new believers again, in the face of powerful satanic opposition (just read the two preceding verses). But interestingly, in the light of my previous paragraphs, if we look at the slightly wider context, we find Paul talking of persecution, and of judgement on those doing the persecuting. Verses 14-16 read:

> *'And then, dear brothers and sisters, you suffered persecution from your own countrymen. In this way, you imitated the believers in God's churches in Judea who, because of their belief in Christ Jesus, suffered from their own people, the Jews. For some of the Jews killed the prophets, and some even killed the Lord Jesus. Now they have persecuted us, too. They fail to please God and work against all humanity as they try to keep us from preaching the Good News of salvation to the Gentiles. By doing this, they continue to pile up their sins. But the anger of God has caught up with them at last.'*

Talking of taking joy and pride in suffering brothers and sisters hardly constitutes conclusive contextual 'proof' of a 'no-suffering-Blessed-Hope' pre-trib rapture position, does it now?

Ah, the 'Blessed Hope'. That brings us on to Titus 2.13, where Paul is telling his student or fellow-worker Titus what to teach to the new churches of Crete, where Paul had left him to consolidate the new body of believers after his evangelistic endeavours there. As ever, LaHaye is taking it out of context – the verse isn't even a whole sentence! So here it is, in its immediate context (v11-14):

> *'For the grace of God has been revealed, bringing salvation to all people. And we are instructed to turn from godless living and sinful pleasures. We should live in this evil world with wisdom, righteousness, and devotion to God, while we look forward with hope to that wonderful day when the glory of our great God and Saviour, Jesus Christ, will be revealed. He gave his life to free us from every kind of sin, to cleanse us, and to make us his very own people, totally committed to doing good deeds.'*

I can't see any 'proof' of a pre-trib rapture here. Can you? You probably think you can if you are a pre-tribber. As with most verses in this book, this is from the New Living Translation, but to understand the nuances of why LaHaye thinks this constitutes 'proof' of a pre-trib rapture, we would do best to use another translation of v13. The King James or Authorized version will allow their reasoning to show – but will also reveal the fatal flaw in their argument...... In the KJV, v 13 is:

> 'looking for that blessed hope, and the glorious appearing of the great God and our Saviour Jesus Christ;'

In fact, let's go wild and add the original Greek (the 1550 Stephanus text for anyone who is interested):

> prosdechomenoi ten makarian elpida kai epiphaneian tes doxes tou megalou theou kai soteros emon iesou christou

Now I suspect that there are some more knowledgeable pre-tribbers who know that this argument is a lousy one, but LaHaye and many others use this verse a lot. They argue that 'makarian elpida' (blessed hope) is here clearly shown to be a separate event from the second coming (described here as epiphaneian tes doxes – 'appearing of glory', or 'glorious appearing') because it is separated by 'kai' which is the Greek word for 'and'. Thus Paul is taking, they claim, a pre-trib position. He is separating an event he calls 'the blessed hope' from the 'glorious appearing'. Having made that assumption, it becomes a weapon and 'proof' in the pre-trib exegetical (allegedly) armoury.

I'm now going to go off on a total (if short) rabbit trail, except, well, it becomes very relevant. Have you ever had the Jehovah's Witnesses knock on your door and try to convert you? I have. If they find out you are a Christian, they will likely immediately try and 'prove' to you that the Trinity is an unbiblical concept. They will say that the Bible never says Jesus is God. They will argue that it is always careful to distinguish Jesus from God himself. You may scramble around for some verse to conclusively show them they are wrong, and you might alight on a verse (depending to some extent on your translation) that appears to accomplish just that..... Titus 2.13! For instance, if you have the New Living Translation, which I have used for most of my bible quotes, it talks of 'our great God and Saviour, Jesus Christ'. Any Jehovah Witness who knows their stuff will immediately use *exactly* the same exegetical manoeuvre that the pre-tribbers use in *exactly the same verse* to get out of this 'proof'. The thing is, in one short verse, Paul uses *exactly* the same grammatical construction *twice*. Let's go back to the Greek original. The phrase in dispute is *megalou theou kai soteros emon iesou christou*. It has just the same construction (two descriptive phrases joined by 'and') as the phrase that these pre-tribbers use to 'prove' that the rapture is a separate event to the second coming. The JW's counter argument if you offer this 'proof' of the divinity of Jesus will be to immediately say

'Ah, but there is the word 'and' in the middle, showing that Paul is talking about two separate persons - Jesus, and God'.

Now in English, we can use the word 'and' in subtly different ways. 'There is a table and a chair' - refers to two objects, whereas 'The amazing device was both a table and a chair' using exactly the same wording, refers to just one object. Hebrew and Greek were no different. Their words for 'and' could also be used in subtly different ways. There have been several debates about the identity of particular kings in the Old Testament over this very issue. For instance, in Daniel 6.28, in the New Living Translation you will read '*So Daniel prospered during the reign of Darius and the reign of Cyrus the Persian*' but the footnote will tell you: or '*of Darius, that is, the reign of Cyrus the Persian*'. Similarly, look at a Greek New Testament with a Greek dictionary in the back and look up 'kai', and you will find a fairly long list of uses and possible translations. It is even sometimes used just to start a sentence - not applicable in our case. A pair of 'kai's in a sentence can be translated 'both... and' or 'not only.... but also' - also not relevant to our case. But 'kai' on its own can also be translated 'also', 'but', 'even', 'that is' and 'namely'. So which is it in our case?

Let's consider this. It is pretty unlikely, almost inconceivable, that Paul would use the exact same grammatical construction twice side by side in the same part of a sentence and not use the two instances in exactly the same way as each other. In fact, there is a well-known grammatical rule in Greek that covers this very construction, known as the Granville-Sharp rule (see the article on Titus 2.13 in the Useful resources at the end of the book). That being so, *either* the pre-trib view separating the blessed hope (aka the rapture in pre-trib interpretation) and the glorious appearing is correct, and so are the Jehovah's witnesses on Jesus not being God, *or* the Christians are right about Jesus being God, and the pre-tribbers are wrong about the blessed hope being a separate event to Jesus visible return. You really can't have your cake and eat it here. It is, though, possible to say that the JW's are right *in this instance*. Other passages may prove the divinity of Jesus, this argument would run, but it is illegitimate to use this verse to prove that position. Let's examine this proposition. Apart from the fact that it violates the Granville-Sharp rule of Greek grammar we mentioned earlier, it would mean that Paul is here arguing that there is going to be a glorious appearing of *both* 'our great God' *and* 'our Saviour Jesus Christ'. This immediately runs into a massive theological problem. It is the unanimous theological position of the New Testament writers that God the Father is invisible, that it is impossible for human flesh to ever see Him! The Synoptic gospels have a couple of moments where God's voice is heard from heaven (at Jesus' baptism and transfiguration), but God is never seen. Near the start of John's gospel we *read 'No one has ever seen God. But the unique One, who is himself God, is near to the Father's heart. He has revealed God to us*', a theme that is echoed in later John passages we have covered earlier where Jesus says things like '*If you have seen me, you have seen the Father'.* Similarly Hebrews 1.3 describes Jesus as being *'the radiance of God's glory and the exact representation of his being'* (NIV), which implies similarly that Jesus is the only sight of God we will get, an implication that gains support from 11.27 which tells us that *'It was by faith that Moses left the land of Egypt, not fearing the king's anger. He kept right on going **because he kept his eyes on the one who is invisible**.'* (And for those of you who think, as I immediately did, of the passage in 12.14 as a possible contradiction, well, it says 'without holiness, it is impossible to see *the Lord'* which is the usual New Testament designation for Jesus.) More to the point, Paul conveys the same message. For instance, he starts his hymn-like paean to the pre-eminence of Christ with the words *'Christ is the visible image of the invisible God....'* (Colossians 1.15). Doubly relevant is 1 Timothy 6.15-6 because not only was it written about the same time as Titus (and even if you are a liberal who believes the pastoral letters are 'deutero-Pauline' then these were written by the same author), but it also refers to God's invisible nature specifically in the light of the second coming. That passage reads:

> *For at just the right time Christ will be revealed from heaven by the blessed and only almighty God, the King of all kings and Lord of all lords. He alone can never die, and he lives in light so brilliant that no human can approach him. **No human eye has ever seen him, nor ever will**. All honour and power to him forever! Amen.*

So, our question then is, how can the intrinsically invisible One ever appear, however gloriously? Unless we are to assume Paul suddenly changed his mind on such a fundamental matter and contradicts himself, then in Titus 2 Paul clearly does not have God the Father (nor for that matter, the Holy Spirit) in mind when he is talking of God's 'glorious appearing'. Thus we have conclusively established that Paul's use of 'and' in the second phrase is one that is emphatically not used to refer to separate elements, but rather to link two descriptive elements *of the same event or object or person*. And therefore the earlier phrase that uses exactly the same construction must be the same. Thus the KJV may accurately reflect the literal word for word Greek when it translates Titus 2.13, but translations that read something like the New International verse does here:

while we wait for the blessed hope - the glorious appearing of our great God and Saviour, Jesus Christ

extremely accurately capture Paul's meaning – he is referring to one and the same event. Jesus' *visible* return is both the 'blessed Hope' and the 'glorious appearing'.

Once more, the very verse and phrase that LaHaye uses to 'prove' that the rapture is a separate event from the second coming actual turn out to emphatically teach and prove quite the opposite. So much for an 'irrefutable proof' of a pre-trib rapture!

PROOF 6

The rapture is imminent – it could happen at any time (Matthew 24.42-4) but the Second Coming cannot happen for at least seven years (Daniel 9.26-9)

PROOF 7

There are no signs before the Rapture, but there are many signs for Jesus' physical coming at the Second Coming (Matthew 24.3-36)

These final two 'proofs' both have to do with the pre-eminent pre-trib concept of 'imminency'. In fact, LaHaye says that of all his 15 'proofs' he believes proof 6 to be the most compelling and unassailable of all.

Let's deal with proof 7 briefly before focusing on the final one. Firstly, yet again, LaHaye uses a passage that explicitly refers to a post-tribulation-at-the-visible-Second-Coming rapture and tries to claim it is a 'proof' that the rapture is a separate event to the Second Coming. Since we have gone over Matthew 24 pretty much to death, we don't need to look any more at this. Secondly – also not for the first time – we find that LaHaye gives absolutely no scripture reference to prove his assertion that 'there are no signs before the Rapture'. He is relying on the concept drummed into his supporters brains that the rapture has to be a pre-trib one because of all the passages that they claim show that Jesus' return will be without any warning whatsoever, largely those passages that refer to Jesus coming as a 'thief in the night'. We will cover these on proof 6, but at this point, all I will say is that – again – just because Paul's rapture passages in 1 Thessalonians 4 and 1 Corinthians 15 do not mention signs that come before the rapture, this does not 'prove' that there are no such signs. Absence of evidence is not evidence of absence, and more to the point, an absence of evidence of a detailed end-time chronology or 'signs preceding' in passages that are focussing on comfort for the grieving or teaching on the nature of the resurrection is *definitely* **not** definitive evidence of absence of such 'signs preceding'. As we have seen, Paul's focus meant he had no need to cover such issues as the signs or timing of the rapture, but his language clearly links them to Matthew 24 which *is* explicit about such signs and chronology. Remember : '*After the tribulation of those days....*'. But, in the one passage where Paul *is* in fact concerned about the timing of the rapture, he does mention such signs – in 2 Thessalonians 2 (see proof 15 above).

So that leaves us with the supposedly massively compelling 'proof 6' where LaHaye actually uses the seminal word 'imminent'. Let's look at the specific passages LaHaye uses first. He says the second coming can't happen for at least seven years (he means from the time of the rapture in a pre-trib scenario). For evidence he cites Daniel 9.26-9. Since Daniel only has 27 verses, this must be a typo, so I will quote v 24-7:

> 'A period of seventy sets of seven has been decreed for your people and your holy city to finish their rebellion, to put an end to their sin, to atone for their guilt, to bring in everlasting righteousness, to confirm the prophetic vision, and to anoint the Most Holy Place. Now listen and understand! Seven sets of seven plus sixty-two sets of seven will pass from the time the command is given to rebuild Jerusalem until a ruler—the Anointed One—comes. Jerusalem will be rebuilt with streets and strong defences, despite the perilous times.
>
> After this period of sixty-two sets of seven, the Anointed One will be killed, appearing to have accomplished nothing, and a ruler will arise whose armies will destroy the city and the Temple. The end will come with a flood, and war and its miseries are decreed from that time to the very end. The ruler will make a treaty with the people for a period of one set of seven, but after half this time, he will put an end to the sacrifices and offerings. And as a climax to all his terrible deeds, he will set up a sacrilegious object that causes desecration, until the fate decreed for this defiler is finally poured out on him.'

(I have, as usual, used the New Living Translation here, but I just want to say that at one point it is probably not the best translation. I think that after talking about the Anointed One being killed, it should read something like 'and the people of the ruler to come will destroy the city and the Temple'. This is not at all central to the case I am making here, but it is basically the translation that pretty much all pre-tribbers would think was correct, and in this case - for once! - I agree with them.)

Now this is clearly something that deals with actual and very specific chronological time periods. On almost everything to do with this passage, I would agree with what I think would be the standard dispensationalist reading of this passage. This passage is specifically to do with Israel. They believe that after the 69th 'week' or 'seven' when the Messiah is killed there is a gap of indeterminate length before the start of the 70th 'week' which describes the actions of the person who in later Christian interpretation would commonly be known as the 'anti-Christ'. After entering into some kind of covenant or treaty with Israel, after three and a half years he puts an end to the God-ordained system of sacrifices and worship, and will set up this 'sacrilegious object that causes desecration', a phrase usually taken to mean setting up an idol for worship in the temple of the one true God. For pre-tribbers, this is a key verse for the pre-trib rapture, and their dispensationalist views are central to why they interpret this passage the way they do. They say that that indeterminate gap is the church age. Often they will say that God's original plan was that Jesus would come as Messiah - and yes, he would still be crucified and resurrected - but the goal was that immediately afterwards Israel would accept the person, work and message of Jesus as their Messiah, at which point God's rule would come to fulfilment on earth. But that Jewish generation's rejection of the gospel of Jesus (foreseen by God) meant that he had a kind of back-up scheme, the church. The message of Jesus' gospel would go out mainly to non-Jews. The Daniel 9 prophetic 'clock' concerning Israel had paused - 'the clock has stopped' as many would put it. But, for these dispensationalists the church age is a kind of hiatus, with God biding his time, preparing to switch his interest back to Israel again. For them the rapture is that moment. The church is whisked out of the way, and the prophetic clock starts ticking again, with the false treaty between the anti-Christ and Israel. This is why they not only believe that there is a fixed 7 year period that LaHaye mentions in this proof, but that this constitutes proof of the pre-trib rapture. The fact that the focus is now on Israel is critical for them. When you combine this understanding with the fact that they believe that the rapture is 'imminent' - in other words, it can happen at any time, without warning, you can see why LaHaye thinks this is the most telling point of all. Since Daniel 9 proves that the Second Coming has a fixed seven year run-up to it, and since - in their view - the bible describes the rapture as somehow part of the Second coming, and yet also describes the Second Coming as something that can happen at any time, then for them the rapture *must* be somehow separate from the visible return of Jesus. But the trouble is, once again you have to *assume* a pre-trib view for this reasoning to in any way 'prove' the pre-trib position. Back to Daniel 9: do you see the rapture anywhere in there? I, for one, do not - not even a hint. Quite frankly, the only thing that could possibly cause anyone to believe that the rapture is in view here is rigid adherence to a dispensationalist position. Dispensationalism was something that I imbibed through what I read as a pre-teen and teenager. Even though I wasn't a believer in a pre-tribulation rapture (I opted for the minority view among dispensationalists - the mid-tribulation rapture, one reason being I figured that the division of Daniel's last 'week' precisely in half *had* to be there for some reason), I accepted without question a lot of dispensationalist rhetoric, thought patterns, broad beliefs and so on. I remember that I pretty much dismissed any notion of a post-trib rapture, probably because I had been so indoctrinated by the repeated assertions - even assumptions - that the rapture was a separate event to the second coming. So for me, it was a choice between a pre and a mid-rapture position. There were various further reasons I chose 'mid-trib' - one being that I thought it terribly unfair that the

Western church appeared to get away with no persecution at all, while the church in the Middle East, China and the like were suffering great tribulations and persecutions. But as I read various materials and arguments around Daniel 9 and other passages, I began to realize that none of my arguments were at all decisive, and neither were those of the opposing pre-trib view. There was nothing exegetically to show support for either, really. I now realize that this is because neither was correct and that Daniel 9 has absolutely no bearing whatsoever on the timing of the rapture. It was all what I now like to describe as an exegetical game of 'eschatological pinyata'. Instead of donning a blindfold and trying to pin the tail on the donkey, we were blindly trying to 'pin' the rapture somewhere on Daniels 70th week. Now, the dispensationalist view at least has the merit of recognizing that the church is not in view in the 70th week, but then in typical dispensationalist fashion they argue that because the church is not in view, this must therefore mean that the church is not there. That's the bit I just don't agree with now.

Let's use an analogy here. I have a now retired friend called Gordon, who, like a good few others, has a model railway in a spare bedroom. And like so many others in that situation, he has solved the space problems by building a mainline loop on a big board on one side. Against the opposing wall he is building another section with a substantial terminus station, and with a removable link section across the doorway. When the link is in place, the two sections are linked. If the link is not in place, then the two railway tracks from the loop that would otherwise be the link function as sidings. The long established loop section has full scenery, whereas the new section has virtually none, at least the last time I saw it. Now let us say I was writing for a model railway magazine and wanted to do a piece on Gordon's railway. They told me that I had to do a piece about scenery, which means that I naturally take photos and write only about the well developed scenic original section. That does not mean that the other section does not exist, even if I don't mention it. Now say someone else went to Gordon's house and through the doorway to that room caught a glimpse of only the other section as he passed, because of the way the door was only half open (and no link section was in place). If he reads my article and realizes it doesn't match up with what he saw, he could think that I am telling porky pies. He saw bare boards with tracks, while I described a layout with full scenery. Alternatively, he could think that I had described a separate layout which has now been sold or dismantled, and that my friend is now working on a brand new project. This would be because he had *assumed* that any layout has the same level of completeness in all its parts, and because he has not *seen* the link position in place that might give him a clue that his assumption is false. He has also assumed that what is *in view* is all that exists of the layout. Similarly, pre-tribbers do not see the link between the rapture passages and Jesus' teaching about his return because they hold to a belief system based on false assumptions. The person in my analogy could compare what he had seen of the model railway layout and my descriptions and photos of the layout and build up a list or chart of differences and contrasts between them that 'prove' that they cannot be the same layout, just as LaHaye does on the rapture and the Second coming here.

	Bare bones layout versus	Fully functional layout
Proof 1	Lots of sidings, no continuous running	Few sidings, continuous running loops
Proof 2	Many trains (sitting in sidings)	Only a couple of trains (running in the loops)
Proof 3	Trains mostly stopped	Trains mostly running
Proof 4	Almost completely flat	Lots of hills
Proof 5	Bare boards, no scenery	Complete set of varied scenery
Two separate layouts – proved beyond all possible doubt!		

But he would have been wrong, just as LaHaye has been proven wrong over and over again as we have moved through these 'proofs'. And so often, the false assumption has been the same – that just because something is not *in view* in a particular passage therefore it must mean that that something *does not and must not exist* in the mind of the author as he describes that event or concept or time.

Quite simply, there is no reference to the rapture in Daniel 9. You can accept - as I pretty much do - all the other elements of the dispensationalist interpretation of Daniel 9, but reject the need for it to posit some definitive end to a church age with the rapture. Nothing in the passage is at all contradictory to a post tribulation rapture position in which the church goes through that final 7 years. They just *aren't in view* in this passage because the focus is on Israel and Jerusalem.

'Ah', I can hear the pre-tribbers reply, 'you might be right about Daniel per se, but placing the rapture before the Tribulation and the fixed final 'Week' of years makes sense of all those other verses that say that Jesus could return at any moment. Your post-trib position where Jesus comes at the end of the final seven years cannot make any sense of those verses, and directly contradicts them.'

So let's have a look at that, starting what LaHaye's claimed 'proof' found in Matthew 24.42-4. It reads:

So you, too, must keep watch! For you don't know what day your Lord is coming. Understand this: If a homeowner knew exactly when a burglar was coming, he would keep watch and not permit his house to be broken into. You also must be ready all the time, for the Son of Man will come when least expected.

For pre-tribbers like LaHaye, the typical argument goes like this. The only reason Jesus would have said to be ready all the time was because he was referring to the 'rapture' that could happen without any pre-warnings or signs. (Funny then, how so many dispensationalists are so obsessed with signs they consider 'prove' that the rapture is close at hand, isn't it?). Since they believe that the visible return of Jesus is preceded by set times and a set chronology, and because they believe that Jesus must mean he can return 'any moment', for them this 'any moment' element must refer to the rapture. This doctrine of 'imminent return' has come to be quite probably the major plank in the pre-tribbers arsenal, which is why – in his mind at least – LaHaye calls Proof 6 the most telling (and presumably 'irrefutable') of them all. For instance, a prominent pre-trib writer and teacher is quoted as saying that imminency is 'the heart of Pre-tribulationism'. He is quite right.

Before we look in detail at this passage, I would like to note that many pre-trib books and websites will unleash a host of quotes that 'prove' 'imminency' as they define it, some so ridiculously not 'proofs' that I will not cover them here in detail. They very often try to use this 'abundance' of texts as 'proof' that no scholar can refute. Take http://www.raptureready.com/rr-imminency.html for instance, which, under the heading 'Scriptures Galore' says :

> *A host of Scriptures indicate the Church should expect an imminent return of their Lord. The opponents of imminency constantly try to pick apart each individual reference, but they should look at the big picture. An overwhelming number of verses in the Bible support imminency.*
>
> *I've been able to easily locate 22 passages that imply that the coming of Christ remains an imminent event. All you really need is one verse to prove a point, but the weight of evidence should cause even the most hard-core imminency foes to rethink their stance.*
>
> *I seriously doubt any scholar or layman could find 22 passages of Scripture that clearly indicate the tribulation or the rule of the Antichrist is the next imminent event facing the Church.*

Notice that the emphasis is on the 'overwhelming number' of texts. To this writer 'one verse' would be enough to 'prove' the point. Also notice that the writer assumes a particular definition of 'imminency', and then holds up a false and double standard. The author first says just one 'scripture' would be enough to 'prove' his view, but then doubts that his opponents could find 22 passages that 'clearly' indicate facts that are necessary for a post-trib position. As we have already seen, there are a number of passages which – when taken *in context* – do consistently teach the very thing he doubts. We won't go over those again, but have you ever heard the phrase 'quality, not quantity'? He could 'easily' find 22 scriptures to support his point, but setting aside for a while the ones that seem at least somewhat supportive of his case, some of them seem bizarre, and taken desperately out of context. For instance (given just one verse is compelling 'proof' for him) he thinks that Romans 16.20 '*And the God of peace shall bruise Satan under your feet shortly*' is proof that Jesus could return anytime. The verse appears in a chapter largely made up of greetings from Paul and Christians to various prominent individuals in the Roman churches. In the middle of this, he issues a final exhortation against false preachers who create divisions and teach doctrines different to what the Roman church has been taught. He praises them for remaining obedient to God, and then comes v20 about God crushing Satan. There is absolutely no mention of the Second Coming of Jesus here in any way, shape or form, yet apparently it is 'indisputable proof' of one very specific end-times scenario. The real context is a promise that God will defeat those false teachers afflicting the church in Rome at the time. That was – let me see now – close to 2000 years ago. Hardly a persuasive argument! But let's just assume for the minute that Paul is in fact referring to the second coming here. Why should this be a 'proof' of the pre-trib position? After all, pretty much every view of the end times envisages Jesus returning with his church, at which time the rule and power of Satan is destroyed. It took me a while to think through why this author thought this was 'proof' of imminency. It is because he assumes the whole panoply of dispensationalist teachings about the anti-Christ, 7 year tribulation and the concept of 'imminency'. This is the *only* way this can constitute the 'proof' he wants. Once again people have to assume the pre-trib position to 'prove' it. (And you know what, when I came to check the final proofs for this book, I read the bit about me taking a while to understand why he thought Romans 16.20 was 'proof' of a pre-trib rapture, and whatever I concluded, it's lost to me now. The only thing I can think of is that because he regards any view other than 'pre-trib' as robbing people of their peace, therefore a reference to 'the God of peace' must 'prove' a pre-trib rapture. Whatever his thinking, well.... when people talk about gossamer thin argument, this is more like the *invisible* argument. Emperor's new clothes, anyone?)

Another alleged 'proof' from the same book of the Bible is 13.11-12 :

> *This is all the more urgent, for you know how late it is; time is running out. Wake up, for our salvation is nearer now than when we first believed. The night is almost gone; the day of salvation will soon be here. So remove your dark deeds like dirty clothes, and put on the shining armour of right living.*

I'm guessing that this is included because it says our salvation is 'nearer now than when we first believed', meaning Jesus' return. But this applies to any view of Jesus' second coming, and to any time period. Now is nearer to that time than a second ago when you read the scripture above, today is nearer than yesterday, this week is nearer.... well, you get the picture.

In fact, if you look through those 22 'easily' found proofs, the vast majority of them only refer to longing for Jesus return, or say that he will come 'quickly', but say nothing about it being 'imminent' in the sense that pre-tribbers claim they do. And at least one more has no reference to Jesus' return at all – Jude 21, which says '*Keep yourselves in the love of God, looking for the mercy of our Lord Jesus Christ unto eternal life*'.

The same pattern of claiming little scripture-snippets as 'proof' of a specific view of imminency while ignoring contexts that say otherwise also appears in the same article when it covers the views of pre 1830 bible teachers on the subject. (This pre-1830 issue is a big deal for pre-tribbers because opponents of the pre-trib rapture mostly argue that it only arose in the 1830's in England, and that no-one held such a view before then). The author assumes that any passage that mentions Jesus returning 'suddenly' or 'speedily' means the author believes that Jesus could come at any time, a tactic which, I have found, is a very typical – and shabby – one used in much pre-trib rhetoric. As another example, the article cites Didache chapter 16 – the teaching of the 12 apostles to the Gentiles that we looked at earlier – as saying:

> Be vigilant over your life; let your lamps not be extinguished, or your loins ungirded, but be prepared, for you know not the hour in which our Lord will come.

But as we saw, this cannot mean 'imminency' in the sense pre-tribbers mean, as the passage goes on to clearly time the rapture after the tribulation and the rise of the anti-Christ. In other words, even though the passage urged readiness because the exact time of Jesus' return was unknown, it went on to teach specific events had to happen before Jesus' return. Again, I have found this taking of snippets of church documents out of context to be typical of many pre-trib arguments and assertions.

Bearing in mind this aptitude to force-fit all sorts of passages to their concept of 'imminency', let us turn back to the passage LaHaye cited as 'proof'. It might seem compelling, until you look at the context. Remember, Jesus had already given an account of the last days which ended with the rapture and his return 'after the tribulation' in 24.3-31. In other words, there were signs, including the actions of the anti-Christ, which have to occur before the rapture/return of Jesus will happen.

However, it is very instructive to see how Jesus applied the lessons of this teaching, in view of the way pre-tribbers are adamant that any verse that talks in terms of the time not being known is 'proof' of imminency and therefore a pre-trib rapture. Jesus seems to alternate between applications that emphasize there are signs to watch for and classic 'imminency' passages that say the exact time is not known by anyone except God.

Immediately after his teaching about the chronology and events of the end days, ending in Matthew 24.31, Jesus goes on to say :

> *Now learn a lesson from the fig tree. When its branches bud and its leaves begin to sprout, you know that summer is near. In the same way, when you see all these things, you can know his return is very near, right at the door. I tell you the truth, this age will not pass from the scene until all these things take place.*

Whatever the particular interpretation we place on these verses – and many dispensationalists believe this is a reference to the resurrection of the nation of Israel – it is quite clear that the emphasis is on a sign or signs that must happen before his return. Given Jesus has just given a whole description of events and signs, including the event Daniel described in the middle of his last 'week' (see Matthew 24.15 on), it is quite clear that they are the 'these things' Jesus is referring to here. He speaks this to his disciples – in other words, the nascent church. This is hardly the 'no-sign-rapture-at-any-moment' imminency teaching we would expect if the pre-trib dispensational position is correct. Jesus immediately follows this by what is a classic 'imminency' text so beloved of pre-tribbers in v36:

> *'However, no one knows the day or hour when these things will happen, not even the angels in heaven or the Son himself. Only the Father knows'*

Given that Jesus has just listed lots of signs, this can hardly mean what the pre-tribbers want it to mean. Notice that Jesus doesn't say that the season is unknown, only the particular day or hour. And 'reconciling' these two back-to-back and allegedly contradictory passages is really that simple!

Jesus goes on to say, (v37-41):

> *When the Son of Man returns, it will be like it was in Noah's day. In those days before the flood, the people were enjoying banquets and parties and weddings right up to the time Noah entered his boat. People didn't realize*

what was going to happen until the flood came and swept them all away. That is the way it will be when the Son of Man comes.

Two men will be working together in the field; one will be taken, the other left. Two women will be grinding flour at the mill; one will be taken, the other left.

These sentences too, are often taken as 'proof' of the rapture by pre-tribbers. They say that since there are signs of the return of Jesus including massive chaos and portents, yet here there appears to be no warning, this must refer to a separate pre-trib rapture, in which the church is taken away, leaving the wicked 'left behind'. Hence, also, the following verses that LaHaye uses as his proof of 'imminency' must also refer to this same pre-trib rapture.

In LaHaye and friends 'chop and dice' approach, you can put these two sets of passages into a table of proofs like we did over the model railway and 'prove' that they 'must' be talking about two different events. But actually reading this particular teaching of Jesus in context as the sustained passage that it in fact is shows the silliness and barrenness of the dispensational 'slice and dice' approach. After all, in 'Proof 7' LaHaye uses v 3-36 as proof of 'many signs of Jesus coming' and yet uses v 42-4 here as 'proof' that Jesus can come at anytime in the rapture. And yet these are part of the same teaching. Methinks LaHaye is a touch confused here.

If Jesus meant to teach what pre-tribbers claim is the true understanding about the rapture, he's made a pretty ugly mess of it. He tells his disciples about the signs of the end, including the tribulation, coming before his visible return, which is described in terms of a rapture event, yet he never mentions anything that even hints of a rapture earlier on in his talk, yet expects them (and us) to understand a rapture happening where he describes none (there is nothing like a rapture event described before the Tribulation in Matthew 24) and not happening where he does describe a rapture event *('After the Tribulation of those days...')*. Not a very good teacher or communicator, if the pre-trib position was what he meant to teach!

Jesus goes on to emphasize that the 'signs preceding' are evidence that the season of his coming is near, even though the exact time is unknown. He says that his return will be like the days of Noah; specifically that normal human social life will continue right up to the moment that the day of judgement arrives, just as it did right up to when the Flood came, destroying the wicked. The only people 'left behind' when the flood waters of judgement swept over the earth were those righteous ones who heeded God's warning and were on Noah's ark. Thus when Jesus talks of one being taken and one being left, the usual pre-trib view of this passage is called into question. For them, those who are taken are the righteous, 'raptured' out of the world, leaving the wicked behind. But the context, where Jesus talked about the flood when the wicked were taken away and the righteous were left to start a new world, strongly suggests that the pre-tribbers may have this verse all the wrong way round. It is more likely that the wicked are taken away, and the righteous left behind. After all, earlier, in Matthew 13, Jesus had depicted the same pattern in his parable of the wheat and the weeds, which concerns the end of the world and judgement day. He said in v40-43 that:

> *Just as the weeds are sorted out and burned in the fire, so it will be at the end of the world. The Son of Man will send his angels, and they will remove from his Kingdom everything that causes sin and all who do evil. And the angels will throw them into the fiery furnace, where there will be weeping and gnashing of teeth. Then the righteous will shine like the sun in their Father's Kingdom. Anyone with ears to hear should listen and understand!*

Pre-tribbers like LaHaye just don't seem to know what to do with a passage like Matthew 24 as a whole, which combines signs before Jesus return, and yet the need to be watchful because the *'Son of Man will come when least expected'* (24.44). How can Jesus return, they argue, only after the preceding signs, and yet his coming be unexpected? They feel they can only make sense of passages like this by their 'slice and dice' approach, in a kind of evangelical 'documentary hypothesis' (don't worry if you don't get that reference, those of you that do will appreciate the irony) in which certain verses are assigned to a pre-trib rapture because of alleged 'imminency' and others assigned to Jesus visible return to earth to rule. (And quite often they can't even get this straight. I have often seen the same verses in one pre-trib author applied to the visible return of Jesus, whilst another teacher is adamant that the very same passage is 'indisputable proof' for a pre-trib rapture.)

But to be fair, in a way they do have a point – sort of. There is some need of reconciliation beyond understanding that just because the hour and day (exact timing) of Jesus' return is not known, the season may be known through the predicted signs. How can Jesus talk in terms of signs that must happen before he returns, and yet social life goes on as normal, and his disciples must be watchful and alert because they don't know when He will return?

We find the clue to resolve this apparent dilemma, I suggest, in the final paragraph in Matthew 24 (from v45 on), where Jesus says:

> *'A faithful, sensible servant is one to whom the master can give the responsibility of managing his other household servants and feeding them.*

If the master returns and finds that the servant has done a good job, there will be a reward. I tell you the truth, the master will put that servant in charge of all he owns. But what if the servant is evil and thinks, 'My master won't be back for a while,' and he begins beating the other servants, partying, and getting drunk? The master will return unannounced and unexpected, and he will cut the servant to pieces and assign him a place with the hypocrites. In that place there will be weeping and gnashing of teeth.'

Neither the faithful nor the wicked servant supervisor knows exactly when their master returns, but his return is a total surprise to the wicked servant, who is given over to moral dissipation and evil deeds, abusing the trust he was given. Now this passage is specifically for the apostles and church leaders (it concerns someone placed in authority over other servants) but the principles contained here apply more widely. Even though Jesus' disciples suffer greatly, for those people who reject God, they will be living their lives as normal, eating and drinking, marrying and partying, and for them the day will come as totally unexpected. But in v42-4 Jesus is warning his followers not be like that, but to be alert and keep watch - watch for the signs, and live rightly, not in unaware moral dissipation.

This pattern runs through so many of the passages that pre-tribbers take to be 'proof' of their specific reading of the concept of 'imminence'. The key is people's behaviour, particularly those of Jesus disciples (because that was whom he was addressing). This link is even more explicit in Luke's account of the same teaching of Jesus in 17.35-48. The context is telling. Jesus warns of the dangers of greed for money and wealth, and of worrying about provision. He says in v29-31:

*'And don't be concerned about what to eat and what to drink. Don't worry about such things. These things **dominate the thoughts of unbelievers all over the world**, but your Father already knows your needs. Seek the Kingdom of God above all else, and he will give you everything you need.'*

Jesus then turns from worry and wealth to his return, linking the two by starting from v34 with

Wherever your treasure is, there the desires of your heart will also be

Be dressed for service and keep your lamps burning, as though you were waiting for your master to return from the wedding feast. Then you will be ready to open the door and let him in the moment he arrives and knocks. The servants who are ready and waiting for his return will be rewarded. I tell

you the truth, he himself will seat them, put on an apron, and serve them as they sit and eat! He may come in the middle of the night or just before dawn. But whenever he comes, he will reward the servants who are ready.

"Understand this: If a homeowner knew exactly when a burglar was coming, he would not permit his house to be broken into. You also must be ready all the time, for the Son of Man will come when least expected."

Peter asked, "Lord, is that illustration just for us or for everyone?"

And the Lord replied, "A faithful, sensible servant is one to whom the master can give the responsibility of managing his other household servants and feeding them. If the master returns and finds that the servant has done a good job, there will be a reward. I tell you the truth, the master will put that servant in charge of all he owns. But what if the servant thinks, 'My master won't be back for a while,' and he begins beating the other servants, partying, and getting drunk? The master will return unannounced and unexpected, and he will cut the servant in pieces and banish him with the unfaithful.

"And a servant who knows what the master wants, but isn't prepared and doesn't carry out those instructions, will be severely punished. But someone who does not know, and then does something wrong, will be punished only lightly. When someone has been given much, much will be required in return; and when someone has been entrusted with much, even more will be required.

People who live in rebellion against God by evil lives, or who are consumed with the lust for wealth, or worry about provision, are those who will not be ready, will not be spiritually awake and alert, and for whom the day will come as a surprise, 'like a thief in the night'.

Whenever the apostles used the same 'thief in the night' imagery, which pre-tribbers make so much of as a proof of an 'any-time' imminent rapture, they followed Jesus in using the same pattern and understanding. For instance, in 1 Thessalonians 5.1-11, Paul is very explicit on this issue:

Now concerning how and when all this will happen, dear brothers and sisters, we don't really need to write you. For you know quite well that the day of the Lord's return will come unexpectedly, like a thief in the night. When people are saying, "Everything is peaceful and secure," then disaster will fall on them as suddenly as a pregnant woman's labour pains begin. And there will be no escape.

But you aren't in the dark about these things, dear brothers and sisters, and **you won't be surprised when the day of the Lord comes like a thief.** *For you are all children of the light and of the day; we don't belong to darkness and night. So be on your guard, not asleep like the others. Stay alert and be clearheaded. Night is the time when people sleep and drinkers get drunk. But let us who live in the light be clearheaded, protected by the armour of faith and love, and wearing as our helmet the confidence of our salvation.*

For God chose to save us through our Lord Jesus Christ, not to pour out his anger on us. Christ died for us so that, whether we are dead or alive when he returns, we can live with him forever. So encourage each other and build each other up, just as you are already doing.

Back in proof 10 LaHaye uses a couple of verses from this passage completely out of context to 'prove' a pre-trib rapture, but as ever, once you take it in context, the passage says something totally antagonistic to pre-trib assumptions and positions.

The apostle Peter also uses the same context of final judgement and the need for right living when he uses 'thief in the night' imagery, in 2 Peter 3.7-15a:

And by the same word, the present heavens and earth have been stored up for fire. They are being kept for the **day of judgement,** *when* **ungodly people will be destroyed.**

But you must not forget this one thing, dear friends: A day is like a thousand years to the Lord, and a thousand years is like a day. The Lord isn't really being slow about his promise, as some people think. No, he is being patient for your sake. He does not want anyone to be destroyed, but wants everyone to repent. But the day of the Lord will come as **unexpectedly as a thief. Then the heavens will pass away with a terrible noise,** *and the very elements themselves will disappear in fire, and the earth and everything on it will be found to deserve judgement.*

Since everything around us is going to be destroyed like this, **what holy and godly lives you should live, looking forward to the day of God and hurrying it along.** *On that day, he will set the heavens on fire, and the elements will melt away in the flames. But we are looking forward to the* *new heavens and new earth he has promised, a world filled with God's righteousness.*

And so, dear friends, while you are waiting for these things to happen, **make every effort to be found living peaceful lives that are pure and blameless in his sight.**

And remember, our Lord's patience gives people time to be saved.

Notice something else here. It is crystal clear that Peter is talking about the visible return of Jesus when the whole earth is judged and transformed. This is most certainly not a 'secret rapture' coming of Jesus, and yet Peter has no problem using 'unexpectedly as a thief' imagery. This utterly disproves the dispensational contention that 'thief in the night' imagery *must* mean their version of 'imminence' and therefore a pre-trib secret rapture.

'Thief' imagery also appears in the Revelation to John. When in 3.1-6 Jesus sends a message to the church in Sardis, the same pattern of immoral living being linked to Jesus coming like a thief appears. Once again, it is worth quoting in full:

I know all the things you do, and that you have a reputation for being alive —but you are dead. Wake up! Strengthen what little remains, for even what is left is almost dead. I find that your actions do not meet the requirements of my God. Go back to what you heard and believed at first; hold to it firmly. Repent and turn to me again. If you don't wake up, I will come to you suddenly, as unexpected as a thief.

Yet there are some in the church in Sardis who have not soiled their clothes with evil. They will walk with me in white, for they are worthy. All who are victorious will be clothed in white. I will never erase their names from the Book of Life, but I will announce before my Father and his angels that they are mine.

Anyone with ears to hear must listen to the Spirit and understand what he is saying to the churches.

This most likely doesn't refer in any way to the return of Jesus, but it does show exactly the same pattern in the mind of the Lord Jesus as in the other passages. The pattern also crops up once more in Revelation 16.15 where it emphatically *does* refer to the return of Jesus. The context is plagues of judgement of God's wrath being poured out on the earth, and demons gathering together all the armies of the world to fight against God at the battle of Armageddon (definitely no pre-trib rapture here then). In the midst of this John is inspired to interject the following:

Look, I will come as unexpectedly as a thief! Blessed are all who are watching for me, who keep their clothing ready so they will not have to walk around naked and ashamed.

Those who watch for Jesus' return are not caught out. Given that (as we have seen earlier) in Revelation clothing stands for the righteous acts of God's people, and given the context of wrath upon the ungodly, even this small isolated verse contains the imprint of Jesus' pattern of teaching – that the day of the Lord comes unexpectedly like a thief for the wicked, but for those who are righteous and godly and alert and not living lives of moral dissipation, well, they won't be caught ashamed on that day of judgement.

Although Luke's version of Jesus' end times teaching doesn't actually use the 'thief in the night' imagery explicitly, what is made explicit are the effects of moral dissipation and the worries of this life on people's alertness and readiness for Jesus' return (21.34-6):

Watch out! Don't let your hearts be dulled by carousing and drunkenness, and by the worries of this life. Don't let that day catch you unaware, like a trap. For that day will come upon everyone living on the earth. Keep alert at all times. And pray that you might be strong enough to escape these coming horrors and stand before the Son of Man.

It is also worth looking a few verses earlier at v27-8. After having talked of the terrible times ahead, Jesus says:

Then everyone will see the Son of Man coming on a cloud with power and great glory. So when all these things begin to happen, stand and look up, for your salvation is near!

Notice that Jesus tells his *disciples* – i.e. the nascent church – that when they see all the signs preceding begin to happen, they need to stand up and look up, because their salvation is near (does the need to stand up imply that the Christians will be bowed down with oppression, hiding as best they can, at this point? Just something to think about). In the context of what has been said before, part of that salvation at least, must be rescue from the great persecution (v12) he warned them about. And notice that their salvation is not by some 'secret rapture' but when every eye will see Jesus coming in power and great glory. Another nail in the coffin of the 'pre-trib rapture' right there.

One thing that should be clear is that Jesus warned his disciples repeatedly of a great persecution before he returned. This rather contradicts the 'pre-tribbers' monotonous mantra that Jesus 'would not let his church go through the tribulation'. And here is where potentially esoteric debates on the end times teaching becomes very practical and relevant indeed. If the pre-trib view were in fact correct, then we can rest easy that whatever we suffer, we will not have to face the time more terrible than any other that Jesus warned about. As we have seen, this does not make sense - why would Jesus warn his disciples of this great suffering if they would not have to undergo it, not because it was far in the future (which it was) but because the church would be raptured out of the way?

Look at Luke 17.22-34 where Jesus answers a question from the Pharisees about the kingdom of God and then turns to his disciples and teaches them about the end times.

> Then he said to his disciples, "The time is coming when you will long to see the day when the Son of Man returns, but you won't see it. People will tell you, 'Look, there is the Son of Man,' or 'Here he is,' but don't go out and follow them. For as the lightning flashes and lights up the sky from one end to the other, so it will be on the day when the Son of Man comes. But first the Son of Man must suffer terribly and be rejected by this generation.

> When the Son of Man returns, it will be like it was in Noah's day. In those days, the people enjoyed banquets and parties and weddings right up to the time Noah entered his boat and the flood came and destroyed them all.

> And the world will be as it was in the days of Lot. People went about their daily business—eating and drinking, buying and selling, farming and building - until the morning Lot left Sodom. Then fire and burning sulphur rained down from heaven and destroyed them all. Yes, it will be 'business as usual' right up to the day when the Son of Man is revealed. On that day a person out on the deck of a roof must not go down into the house to pack. A person out in the field must not return home. Remember what happened to Lot's wife! If you cling to your life, you will lose it, and if you let your life go, you will save it. That night two people will be asleep in one bed; one will be taken, the other left. Two women will be grinding flour together at the mill; one will be taken, the other left.

Notice firstly that his disciples will long to see the coming of the Son of Man but won't see it. Now, this is hardly conclusive, but that reads to me most naturally as the church so suffering that they long for the day of Jesus' return to save them from it, but it doesn't come as they wish. Not exactly consistent with a pre-tribulation rapture, for sure! More to the point, once again Jesus emphasizes that normal social life will continue right up to the day of judgement. This seems to have been a central point of his teaching about the end times. Yes, there were dire times ahead, but not so apocalyptic that the normal social practices are abandoned. As this translation has it, it will be *'business as usual' right up to the day when the Son of Man is <u>revealed</u>* (not 'right up until when the invisible Son of Man sneaks in to secretly rescue his church and then returns to heaven leaving chaos behind').

Jesus also gives some very practical instructions on what to do and what not to do on that day. His disciples are warned not to go downstairs to pack, nor to return home, but rather to flee. He urges them to remember Lot's wife, who had such a longing for her old lifestyle that she hung back and gazed on Sodom and was fatally caught up in its judgement. They must flee from those about to fall under judgement, just as Lot and his daughters fled from the wicked cities out into the countryside. Such a teaching would hardly be necessary if everyone was going to be somehow magically raptured out of the way, which is how pre-tribbers would interpret this passage, given it goes on to use the classic 'one will be taken, one will be left' motif so beloved of their dramatic reconstructions of the alleged 'rapture'. Several times Jesus teaches the paradox of losing your life if you cling to it, but saving it if you let it go. Here Jesus says exactly the same thing but applies it in a very practical way to how to respond to his return. If people try and cling to their accustomed lifestyle and pattern of living, they will lose their lives, but if they are willing to heed Jesus warning and flee, then they will save their lives. The point is that if a whole generation of churches have been brainwashed by the pre-trib lie, then they have been brought into a false hope that will preclude the cultivation of this attitude that Jesus encourages here. They will be chained by a complacency that will - except for the grace of God - condemn them. They will have been insulated against Jesus' forceful warnings to his disciples that they will go through great persecution in the end times, and only those who persevere and endure to the end will be saved (e.g. Matthew 24.13 and Mark 13.13).

This is why the issue is so vital, not an obscure matter for esoteric debate. If these are the very last days, then it really matters what we believe on the issue of rapture timing. It has massive practical and real ramifications. The evangelical church needs to stop heeding the seductive siren calls of the pre-trib position promising escape, and listen to Jesus' passionate warnings about what is to come and what we must endure.

One final point on the question of 'imminency'. It is quite possible that there is a passage in scripture that directly refutes and warns about the pre-tribbers doctrine of 'imminency' – the teaching that the day of the Lord / rapture can occur at any moment. Let's go back briefly to a passage that we have already looked at, 2 Thessalonians 2. This passage is responding to a false teaching that the day of the Lord had already come and gone, and it does so by saying that certain events must happen before that day can come. Since those events had not happened, ergo, the day of the Lord (Jesus' return) had not happened. Specifically, v2 in the New Living Translation reads

> *Don't be so easily shaken or alarmed by those who say that the day of the Lord has already begun. Don't believe them, even if they claim to have had a spiritual vision, a revelation, or a letter supposedly from us.*

Now, we may wonder why on earth anyone would believe that the day of the Lord had already come or begun. After all, pagan Rome still ruled, Israel was still conquered, the church was still persecuted. We don't know how the false teachers justified such an assertion, or what specific teaching they were using, but there are surely parallels with the pre-trib position. After all, for pre-tribbers, people on earth after the rapture can realize that they have been left behind, that the 'day of the Lord' (meaning the final 7 year period) has already come.

But there is more. A number of other translations, such as the King James Version, read slightly differently (and this is especially interesting because so many pre-tribbers also insist that the KJV is the only valid and uncorrupted translation):

> *That ye be not soon shaken in mind, or be troubled, neither by spirit, nor by word, nor by letter as from us, as that the day of Christ is at hand*

This is even stronger. If this translation is correct, then the false teaching faced by the Thessalonian church is even more relevant to the equally false pre-trib teaching we face today. If it is correct, then Paul is refuting the idea that the day of the Lord is imminent – that it could come at any time, by reminding his hearers of the actions of the anti-Christ and other events that must happen before Jesus' return. Obviously the word 'if' is key. Why the two different translations of this word? I am no Greek expert, but to find out, I turned to my Greek New Testament and its dictionary. The Greek word Paul used here is *enestayken*. When I look it up in the dictionary, I find that it is the 'perfect tense' of *evistaymi* which the dictionary defines as 'be impending, be present'. It goes on to say that in the perfect tense it means 'have come, arrived' and that when it is used in the perfect participle form, it means 'present' or 'imminent'. Thus we can see why some translations differ in how they translate the word. 'Imminent' or 'at hand' is a viable translation, and arguably is the better translation when you consider the underlying concerns Paul seems to be responding to (see the links about 2 Thessalonians in the additional resources section at the back). But as we have already seen when we discussed proof 15, even if we use the other translation – which is weaker in terms of its usefulness for my argument here – then the passage as a whole still undermines the pre-trib position, particularly when we take it in conjunction with Jesus' teaching on the matter. The pre-tribbers' notion of 'imminence', we find, is not supported by the very passages and imagery they claim for its defence. And if, as seems quite probable, the 'at hand' or 'imminent' translation does turn out to be the better one, then here we have an extremely direct, and complete and utter, biblical refutation of this central pre-trib pillar.

WRAPTURING IT ALL UP

So let's summarize. Firstly, in the two unequivocal rapture passages in Paul - 1 Corinthians 15 and 1 Thessalonians 4 - the apostle uses language that points directly and uniquely, once we understand Jewish idiom and interpretational techniques, to Jesus' teaching on the last days in Matthew 24 and parallel gospel passages. In this teaching, Jesus describes the rapture in the same terms as Paul uses, and is absolutely explicit in placing it *at his visible return and after the tribulation.* For the pre-trib position to be correct, we would have needed some sign of a disruptive key rapture event *before* the tribulation, but such a hint is not found, even in cryptic terms, anywhere in Jesus' teaching on the end times.

Secondly, we have found that when we examine scriptures that pre-tribbers claim as 'proof' of their position, they pretty much always turn out to have multiple problems involving:
a) having to assume a dispensationalist pre-trib position before they can in any way remotely 'prove' such a position - in other words, circular argument is rampant,
b) these circular arguments often involve a false assumption that absence of a particular concept or event in a passage means that that event or concept cannot happen, and this is then used to 'prove' a contradiction with other passages where none need exist, in ways that evangelical apologists would rightly call out if the same false arguments were used elsewhere in Scripture, such as the accounts of Jesus' birth, and
c) a slice and dice approach to scripture that involves taking verses wildly out of context, so that carefully snipped out verses are taken from within passages which, when read as a whole teach pretty explicitly the opposite of what pre-tribbers require, and in a few cases these little scripture-snippets don't even refer to the second coming of Jesus at all. On occasion LaHaye uses snippets from the very same passage to 'prove' both 'phases' of the pre-trib second coming scenario, even though when read in context, there is nothing to justify the separate-events interpretation.

These false arguments and dubious tactics are not at all unique to LaHaye and are rampant throughout virtually all pre-trib apologists. (Also watch out in popular literature for the following trick : describe dramatic scenes of chaos after a pre-trib rapture, and only then say this is what the bible teaches, followed by quotes from relevant passages, but no actual discussion of the timing, or at least, no discussion that even considers alternative interpretations). If you can grasp the falsity of these tactics you can debunk at least 90% of all pre-trib arguments.

Moving specifically to LaHaye's allegedly 'irrefutable' 15 'proofs', let us summarize.

Proof 1. In the Rapture, Christ comes in the air *for* his own (1 Thessalonians 4.14-17) but at the Second Coming Christ comes to earth *with* his own (Revelation 19.11-16).

Here is a typical false dichotomy, where LaHaye forces the two passages to contradict one another by ignoring the purpose of the 1 Thessalonians passage (to encourage those grieving dead Christians, not to give a full-blown account of the end times), ignoring the actual content of the same passage, which, when examined closely, indicates the resurrected saints meeting with Jesus and accompanying him back to earth, and by assuming that just because Jesus' return to earth is not explicitly mentioned in one passage, that means it cannot be in view. Similarly it *assumes* that just because Revelation 19 doesn't mention resurrected saints meeting Jesus as he returns that it is impossible for this to happen here.

Proof 2. At the Rapture, all the Christians are translated or raptured (1 Thessalonians 4, 1 Corinthians 15), but at the Second Coming no-one is raptured.

Here LaHaye's assumption of dispensational / pre-trib interpretation is so absolute that he doesn't even mention any scripture to support his second contention. If he had actually genuinely considered Jesus' teaching on the end times in Matthew 24 and parallels, he would find that Jesus graphically describes the rapture at his second coming, which he absolutely explicitly says is '*After the tribulation...*'

Proof 3. At the Rapture, Christians are taken to the Fathers House (John 14.1-3) but at the Second Coming the Resurrected saints do not see the Father's House.

Similarly, LaHaye uses no scripture to back up his second assertion, but just resorts to gratuitous assertion. For instance, in LaHaye's version of events, the Fathers house is a reference to heaven, to which he has the church flee for the seven years during the tribulation. But when we consider the fact that the bible repeatedly teaches that Jesus returns to rule on earth, is it any surprise that no passage about his Second Coming refers to saints in the Father's House - i.e. heaven. Again, this proof only 'works' - and barely even then - if we accept the pre-trib concept of a separate group of 'Tribulation Saints'. Furthermore, the passage he quotes in John's gospel about the Fathers House not only cannot refer to a rapture as a separate event to the Second Coming, *in context it doesn't even refer to Jesus' second coming at all!!!*

Proof 4. At the rapture, there is no judgement on earth, but at the Second Coming Christ judges the inhabitants of the earth (Matthew 25.31-46).

Yet another case of a gratuitous assertion with no scripture to back it up. The two unequivocal rapture passages in Paul were meant to a) refute false teaching in a church about the resurrection (1 Corinthians 15) and b) encourage new Christians grieving over their dead that they would see them again at the return of Jesus (1 Thessalonians 4), so to use these as 'proof' that there is no judgement involved when the context and purpose was not concerned with unbelievers at all is absurd in the extreme. Yet again, such an approach *assumes* that just because something is *not in view* therefore it must not exist. And anyway, given that, as we have seen, Jesus actually places the rapture at the time of his visible coming, this is a moot point – rapture, second coming and judgement are all demonstrably part of one event anyway.

Proof 5. In the Rapture, the church is taken to heaven (1 Thessalonians 4.16-17), but at the Second Coming Christ sets up his kingdom on earth (Revelation chapters 19 and 20)

Quite simply, this involves making 1 Thessalonians 4.16-7 say something that it absolutely does not say. It says that Jesus comes *from* heaven, that the saints meet him in the air, and are with him forever from that point on. It says nothing about Jesus returning *to* heaven, and nothing about the church being taken *to* heaven, either. In fact, it uses a word for 'meet' that was used of a crowd coming to greet a conquering military figure and escort him into the city that the crowd originally surged out from. In other words, yet again, you have to *assume* a pre-trib position to *distort* this passage of scripture into fitting the pre-trib scenario.

Proof 6. The rapture is imminent – it could happen at any time (Matthew 24.42-4) but the Second Coming cannot happen for at least seven years (Daniel 9.26-9)

LaHaye, as is typical for pre-tribbers, here has to execute a number of energetic exegetical gymnastics over Matthew 24. His brainwashing in the 'imminent – could-happen-at-any-moment' concept is so strong that he is forced to take these few verses completely out of context. He uses the bulk of the rest of the passage in the very next 'proof' to 'prove' that there are many signs for Jesus' physical return. Jesus not only made it explicit that the rapture was 'after the tribulation' in the very same passage of scripture, but he goes on to emphasize that there were signs to look out for that showed the season of his return was near, even though the exact timing would be unknown. In the midst of this teaching, LaHaye snips out a couple of verses and claims that they mean something directly contradictory to their context.

Proof 7. There are no signs before the Rapture, but there are many signs for Jesus' physical coming at the Second Coming (Matthew 24.3-36)

Once again, LaHaye makes a gratuitous assertion about the lack of signs for the rapture, without any scripture to back it up. If we assume he is referring to Paul's teaching in 1 Corinthians 15 and 1 Thessalonians 4, then the fact that he mentions no signs is irrelevant, for the same reasons as the fact that he mentions no judgement on earth is irrelevant. Giving a detailed account of the end times is not the purpose of such passages, debunking specific false beliefs about the resurrection are. If we actually look at the context, we could reasonably expect no discussion of matters such as signs of the end times. And, as we have seen, the very passage that LaHaye uses to 'prove' that the second coming is separate from the rapture explicitly states the opposite.

Proof 8. The rapture is for believers only (1 Thessalonians 4.14), but the second coming affects all humanity (Revelation 1.7).

Firstly, 1 Thessalonians is written to believers, and chapter 4 concerns an issue with believers, so this is a spectacularly weak argument. The rapture is for believers only, but that does not mean that it can't happen as part of Jesus' visible return, seen by the whole earth. Secondly, the fact that in both Revelation 1.7 and 1 Thessalonians 4.17 Jesus is described as coming with the clouds strongly suggests that it is talking about the same event, especially since Matthew 24.30 describes the rapture as happening when the whole earth sees the 'Son of Man coming in the clouds of heaven with great power and glory'. Not only that but v30 says the nations of the earth mourn at Jesus' return, while the elect are raptured, and Revelation 1.7 also says the nations mourn, which is a clear and direct allusion to Jesus words in Matthew 24.30. The implications could not be clearer. Far from being a proof that the rapture must be separate from the second coming, these two 'proofs' actually demonstrate the opposite, that the rapture and Jesus' return are one and the same event.

Proof 9. The rapture is a time of joy (Titus 2.13, 1 Thessalonians 2.19-20, 4.18) but the Second Coming is a time of mourning (Revelation 1.7).

This is a similarly numbskull argument. Even if we take the pre-trib position that there will be 'Tribulation saints' then surely these will rejoice when Jesus comes again? In his Left Behind series, this is precisely how LaHaye depicts them, despite his claim here that the Second Coming is a time of mourning for all the earth, and that therefore this must make it distinct from the rapture. In actual fact Revelation 1.7 has elements both of rejoicing 'Look, he is coming.... Yes, Amen!' framed around a depiction of the nations (assumed to be enemies of God) mourning.

1 Thessalonians 2.19-20 talks of Paul's expectation of rejoicing before Jesus at his second coming. To claim that this is clear 'proof' of a separate pre-trib rapture is utterly inadequate. Any believer will look forward to rejoicing when Jesus returns, regardless of their 'trib' position. It proves nothing. Similarly 1 Thessalonians 4.18 is irrelevant to this issue, apart from the fact that it occurs in a rapture passage. It just commands the Thessalonian believers to encourage each other with the words Paul has spoken, which yes, are about the rapture / second coming of Jesus, but specifically in the context of grief and theological questions over recently deceased fellow believers. It proves nothing about the timing of the rapture in any way shape or form. To use this verse as a 'proof' is a desperate clutching at straws.

Most spectacularly of all, Titus 2.13, so often used to 'big up' the pre-trib rapture with the title of 'the Blessed Hope' turns out on close linguistic examination to utterly undermine the pre-trib position. Lahaye and pre-tribbers who use this verse as 'proof' that the rapture is separate to the second coming have clearly just not thought it through, but operated on brain-washed repetition. This is so important that I will cite the verse in full and summarize the argument. Titus 2.13 reads (here using the KJV):

...looking for that blessed hope and the glorious appearing of the great God and our Saviour Jesus Christ

Lahaye and friends say that the blessed hope is the rapture, and the glorious appearing is the second coming. To them the 'and' here indicates two separate events or concepts. However, Paul uses the exact same linguistic formula in the next section about *who* is gloriously appearing. Many apologists and scholars say this phrase indicates a belief in the full divinity of Christ – in other words that it is saying Jesus is both 'the great God', and our Saviour, with 'and' here joining the two short phrases, not separating them. Paul must have used the linguistic formula the same way in both halves of the verse. If he was using the word 'and' to separate two events or concepts, as the pre-trib position requires, he must here be picturing the 'glorious appearing' of *both* Jesus Christ *and* 'the Great God' which would then have to mean God the Father, but as we know from other New Testament passages, including from at least one other pastoral letter Paul was writing *at the same time,* God the Father, however glorious he is, is invisible to the human eye, and therefore cannot 'gloriously appear'. And there is no other verse that depicts the Father appearing at Jesus' return, only Jesus the Son. Thus the only way that pre-Tribulationists who use the verse the way LaHaye does can do so *consistently* is by propagating grave theological error – amounting to outright heresy – in the very same verse.

Proof 10. The rapture occurs before the 'day of wrath' (Revelation 3.10, 1 Thessalonians 5.8-9), but the second coming occurs immediately after the Tribulation (Matthew 24.29-36).

This demonstrates the typical LaHaye / pre-trib tactics of a) using irrelevant passages or taking them out of context, and b) using as 'proof' a passage that clearly states the exact opposite of what he is claiming. As we saw in proof 7, Matthew 24.29-31 has Jesus clearly describing the rapture as happening at the same time as his visible return and explicitly saying it happens 'After the tribulation...'. Hardly very conducive to a 'pre-trib' rapture position! Revelation 3.10 is taken completely out of context, despite LaHaye's and pre-tribbers' repeated claim that their position and interpretation is the only one that 'truly takes the bible literally'. Here they take a promise given to one particular church in Western Turkey in the 1st Century AD in one particular historical situation and try and claim it as 'proof' of something thousands of years later for the whole church. 1 Thessalonians 5.8-9 (sic – probably he meant to say v9-10) is a passage that in the context of the Second Coming describes a) the need for Christians to live righteously and spiritually alert, and b) the fact that God had chosen believers for salvation, not for wrath. For this to constitute 'proof' you have to assume the pre-trib assumption that the 'wrath' here refers specifically and narrowly to the wrath of God in the seven years before Jesus' return, rather than, say, the eternal wrath of God in judgement (i.e. hell). LaHaye also uses this little snippet, but ignores the earlier verses that form the context, and which undermine his position as they allude to Jesus' explicit teaching in Matthew 24 that places the rapture as exactly contemporary with his return and after the Tribulation (a Tribulation which most pre-tribbers believe also coincides chronologically with the wrath of God).

Proof 11. At the rapture, there is no mention of Satan, but at the Second Coming, Satan is bound in the abyss for 1000 years (Revelation 19.20-20.3)

Yet another case of LaHaye violating the dictum that absence of evidence is not necessarily evidence of absence. In this case this kind of argument is particularly useless, as these 'rapture passages' have no need to mention Satan since their focus is on either the *nature* of the final resurrection of the elect (1 Corinthians 15) or the *fact* of the final resurrection of the elect (1 Thessalonians 4). There was therefore no need for Paul to mention the *enemy* of the elect here.

Proof 12. At the rapture, there is the judgement seat of Christ (1 Corinthians 4.5, 2 Corinthians 5.9-10, but at the Second Coming, there is no time or place for the judgement seat of Christ.

This is a classic example both of a 'gratuitous assertion' without any scripture to back it up, and of only being able to 'prove' the pre-trib position by assuming it. Both the Corinthian passages are simple references to the fact that Christians will be judged for their actions, and instruction on how to live in the light of this. There is nothing in their context to indicate any concern for the particular timings of the return of Jesus and can fit just as well, if not better, in a post-trib scenario. The reason LaHaye and those who believe similarly think this constitutes proof for a pre-trib rapture is because they are a) assuming that this judgement happens in heaven, which is their assertion as a result of their pre-trib position (it's really circular reasoning) and b) because their position means they are adamant that a judgement of believers and non-believers does not happen at the same time, despite the clear contrary indications in, say, the parable of the sheep and goats in Matthew 25, to give just one example. The passages do not say *where* the judgement happens, only that it happens when the Lord returns (1 Corinthians 4.5) – and where does the Lord return *to*? Earth. And 2 Corinthians 5.9-10 also may hint at the same earthly setting when it says judgement is for deeds done in the earthly body. Just because only believers are mentioned or in focus does not mean that this judgement is only for them. Paul is, after all, writing to believers, not unbelievers.

The 'gratuitous assertion' is where LaHaye says there is no time for the judgement seat of Christ at the second coming, again, despite Matthew 25 describing a Jesus enthroned in judgement when he returns, and despite the fact that Revelation 20 has a scene immediately after Jesus' return to earth that has the same elements of thrones and judging / authority to judge, and mentions believers. In point of fact, not only is there time and place for a judgement seat of Christ at the Second Coming, but both Revelation and especially Jesus in Matthew 25, actually *describe and place* the judgement seat of Christ at precisely that point in time! Quite frankly this is where LaHaye and the pre-tribbers behave exactly like the Pharisees, in that just as the Pharisees were condemned by Jesus for placing their own rules and interpretations over the commands of God and in effect subverting them, so to hold to a (man-originated) pre-trib doctrine with the 'judgement seat of Christ' in heaven seven years before Jesus return is in actual fact to call Jesus a liar and ignore his teaching that sets his judgement seat as being *at* his visible return and *not before*. That is very serious stuff. Not only do they believe it, but they teach others to believe the same and attack those who rightly adhere to Jesus' true teaching!

Proof 13. The rapture is the marriage of the Lamb (Revelation 19.7-10), but at the Second Coming the bride descends with the Lamb as an army (Revelation 19.11-14, Jude 14).

First, let's deal with Jude 14. In the pre-trib scenario, when Jesus returns, he brings the previously raptured church with him. The church will already have been cleansed of all false believers because only those truly his will have been raptured, and God's wrath in judgement has been poured out on all the wicked during the tribulation. However when examined in context, Jude 14 rather tends to undermine this picture. The reason is that the letter up to that point has been devoted exclusively to dealing with evil people / corrupting teachers *within the church*. And it is precisely 'these people' that Jude says Enoch is prophesying about when he describes God and his 'holy ones' returning to execute judgement on ungodly people. There is not even a hint that the church has already been cleansed by the rapture. Technically you could say 'absence of evidence is not absence of evidence', and claim that Jude still believed and held to a pre-trib rapture, but given the clear teaching elsewhere in Scripture on the issue, this seems just a tad unlikely.

As to Revelation 19, this is yet another example of LaHaye and dispensationalists engaging in inappropriate atomizing of passages, as well as ignoring context. Claiming that the rapture is the 'marriage of the Lamb' they proceed to take one continuous passage, Revelation 19.7-14, and chop it right down the middle, taking the first half and making it apply to an event 7 years earlier in time than the rest of the passage, despite there being not a hint of such a time break. For instance, when the passage mentions the 'marriage feast of the lamb' it never uses the past tense, but rather at the very point where Jesus is about to return in glory, an angel proclaims that the *'time has come for the wedding feast of the Lamb, and his bride has prepared herself'*

Notice, if the pre-trib position were true, this should read 'the time has passed for the wedding feast of the Lamb'. In the pre-trib position, the bride, aka the church, will already have been prepared by the rapture, which would have purified and perfected them, but in reality in Revelation 19 it is only at the very moment of Jesus' visible return that the bride has actively prepared herself. And the imagery of a marriage supper of the Lamb perfectly fits here, with the return of Jesus when heaven and earth are wedded into one; Jesus descends from heaven and the church ascends from earth to be joined together in the air in consummation of all history and the promises of God.

Proof 14. At the rapture, only His own see Him (1 Thessalonians 4.14-17), but at the Second Coming every eye shall see Him (Revelation 1.7)

Here again we see a subtle slipping in of a word or concept not in the passage, a tactic which is so typical of pre-tribulation rhetoric. 1 Thessalonians never says that *only* his own see him. Rather, because it is written specifically *to* believers about something that *concerns only* believers (the resurrection of the righteous / believing dead) there is no need to mention how the coming of Jesus affects the world and the unbelievers, especially since the Thessalonians would almost certainly have been taught the basics of Jesus' teaching in Matthew 24. They knew that the rapture happened at the same time as Jesus' visible return, and would not need reminding. One additional thing to note. The invisible pre-trib rapture sounds suspiciously like the Jehovah Witnesses' invisible coming of Jesus to earth in judgement in 1914, a device used to mask the fact that their prophecies of the date of Jesus' return were not accurate. This invisible pre-trib rapture is hardly the 'glorious appearing' (Titus 2.13) that the scriptures speak of.

Proof 15. At the rapture the Tribulation begins (Matt 24.9-32, 2 Thess 2.3-12), but at the Second Coming the 1000 year kingdom of Christ begins (Great White Throne) (Rev 19.11-15, 20.4-6).

Once again we have LaHaye being so blinded by the doctrinaire dispensationalist position that he uses Scripture passages that say the exact opposite of what his position requires. In Matthew 24, if the pre-trib rapture were true, we would expect any rapture-type event to be described sometime before the account of the last days tribulation – but it simply isn't there; there is not even a hint of some such break in God's activity and focus. Instead there is only a continuous narrative that describes the tribulation and the desecration of the Temple, and then says (v29) *'After the Tribulation of those days....'* and goes on to describe the visible return of Christ accompanied by (even followed by in a sense) an event that matches up with Paul's description of the rapture in 1 Thessalonians 4 - trumpet blast, angels and the gathering of all the elect from across the world.

On 2 Thessalonians 2.3-12, despite the difficulties in understanding and interpreting v5-7, the whole thrust of the passage is much more consistent with a post-trib position of some kind, so it is hardly compelling 'proof' of a pre-trib position. Specifically, Paul was writing to address concerns caused by false teaching that said either that the 'Day of the Lord' had already come, or was right at the door – 'imminent', in other words. He says that the Day of the Lord only comes after a great apostasy or rebellion or falling away in which the anti-Christ is revealed and sets himself up in the Temple as God, an event described in Daniel 9, as well as placed by

Jesus as part of the tribulation in Matthew 24 and parallel passages. In the pre-trib position, all of these things happen *after* the rapture, so if Paul was teaching the pre-trib rapture, then the reasons he gives as to why the Lord can't have come yet are irrelevant to the new disciples at Thessalonica. All he needed to say was something along the lines of 'You and I are still here, we haven't been raptured, and nor has the rest of the church, so you're alright.' But if Paul teaches a post-trib scenario in line with the teaching of Jesus in Matthew 24, then the passage makes perfect sense – he is arguing that the events of the tribulation with the rise of the anti-Christ must happen before Jesus returns to '*kill him with the breath of his mouth and destroy him by the splendour of his coming*' (v8), and therefore the Thessalonians can rest assured that the day of the Lord has not come yet, despite what the false teachers then were teaching – and still teach today – on the issue.

Finally using Revelation 19 and 20 as proof of the rapture and the second coming as separate events is irrelevant in light of the clear teaching elsewhere (often in the very passages LaHaye claims 'prove' a pre-trib position) that they are one and the same event. Rather bizarrely, LaHaye in this 'proof' refers to 'the Great White Throne' as being associated with the return of Jesus and the start of the Millennium (1000 year reign of Christ) and cites Revelation 20.4-6 as proof. This passage contains elements of judgement, but in actual fact Revelation 20 has the 'Great White Throne judgement' at the end of the Millennium, in v11-15. You know there is a problem when a teacher who boasts about the 'literalness' of his scheme makes basic errors like this, that directly contradict the most basic literal reading of the bible. I mean, come on. A teacher with a focus on literalness and detailed chronology, yet gets an event a whole thousand years out of sync! If you are going to mess up, do it properly, I guess.... Unfortunately, when you are a teacher who influences multi-millions, then messing up like this in an 'irrefutable proof' has disturbing implications.

So to (really this time) conclude, these 'proofs' are typical of the flawed logic used in the pre-trib camp as a whole, and involve persistently and consistently perverting the word of God, forcing it to fit the doctrines of man, rather than letting the bible speak for itself. *Every single* 'proof' turns out to be *anything* but a proof for the pre-trib position. They only 'prove' such a thing if you are already brainwashed into the dispensationalist pre-trib position, and even a very cursory reading of content and context reveals that LaHaye and the pre-tribbers actually go against clear teaching from Jesus and the apostles that *absolutely explicitly and unequivocally* place the rapture at the visible return of Jesus and *after* the Tribulation. **In other words, LaHaye and the pre-tribbers, however sincere they may be, are – on this point at least – false teachers who are leading the church astray into a doctrine of demons that will have devastating effects on their followers when they face the Tribulation utterly spiritually and mentally and practically unprepared.**

(Exactly such a disaster actually happened to Chinese Christians taught the pre-trib position when the Communists came to power – huge numbers of these Christians abandoned the faith, such was their shock and disillusionment.)

Thus, I call on bible teachers and ministers and Christians everywhere who teach the pre-trib position to give up this false and ungodly doctrine, and start teaching truth. In particular I publicly call on LaHaye to desist from touting his 'proofs' because they are anything but, and involve a distortion and corruption of bible teaching so profound that in effect they call Jesus a liar over his end times teaching in Matthew 24. Any doctrine that so distorts the word of God and yet claims to be 'biblical' is from the pit of hell, not the palm of heaven, and must be repented of, publicly and thoroughly, as a matter of grave urgency, and I call on LaHaye and his followers to do so *now* and stop crippling the church with demonic doctrines. Come back to the truth and may the church be set free from these lies, in the name of Jesus Christ, Amen!

AFTERWORD

After writing the first draft of this book, and just before writing the second, I got involved in a ding-dong debate over the rapture with a guy on a Facebook group I helped moderate. Guess what? He was taking scriptures out of context to 'prove' the pre-trib rapture. Yes, apparently Isaiah 26.19 (actually from a passage all about Israel and the Jews) is actually really about the rapture of a largely Gentile church. And when v20 warns Jews to shut themselves into their houses while the wrath of God strikes the enemies of God (shades of the Passover anyone?), really it is referring to the fact that Gentile Christians are raptured to heavenly homes to avoid the wrath of the 'Tribulation'. It kind of went downhill from there. When challenged, up came yet another verse taken out of context and when that was debunked, then yet another. And then, twenty posts down the line, the same (ab)use of the scripture passage is raised again, without addressing the refutation. *Very* exasperating. Lessons learned : telling people to repent and stop teaching the doctrines of demons is not always helpful, although I think the evidence of extreme deception I've detailed in this book documents that is exactly what is going on. I also learned again how people can go through incredibly energetic gymnastic contortions in defending a false belief.

In at least one point in this book, I have noted how the teaching of the doctrine of a pre-trib rapture operated to subvert God's word in much the same kind of way that many of the Pharisees did in Jesus day. Like many dispensationalist-system teachers today, the Pharisees were ardent students of God's word, dedicated to searching out its meaning and with a focus on a system where the minutiae of details were all worked out to a high degree, even if there was disagreements over the exact details, and yet Jesus said that by and large, the Pharisees blew it. For today's dispensationalist pre-tribbers, the focus is on the exact working out of end time prophecy, whereas for the Pharisees it was the exact working out of God's commands in the Law so that there was not a chance of inadvertently breaking God's law. Interestingly, Jesus could in many way be classed as a Pharisee himself, and he went so far at one point at the start of a condemnation of the Pharisees as to tell his disciples to carefully obey the Pharisees and the teachers of the law as they 'sit in Moses seat', meaning they were in a genuine authoritative position of authority (Matthew 23.2-3). Jesus insisted that they missed God's heart, so that tithing the tiniest garden herb - which Jesus had no problem with and commended - took precedence over issues of justice, mercy and faithfulness. He roundly condemned them for hypocrisy (something that other Pharisees did at times too). But what struck me during this debate is the way that the pre-tribulation / dispensationalist exactly parallels something that Jesus roundly condemned in the Pharisees - namely putting the religious traditions of men above the commands or word of God. The specific example he gave was 'korban', which you can read about in Mark 7.1-13, particularly the latter part of the passage. Korban (sometimes also spelt corban or karban) is the Hebrew word for 'offering', and in the bible is used mainly in Leviticus and Numbers. However, the word came to be used of anything dedicated or set aside for use in the temple, and therefore not available for personal use. Jesus noted that the way the Pharisees used this concept of dedicating something to God and the Temple was violating the commandments of God, namely one of the ten commandments – that of honouring your mother and father, and another commandment not to 'curse' your parents, a crime punishable by death, a command that was repeated in both Exodus and Leviticus for emphasis. 'Honouring' parents was more concrete than just words, it included providing financially for those who had provided for you as a child. In such a culture, refusing to do so was in effect to 'curse' them, to insult them outrageously. The particular extension or application of a biblical concept as taught by the Pharisees, which seemed so noble and pious, dedicating wealth or assets to God, was in fact a violation of some key commands of the God they sought to honour. In the same way, the pre-tribulation / dispensationalist position that has grown up over the last two hundred years or so that so many claim is *the* truly biblical way to understand the structure of scripture is a tradition of man that nullifies the actual words of our Lord and Saviour Jesus Christ. When, in Matthew 24 and parallels, Jesus taught about the end times, he massively emphasized the suffering that his church, or disciples, would go through in the last days, including the period right up to his return. However, belief in a pre-tribulation rapture effectively nullifies the solemn warnings of Jesus to his disciples (and us) by claiming that the rapture happens before the 'Great Tribulation', even though there is no warrant anywhere in Matthew 24 to say this, and even though Jesus *unequivocally and precisely* pinpointed the timing of the 'rapture' as happening 'After the tribulation' and at the time of his visible return. Just like the Pharisees concept of korban eviscerated central commands of God's law, so too the pre-tribulation / dispensationalist system guts Jesus' solemn teaching on the church and the last days. And just like the Pharisees who condemned Jesus for not carrying on 'the traditions of the elders', so pre-tribulationists condemn those who pay attention to Jesus' true teaching *and* what is worse, effectively call Jesus a liar by directly contradicting his clear teaching.

In other words, the pre-tribulation / dispensationalist teaching functions as an idolatrous lens that gravely distorts the teaching of the bible. Jesus warned about 'false prophets' that 'by your fruits you shall know them'. The same can be applied to doctrine. Despite the utter and sometimes fanatical and almost violent conviction among large swathes of the evangelical and fundamentalist churches that the pre-tribulation belief (and the dispensationalist system of which a pre-tribulation rapture is the climax) is the only truly biblical approach to the bible and any attack on it is the work of the devil, we have shown that the opposite is true. A doctrine which requires such mental gymnastics and such distortions of bible passages as we have seen is fruit that is bad by any remotely objective standard. Dispensationalism and especially the pre-tribulation rapture have become idols which block people from receiving and benefitting from the true teaching of Jesus and the apostles and the New Testament about the last days. They are most pernicious and demonically deceptive precisely because they lead people to believe that they are being biblical and godly and are on the right track when in actual fact they are being lured into a spiritual trap of global proportions. I've already mentioned China in the 1950's and the disaster that befell the church there after the communists took control and huge numbers of Christians apostasized from the true faith. No doubt under suffering some would have fallen away anyway. But huge swathes of evangelical Chinese Christians had been taught that the dispensational view that they would be raptured out of the way before 'serious' suffering afflicted them was truly the biblical teaching. When reality exposed that lie, the disappointment was so great that many thousands upon thousands of disillusioned Christians abandoned the faith entirely. The key word is that they were disillusioned – the illusion had been exposed. But that same illusion is entrenched, insinuated among huge swathes of the world church, particularly in the West that has to an extent taught the rest of the world (just as they did in China). Now, the Chinese church has managed to escape from the illusion, the delusion, and recovered from the effects, but it has taken *decades*, arguably a half century. If we are to take the prophecies of the end time tribulation seriously, the church as a whole will not *have* decades to recover from the illusion, we won't even have *one* decade. If we are to avoid seeing a global repeat of the disaster that afflicted the Chinese church, we need to 'dis-illusion' ourselves *now*, with great urgency repenting and turning back to the true teaching of Jesus and the apostles. **The idol of pre-tribulationism must go down and go down hard, go down fast, go down now! There is no time to lose.**

Look at what is happening in the Middle East and Africa right now. In the United States, the Muslim Brotherhood, the group that spawned both Hamas and to an extent Al-Qaeda, already has people in senior positions in the formidable intelligence and security apparatus, and has had for several years. In the UK, I've been told by a knowledgeable source that police forces are infiltrated and compromised, and they don't know precisely by whom, nor what to do about it. Already across Europe many cities have no go areas where sharia law is being implemented. Violent anti-semitism is on the rise everywhere, even in my city, the Oxbridge of the ultra-orthodox world. Across many European countries Jews are fleeing or thinking about it – they know what is coming, and have done for some time. There is at least one city in Europe – Marseilles – where Islamists have even taken to setting up their own road blocks to check and monitor vehicles in and out of 'their' territory. I personally have talked to

Pakistani Christians in the UK who have had to flee to the UK, and have faced the same kinds of attacks they faced in Pakistan within a month of getting out of the asylum system.

Jesus warned that only those who 'persevere to the end will be saved' (Matthew 24.13). Persevering to the end requires at least some level of mental and spiritual preparedness for the harsh times that not only Jesus, but also the apostles, warned would come in the last days (see for instance 1 Timothy 4.1-2 and 2 Timothy 3.1-4). But if people are enraptured by a false vision that teaches that all the things Jesus warned about they will escape by virtue of a mythical 'secret rapture', how will they even consider such preparedness? **Thus this issue is not just a fine point of doctrine, but a matter of intense and urgent practical relevance.**

For a long time, science in the West was enslaved to an incorrect notion of the nature of the universe derived from the world view of ancient pagan Greek philosophers. They believed that the earth was at the centre of a celestial sphere in which the planets, sun, moon and stirs circled the earth. Even though observations contradicted the predictions that the theory necessitated, yet the false theory was still upheld by inventing more and more complex 'fixes' to make the theory fit the facts. And yet more fixes to 'fix' the fixes when things still didn't fit the observations of reality. In precisely the same way, dispensationalists teach these false doctrines, ripping verses and passages apart, out of context to mine them for 'proofs' of their theory. Just as King Nebuchadnezzar built a statue that all his civil servants had to bow to and make obeisance and declare loyalty by, so the idol of pre-tribulation rapture and dispensationalism has become the master, to which Scripture must be the slave, and to which all scriptures must fit, however absurdly or awkwardly, no matter the exegetical cost. The concepts of dispensationalism become the prism through which scripture is viewed, and the fruits are direct contradictions. For instance, in the online debate I had, frequently phrases like 'Jesus said he would never let the church suffer the wrath of the Tribulation' were stated to condemn my position without even a single verse to back it up. I was told that I could not comprehend the true teaching of the bible because I kept together things that should be kept strictly separate – namely Israel and the church. (This guy was big on engineering analogies and an emphasis on precision – I think he must come from an engineering background, which fits very nicely with the dispensationalist approach that takes passages out of context and engineers them into an artificial edifice.) Now it so happens that there is at least one whole book of the bible that actually teaches the opposite – namely the book of Romans. Even if you don't think that is the main purpose of the book, what is indisputable is that chapters 9-11 of Romans deal with the issue of the relation between the church and the Jewish nation that as a whole rejected Christ. And what is striking is that there is not even a hint of the 'strict-division' approach that is so beloved of the dispensationalist movement. Yes, Paul talks about how God has used the partial hardening of Israel to privilege the mission to the non-Jews, but when he talks of the relation of Israel and the church, in chapter 11 particularly, he uses imagery of *organic unity*, not some cast-iron division. When I pointed this direct contradiction to his dispensationalist approach, he had no reply, yet *still* continued using that approach to try and argue his case. It got so bad that at the end that just before I blew my top in frustration, this guy actually said something like 'If you really knew the bible so well and precisely, you would know that Matthew 24 teaches about before the tribulation and Luke 21 teaches about after the tribulation'. He didn't give even a smidgen of an attempt to justify this bizarre assertion by any analysis. Just that bald assertion was enough in his eyes to condemn me as biblically ignorant. I felt like asking if the other parallel passage that reports Jesus' end-times teaching - Mark 13, in between Matthew and Luke - is mid-tribulation! Now, whatever the differences in emphasis between Matthew and Luke's account of Jesus teaching - and there are a couple - to make claims like this is a tad unhinged (translation of British idiom for American readers - 'about as nutty as a squirrel binging in the Fall'). I should add that I'm not claiming my 'worthy opponent' needs a visit to a psychiatric hospital, but I am saying the justifications for clinging on to a pre-tribulation position in the face of contrary evidence in the bible quickly get completely nuts!

Early on in the debate, the bloke claimed justification for taking verses from here and there all over the bible and ripping them out of context by saying that not only was it the way that the New Testament does it (which we have seen is by and large about the opposite of the truth), but also that it was the way God commanded us to approach the bible, citing Isaiah 28.10 or v 13, I think from the King James Version, which reads

> But the word of the Lord was unto them
> precept upon precept, precept upon precept;
> line upon line, line upon line;
> here a little, and there a little

He also said that because of the way Satan always attacked God's word, God had made the bible according to an engineering design using 'message width' so that each doctrine of the bible was split all around the bible, so that if some part of the bible was 'taken out', the doctrine could still be deduced from other parts of the bible. It's a nice analogy, and it exactly fits how pre-tribulationists and dispensationalists almost invariably approach the bible on this matter. However, a look at the context of Isaiah 28 blows this approach completely out of the water and raises serious questions as to whether this kind of dispensationalist approach to scripture is not just in grave error, but a sign of divine judgement and displeasure.

Isaiah 28 contrasts the good promises and purposes of God with the degradation and immorality of his people, Israel, and in particular the religious leaders – the priests and prophets (v7-8). The 'line upon line' method of teaching is used because they are like little children unable to understand (v9-10). It could well be that the prophet is depicting the attitude of his contemporaries to God's word. They feel like God is treating them like little children, learning by rote. But they have refused to accept God's offer of rest (v11-2), so in judgement God says he will speak to them in strange languages, and as part of that judgement, God's word would become to them what they had said it was – 'line upon line, line upon line' for the purpose of making them stumble and fall, and 'be broken, snared and taken' (v13). I should say at this point that a lot of translators are unsure what these phrases mean in the original Hebrew, and actually think they may be words of a kind of meaningless nursery rhyme type chant. But assuming that the 'precept upon precept, line upon line' accurately captures the intended meaning, this means that the word of God being interpreted in this way (the way the pre-tribulationists do it, as we have seen) is actually a sign of spiritual immaturity and of divine judgement. Given that pre-tribulationism is an illusory concept that causes people to avoid facing up to future suffering, it is interesting that the Isaiah passage goes on to deal with a very similar illusionary belief among the rulers and leaders of Jerusalem in v14-5 which is about avoiding death and suffering.

> *Therefore hear the word of the Lord, you scoffers*
> *who rule this people in Jerusalem.*
> *You boast, "We have entered into a covenant with death,*
> *with the realm of the dead we have made an agreement.*
> *When an overwhelming scourge sweeps by,*
> *it cannot touch us,*
> *for we have made a lie our refuge*
> *and falsehood our hiding place"*

Just like the believers in a pre-tribulation rapture, these religious leaders believed an illusion that they would escape suffering. God's response in v 16-22 is sobering:

> *So this is what the Sovereign Lord says:*

> *"See, I lay a stone in Zion, a tested stone,*
> *a precious cornerstone for a sure foundation;*
> *the one who relies on it*

will never be stricken with panic.
I will make justice the measuring line
and righteousness the plumb line;
hail will sweep away your refuge, the lie,
and water will overflow your hiding place.
Your covenant with death will be annulled;
your agreement with the realm of the dead will not stand.
When the overwhelming scourge sweeps by,
you will be beaten down by it.
As often as it comes it will carry you away;
morning after morning, by day and by night,
it will sweep through."
The understanding of this message
will bring sheer terror

The bed is too short to stretch out on,
the blanket too narrow to wrap around you.
The Lord will rise up as he did at Mount Perazim,
he will rouse himself as in the Valley of Gibeon—
to do his work, his strange work,
and perform his task, his alien task.
Now stop your mocking,
or your chains will become heavier;
the Lord, the Lord Almighty, has told me
of the destruction decreed against the whole land

While the passage is about Jerusalem at the time of the prophet, it has meaning for us. Firstly, the New Testament applies this passage about the 'tested stone' to Jesus (2 Peter2.6-8) - and by extension we can take it to also refer to his true teaching. (As an interesting side note, Peter combines it with a very similarly worded quote from Psalm 118 which Jesus applies to himself in Matthew 21.42 and parallels, and significantly does so in a parable aimed at the corrupt religious hierarchy of his day). Those who rely on Jesus' true teaching about the end times 'will never be stricken with panic'. God will sweep away the lie, the illusionary hiding place that the corrupt religious leaders have set up, and he will cancel their 'covenant with death'. The scourge they thought they would escape would sweep them away. In the same way, those who cling to the false method of 'line upon line' taking verses out of context are exhibiting signs of divine judgement. (And it is also interesting to note that when talking about the end times, 2 Thessalonians 2.10-12 warns of a dynamic which, although meant to apply to those who outright disbelieve God, might also apply in principle to the church, in which God sends a powerful delusion on those who perish because they have not loved the truth. The delusion causes them to believe the lie so that those who don't believe the truth will be condemned, just as these religious leaders who believe the delusion in Isaiah 28 suffer judgement.) But as we have seen, those who believe in God's tested cornerstone are the ones who don't panic in the time of trouble. The implications of this passage should be a sobering and deathly solemn warning to all those who believe and teach that the church will escape suffering via the illusion of a pre-tribulation rapture.

APPENDIX 1:

Why does Paul imply Jesus taught that dead saints come before the living in the rapture?

Central to my argument has been the role of 1 Thessalonians 4.15-17, and the fact that it says it is 'according to the word of the Lord' (i.e. Paul's account comes directly from the teaching of Jesus), and that the only possible teaching of Jesus that can be in view is that of Matthew 24.30-1. However, the passage seems to imply that the dead being raised before the living are taken to be with Jesus is also part of the 'word of the Lord'. The full text is as follows:

> *According to the Lord's word, we tell you that we who are still alive, who are left until the coming of the Lord, will certainly not precede those who have fallen asleep. For the Lord himself will come down from heaven, with a loud command, with the voice of the archangel and with the trumpet call of God, and the dead in Christ will rise first. After that, we who are still alive and are left will be caught up together with them in the clouds to meet the Lord in the air. And so we will be with the Lord forever.*

However, there is no sign of an assertion that the dead are resurrected and taken to Jesus before the living anywhere in Matthew 24.30-1 or the surrounding passage. We know that Paul had plenty of theological grounds for arguing that the dead will arise before the living Christians join them in meeting Jesus, because he argues those grounds in some detail in his other 'rapture passage' in 1 Corinthians 15.50-8, plus there are logical grounds for such a belief in earlier arguments in 1 Corinthians 15 – namely that all believers will have bodies like Jesus' resurrected body, as he is the first-fruits of the resurrection, but even that doesn't explain why the dead have to come first. But here he clearly seems to imply he is relying on a specific teaching of Jesus, something he doesn't do in 1 Corinthians 15. What are we to make of this?

Firstly, is there any possible way Paul could have divined this detail from the words of Jesus in Matthew 24? I think it may just be possible, but only if Paul and /or Jesus expected deep background knowledge of Jewish thought and interpretation of the Old Testament. In Matthew 24, Jesus describes his coming by a clear allusion to Daniel 7.13-4, where God gives the 'son of Man' great glory and authority as he comes with the clouds of heaven. Indeed, we might call Jesus 'the glory of God', and Jesus is repeatedly associated with the glory of God in the New Testament. Paul talks of 'the riches of his glory in Christ Jesus' in Philippians 4.19 and in Titus 2.13 of 'the appearing of the glory of our great God and Saviour, Jesus Christ'. When John quotes a passage from the prophet Isaiah about the actions of God, he applies it directly to Jesus 'Isaiah said this because he saw Jesus' glory and spoke about him' (John 12.41). A chapter earlier, Jesus intricately links God's and his own glory 'it is for God's glory so that God's Son may be glorified through it' (11.4). Finally, the first martyr, Stephen, at the moment of his death saw 'the glory of God, and Jesus standing at the right hand of God' Acts 7.55. In the light of this, we could reasonably assume that Jewish hearers or readers such as Paul, on hearing Jesus' teaching in Matthew 24 would immediately associate the themes of glory and seeing the glory with passages from the Old Testament about all people seeing God's glory of experiencing unity with God. There is, for instance – and I start with the weakest argument first – Isaiah 40.5, which states:

> And the glory of the Lord will be revealed,
>   and all people will see it together.
> For the mouth of the Lord has spoken.

The passage goes on to compare the way humans die with the fact that the word of the Lord (and by extension those who rely on the word of the Lord – Jesus, as Christians would say?) lasts forever (v6-7). If the righteous all see God's glory *together*, then surely they must be in the same state – and surely to see the living God you must be alive? This might seem fanciful, but there are several other passages that are much stronger in suggesting the same line of thinking. For instance there is the famous stirring declaration in Job 19.25-7 where he speaks of having a body in the future after his present body has decayed, and seeing God as the Redeemer standing on the earth, which fits perfectly with the idea of a resurrection at the coming of God's glorious Messiah, the Redeemer of all:

> I know that my vindicator lives,
>   and that in the end he will stand on the earth.
> And after my skin has been destroyed,
>   yet in my flesh I will see God;
> I myself will see him
>   with my own eyes—I, and not another.
> How my heart yearns within me!

There are also several other passages in Isaiah that make such an interpretation likely. Isaiah 66 talks of God's final judgement when he comes to slay the wicked, and at the same time will:

> gather the people of all nations and languages, and they will come and see
> my glory .... I will set a sign among them, and I will send some of those who

survive to the nations... and to the distant islands that have not heard of my fame or seen my glory. They will proclaim my glory among the nations. And they will bring all your people, from all the nations, to my holy mountain in Jerusalem as an offering to the Lord—on horses, in chariots and wagons, and on mules and camels," says the Lord. "They will bring them, as the Israelites bring their grain offerings, to the temple of the Lord in ceremonially clean vessels. And I will select some of them also to be priests and Levites," says the Lord..... (v18-21)

Here God not only rescues Israel and destroys the enemies of God and his people, as Zechariah 14 depicts, but there is a gathering of 'God's people' from all the nations to God in Jerusalem, a similar concept to Matthew 24 when all 'the elect' are gathered to Jesus as he returns to the Jerusalem. In Matthew 24, Jesus' language suggests something absolutely universal in scope - the elect are gathered from 'the four winds, from one end of the heavens to the other' which could easily be read as referring to both the dead and the living. In this Isaiah 66 passage (read the wider context) the wicked are dead, but the righteous live and serve God. Since all mankind - at least the righteous - see God's glory together and live, and God will hardly slay the living righteous, then the dead must be raised to be together with the living. Isaiah 25.6-8 is also highly relevant. Even though it does not speak explicitly of seeing God's glory, it does speak of a time when godless nations are punished, and when all peoples will eat a covenant meal 'on this mountain' - i.e. Mount Zion (and could this be the wedding supper of the lamb? - just a thought) - prepared by God himself, and at the same point God destroys death forever:

> *On this mountain the Lord Almighty will prepare*
> *a feast of rich food for all peoples,*
> *a banquet of aged wine—*
> *the best of meats and the finest of wines.*
> *On this mountain he will destroy*
> *the shroud that enfolds all peoples,*
> *the sheet that covers all nations;*
> *he will swallow up death forever.*
> *The Sovereign Lord will wipe away the tears*
> *from all faces;*
> *he will remove his people's disgrace*
> *from all the earth.*
> *The Lord has spoken*

Taken together, all this - I suggest - would indicate to a Jewish thinker like Paul that the dead had to rise to life at the time when God effects the consummation of all things - and for a follower of Jesus, that had to be when Jesus returns. (Additionally there are several other Old Testament prophecies that similarly associate God sounding a trumpet and the deliverance of his people at Jerusalem - Zechariah 9.14 and Isaiah 27.13.) The 'great trumpet call' in Judaism was associated with the Feast of Trumpets, also known as Rosh Hashanah (the head of the year), when a pattern of trumpet calls - mostly short - were sounded, 99 of them in varying patterns. Then the 100th trumpet blast - the great or last trump was sounded. In the Talmud, an ancient Jewish holy writing, the resurrection of the dead is associated with this Feast of Trumpets (if you want to know where, then it's in a section designated Rosh Hashanah 16b). In Matthew 24.30-1, the trumpet blast occurs before the angels are sent out to gather all the elect. Similarly in 1 Thessalonians 4.15-17 the trumpet call is associated with the dead being raised, and it is only after that that the living believers go to be with Jesus too.

The other alternative explanation (other than that Paul knew Jesus' original teaching which had been more extensive and the gospels only recorded some of it - an idea that is possible, but unprovable) is that Paul here is citing two separate teachings of Jesus and bringing them together. This is the solution I first thought of, but on reflection about the Jewish background I came up with the ideas I have just detailed, where Matthew 24 itself contains the clues. In Matthew 22, Jesus has a debate with the Sadducees about the resurrection (v23-33) and Jesus ends up by using a linguistic detail in the book of Exodus to 'prove' by Jewish exegetical standards, that there was in fact a resurrection. We've already noted it in the introductory section. God told Moses that *'I am'* - not *'I was'* - *'the God of Abraham, Isaac and Jacob'* even though these three had died long before Moses time. Jesus' comment was *'God is not the God of the dead, but of the living'* (v31-2). One of the ancient titles for God was 'the Living God', as shown by the words of the chief priest (ironically a Sadducee whose doctrine Jesus refutes here) to Jesus at his trial in Matthew 26.63. Since God is a God of the living, not the dead, then surely the dead must be transformed to life to meet God in the person of his Son as he returns? Thus, even aside from the implications of the timing of events in Matthew 24, this was a 'word of the Lord' that intrinsically implied that a resurrection must take place when God and humanity were united at Jesus' return. What makes it even more likely that Paul could have both these teachings in mind simultaneously, is that in Matthew, these teachings were all given by Jesus on the same day, since Matthew 21.18 to at least 26.2 contain an account of one day in the life of Jesus. (And another apostle also implied that the followers of Jesus would be like him - resurrected - at his return, as per 1 John 3.3 *'Dear friends, now we are children of God, and what we will be has not yet been made known. But we know that when Christ appears, we shall be like him, for we shall see him as he is.'*)

Thus, Paul's emphasis that the believing dead are raised to life and go to be with Jesus entirely fits with Jesus' teaching on the details and chronology of his visible coming in Matthew 24, and are not evidence of a separate 'rapture event'.

APPENDIX 2:

Do Jewish wedding practices of Jesus' time support a 'pre-trib rapture'?

Pre-tribulationist proponents often make the ancient Jewish wedding practices a central plank of their position. Amongst fundamentalist / evangelical websites and books on this topic this is often combined with a scheme which matches up the key events of Jesus first and second comings with the Old Testament feasts. It is certainly reasonable to examine Jesus' teaching through the lens of the wedding practices of the time, especially in relation to his second coming, because he very often did use wedding imagery in relation to his return.

A typical presentation might say something like this (actually, this is more detailed than many presentations of this concept): An ancient Jewish wedding had three stages – intention, betrothal and marriage, stages that normally covered at least a year. The announcement of intention might be seen in either Jesus' incarnation, or his baptism (i.e., his becoming human and/or his being baptised for forgiveness of sins announce his intention of becoming 'one' with humanity). The actual betrothal – which was so binding as to need a legal bill of divorce to break it off – made with a covenant meal, is the whole last-Supper, crucifixion and resurrection sequence, where Jesus committed himself irrevocably to saving a body of people from sin and winning them to himself. After the betrothal, the groom would go back to his father's house, and prepare a house / a room for the bride, which would take about a year normally. Everyone knew the rough time of the wedding, but the exact time wasn't known, because it would only happen when the father of the groom decided that the new dwelling was fit for the bride, which – it is usually said in such arguments – parallels Jesus actions in John 14.1-3 about going to 'prepare a place' for his disciples, and the fact that he said that no-one, including himself, knows the day or hour of his coming, except for his Father in heaven (Mark 13.32). The bride would have her wedding clothes ready, and when the groom's party approached – almost always in the middle of the night – it would be announced by his friends coming in advance and shouting 'The Groom is coming' and perhaps blowing trumpets. The bride would then be taken back to the groom's Father's house, where there would be a seven day feast – the marriage supper. This represents Jesus coming and taking his bride – the church – back to his Father's house – heaven, in the pre-tribulation rapture, and the seven days feasting represents the seven years of tribulation on earth while the church celebrates in heaven. After that, Jesus and the church together return to earth at the start of their 'marriage'. It sounds very convincing and neat, especially, since Jesus repeatedly used wedding imagery to describe his second coming.

However, as we discussed in the body of the book, there are severe problems with taking John 14.1-3 as wedding imagery, and there are serious problems with the pre-tribulation interpretation of the 'Wedding Supper of the Lamb' in Revelation. In Revelation, this wedding supper does not occur in Revelation 4, where pre-tribbers argue the rapture – and the start of the Wedding Supper – begins, but in Revelation 19, at the moment of Jesus' visible return to earth. But still, despite this, you get many people who remain adamant that the only correct way to interpret the end times and wedding imagery is the idea that the 'Wedding Supper of the Lamb' is the church being in heaven for seven years during the tribulation. In other words, once again the concepts and ideas behind a pre-tribulation rapture have been made into a kind of template against which Scriptures are made to conform; here a particular very dogmatic and rigid conception of Jewish wedding practices becomes the template to which all else must conform.

I examined a number of online expositions of this concept, and despite the variations, one thing I noticed was that in pretty much every case – as so often is the case in pre-tribulationist argumentation – the wedding scenarios are simply stated as hard and undeniable fact, and there is absolutely no actual citation to back up these claims. It was just stated 'this is how Jewish weddings were done, and this is how it matches the pre-trib scenario'. It rather looks to me like people have just copied the argument and adapted or embellished it for their own particular perspectives or devotional purposes – and as it happens – see the last couple of paragraphs – this is precisely the pattern that other researchers have actually documented. Readers will just accept these 'gratuitous assertions' as fact and accept them as powerful evidence for the pre-trib position.

I'm no expert on Jewish customs, but when I read such authoritative assertions, I smell a rat, for the simple reason that evidence for Jewish wedding customs must come from multiple sources over a long period of time. There is no text or document that outlines comprehensively Jewish wedding customs, otherwise – believe you me – scholars and especially pre-tribulationist teachers would cite it. What we have is a morass of little snippets and clues over a period of centuries and from a wide geographical range. They are contradictory in parts because practices varied over time and distance. Much of the material will come from the Mishnah and especially the Talmud, Jewish holy books that consist of the written down discussions of 'Oral Torah' by rabbi's. These texts were not concerned with laying out wedding practices in detail for outsiders, but rather very densely written summaries of legal debates on specific points. They come from several hundred years after the time of Jesus, and after the intense social upheavals caused by the Jewish revolts in Rome in AD70 and AD135, and the ensuing consequences of defeat. And yet, these writers dogmatically and baldly assert detailed and rigid wedding practices that oh so conveniently back up their notions about the rapture!

In fact, when we examine the New Testament passages that use wedding imagery, a rather contrary position emerges. We have already covered Revelation 19, but there is another passage where Jesus used wedding imagery to describe his second coming, and that is the parable of the wise and foolish virgins found in Matthew 25.1-13. There are ten virgins, which was quite a standard number for such occasions. They would be friends of the bride appointed to be witnesses to the marriage (the groom would typically bring along ten of his friends to be witnesses also). Firstly, contrary to the assertion that the bride did not know the day the groom was coming, these virgins assembled on the day groom came. In other words, the day was known, or rather the night, as the groom usually came a little before midnight. (Typically this was a Wednesday - it gave the bride several days to prepare after the Sabbath, and also was timed so that if the groom came to doubt his bride's virginity, he could immediately take the issue before the religious courts, who met on a Thursday.) The groom in Jesus' parable delayed and didn't arrive until midnight, the deepest part of night (we could perhaps say that this indicates that Jesus will come for his church in the darkest hour of her tribulation). The consummation of the marriage along with the seven day period in the bridal chamber, were held in the bride's home and the wedding feast went on at the groom's house. They happened at the same time. So when Revelation 19 refers to the Wedding Feast of the Lamb being about to happen because the bride has made herself ready, it can't mean that there has been 7 'day-years' of consummation in heaven before the feast begins, nor can it mean a 7 year feasting period before the consummation - it can only refer to that day's events, the visible and bodily return of Jesus to earth to be united with his bride, the church. In addition, if you look at the Matthew 25 parable, the virgins go out to meet the groom and escort him back, just like in the post-tribulation scenario where the church rises to meet Jesus in the air and then escort him back to earth.

Now, you will have noticed that I have not provided many citations for my assertions. Well, for the basics, try http://olivetdiscourse.com/index2.php?option=com_content&do_pdf=1&id=273 from someone who has given citation and evidence from scholarly works, and also has tracked and detailed the way pre-tribulationist teachers invent or distort the evidence on this issue. (There is also a fuller version of this document in the useful sources below). Interestingly enough, while he believes - unlike me - that John 14.1-3 does use primarily wedding imagery, he demonstrates how it is *also* temple imagery and how the wedding theme interlinks with temple or tabernacle imagery in Old Testament prophecies that relate to Jesus' return and the Messianic age. For those of you who are reading paper copies of this work and don't have internet access, the scholarly works he cites are as follows (unfortunately he doesn't specify which editions) :

Edersheim, Alfred, *The Life and times of Jesus the Messiah* Chapters 5 and 7, and p663-4
Edersheim, Alfred, *Sketches of Jewish social Life in the days of Christ* Chapter 9
Gundry, Robert, *First the Antichrist: Why Christ Won't Come before the Antichrist Does* p94-5
Jeremias, Joachim, *Parables of Jesus,* p72-3

Although mostly focusing on the Medieval period, the following article from an Orthodox Jewish website contains interesting insight as to how and why Jewish marriage practices could change.
http://www.chabad.org/library/article_cdo/aid/465162/jewish/The-Jewish-Marriage-Ceremony.htm

But the bottom line is, Jewish wedding practices emphatically don't support a pre-tribulation rapture position, and if you read something that dogmatically asserts they do and presents a seemingly neat and tight argument where Jewish practices exactly match the pre-tribulation structure, remember that it will be effectively made up and without genuine evidence at the key points that allegedly support the pre-trib position. In fact, the pre-tribulation position essentially entails completely contradicting Jewish wedding customs – see the last few paragraphs of the link entitled 'Double talk : How Many second comings' in the useful information section at the end of this book.

APPENDIX 3.

What does Jesus mean when he says in Luke 21.36 about praying 'that you may be able to stand before the Son of Man'?

And another thing that came up after I finished the book. I got involved in a debate on LinkedIn on this issue and it sparked off some thinking about the meaning of the phrase 'able to stand before the Son of Man' in light of its context and Old Testament background. I give the original post and the entire thread – (most) typos and all – apart from one irrelevant comment. (You will need to have a bible at hand, because I don't always quote the bible verses I cite). Oh, and at the end, there is a useful link about a perennial 'proof text' that pre-tribbers bring up – that Christians can't undergo the Tribulation as they are 'not appointed to wrath'.

The Original Question :
Hi I have a question and I'll explain my theory behind why...

Matthew 24:36-44

> "But concerning that day and hour no one knows, not even the angels of heaven, nor the Son, but the Father only. For as were the days of Noah, so will be the coming of the Son of Man. For as in those days before the flood they were eating and drinking, marrying and giving in marriage, until the day when Noah entered the ark, and they were unaware until the flood came and swept them all away, so will be the coming of the Son of Man. Then two men will be in the field; one will be taken and one left. Two women will be grinding at the mill; one will be taken and one left. Therefore, stay awake, for you do not know on what day your Lord is coming. But know this, that if the master of the house had known in what part of the night the thief was coming, he would have stayed awake and would not have let his house be broken into. Therefore you also must be ready, for the Son of Man is coming at an hour you do not expect. "

Is this talking about the rapture?
If it is, then the ones taken away, are the unrighteous right? Noah was left and the unrighteous were swept away and it says that it will be the same?

Also Luke 17:22-37

And he said to the disciples, "The days are coming when you will desire to see one of the days of the Son of Man, and you will not see it. And they will say to you, 'Look, there!' or 'Look, here!' Do not go out or follow them. For as the lightning flashes and lights up the sky from one side to the other, so will the Son of Man be in his day. But first he must suffer many things and be rejected by this generation. Just as it was in the days of Noah, so will it be in the days of the Son of Man. They were eating and drinking and marrying and being given in marriage, until the day when Noah entered the ark, and the flood came and destroyed them all. Likewise, just as it was in the days of Lot—they were eating and drinking, buying and selling, planting and building, but on the day when Lot went out from Sodom, fire and sulphur rained from heaven and destroyed them all— so will it be on the day when the Son of Man is revealed. On that day, let the one who is on the housetop, with his goods in the house, not come down to take them away, and likewise let the one who is in the field not turn back. Remember Lot's wife. Whoever seeks to preserve his life will lose it, but whoever loses his life will keep it. I tell you, in that night there will be two in one bed. One will be taken and the other left. There will be two women grinding together. One will be taken and the other left." And they said to him, "Where, Lord?" He said to them, "Where the corpse is, there the vultures will gather."

Again it talks similar but in the last verse it says

And they said to him, "Where, Lord?" He said to them, "Where the corpse is, there the vultures will gather

So if that's the case then the ones taken are again the unrighteous right? I'm guessing when the disciples ask "where Lord" they are asking where they will be taken to...

I was under the impression that in the rapture the ones taken... (and this is from my old church) were the righteous... My old Church used to say that you didn't want to be the one left behind grinding at the mill, that you wanted to be taken... But I don't see that in the scripture, I see the vultures and the water sweeping the unrighteous away...

OR am I looking at it all wrong? Is it even about the rapture? Is there even a rapture? Why does the bible have to be so complicated?

Nathanael Lewis

An awful lot of the problems about the last days are because people believe the unbiblical doctrine of the rapture - as in, the belief in the 'secret' rapture as a separate event from the visible return of Jesus. Particularly in the Luke 17 passage, I think Jesus' teaching is very practical - to run from places of evil (i.e. cities, civilization) on the day of the Lord - hence the need to remember Lot's wife.

Other Guy

Nathanael,

> *1. And take heed to yourselves, lest at any time your hearts be overcharged with surfeiting, and drunkenness, and cares of this life, and so that day come upon you unawares. 35 For as a snare shall it come on all them that dwell on the face of the whole earth. 36 Watch ye therefore, and pray always, that ye may be accounted worthy to escape all these things that shall come to pass, and to stand before the Son of man. Luke 21:34-36 (KJV)*

I don't know about you; but, I am making preparations to ESCAPE. Jesus indicated that we could do that if we were accounted worthy. Since all my sins are under the blood; there should not be any negatives in my account. I don't know how many positives are required to become worthy; but, that should be all that's written there.

Me

And yet, your interpretation ignores and directly contradicts key parts of Jesus words in just these few verses. Did Jesus say 'Put it under the blood' to be counted worthy or some equivalent like 'Just believe'. No! He said there were things to DO to be counted worthy. Watch and pray.... If you've got that so wrong, then maybe you're assumptions about what 'escape' means here. What is the context? The context is not 'escaping tribulation' as pre-tribbers claim. What is escaped is what Jesus warned us to 'take heed' about - surfeit and drunkenness and cares of this life causing us to be dull so that Jesus' return comes on us unawares.......

OG

Nathanael,

Don't limit yourself to "these few verses". Read the whole context. Jesus was talking about the troubles that would come to "all them that dwell upon the face of the whole earth." The description of those troubles consumes about 25 of the earlier verses in this same chapter.

I didn't even attempt to interpret this passage. I just told you what I am hoping and doing about it.

If there was an interpretation, you must have read it yourself.

Me

I did read the whole context. The fact remains that a) Jesus said these times were to come on ALL people on the face of the earth - not 'on everyone except those who kept zapped out of the way'. He does describe what precedes his visible return that all will see (v27-8) and says that his disciples should look up when they see these things begin to happen. No mention of a 'secret rapture'. And if you are claiming that Jesus words about 'escape' mean a 'beam me up out of here' rapture, you haven't paid attention to the implications of v16-19. Jesus tells his disciples that they will be betrayed and put to death, but yet not a hair on their heads will perish, and if they stand firm (even while being slain) they will find life - i.e. that they won't deny their faith or Christ - as Jesus said in the equivalent passage in Matthew 24 only 'those who endure to the end will be saved'. No need to endure to the end if you are getting zapped out of the world some years before the end.

OG

What are we to pray that we be counted worthy to escape? Is this just a word game He was playing? Are you saying the only escape will be physical death, (even by torture)? I'm sure it would be an honour to be counted worthy to become a martyr. But, it is not a privilege I am praying to receive.

Me

As ever, the clue is in the context. I've already given you some, but let's look at just v36 - we are to pray to be counted as worthy to escape by being able to 'stand before the Son of Man' - which matches the teaching in Matthew 24 about only those who 'endure to the end will be saved'. That's without looking at v34 which, as I've said, links being careful with the warning not to be weighed down with carousing and drunkenness and anxieties of this life. It is no word game, but deadly real....
Remember, Jesus warned his disciples elsewhere of his second coming that a key criteria is whether they have been ashamed of him and his words in a sinful and adulterous generation (Mark 8.38) - if they have, Jesus will be ashamed of them at his visible coming in glory with angels (not at a 'secret' rapture). Jesus teaching was to be holy and not worried by the affairs of this life (e.g. Matthew 5-7). This is what being able to 'stand before the Son of Man' means – not to have to shrink away in shame because you have denied his words and teaching by your life. (Oh, and before I forget, did you know that in the Judaism of Jesus' day to 'hallow God' meant to give your life as a martyrdom. So every time you pray the Lord's prayer, you could be said to be praying for martyrdom!).

To understand this being 'able to stand before the son of Man', as ever with Jesus' teaching, you need to understand what it means from the Old Testament, where the phrase to 'stand before the Lord' had great significance. He taught as a rabbi, and the phrases he used come from Scripture and so to Scripture we must turn.

As ever, the first usage is key. Genesis 18.22 - Abraham stands before the Lord in a place of intercession / shared governance. Look up at v 17-19, especially v 19, which says why the Lord privileged him - it was because of faithfulness to the Lord and his promise and his teaching - living holy and teaching others to do the same - to direct his household in 'the way of the Lord' by doing what is 'right and just' - living righteously.

Deuteronomy 10.8 - the Levites have been set aside to '*stand before the Lord to minister*'

1. Samuel 6.20 is linked also to the 'ark' or presence of God - after irreverently looking inside, the inhabitants of Beth Shemesh say '*Who can stand in the presence of the Lord, the Holy God?*' again linking holy living with standing in the presence of / before the Lord.

Ezra 9.15 '*Lord, the God of Israel, you are righteous! We are left this day as a remnant. Here we are before you in our guilt, though because of it not one of us can stand in your presence.*' Again the link between holy living and standing before the Lord

Psalm 24.3-4 has similar language and message '*Who may ascend the mountain of the Lord? Who may stand in his holy place? The one who has clean hands and a pure heart, who does not trust in an idol or swear by a false god.*'

Psalm 130.3 '*If you, Lord, kept a record of sins, Lord, who could stand? But with you there is forgiveness, so that we can, with reverence, serve you.*'

Jeremiah 15.1 is an especially strong thematic parallel. '*Then the Lord said to me: "Even if Moses and Samuel were to stand before me, my heart would not go out to this people. Send them away from my presence! Let them go!"*'. The Lord says his people, Israel, will not stand before him, and he will send them away from his presence (by the Temple) because of their sins and unrighteous living. A sober warning to us (and remember that Hebrews takes up this general theme - warning not to fall away from Christ, because if we reject such a salvation, our punishment will be greater than those who broke the first covenant - see especially the last part of chapter 10 and also chapter 12. And Jesus and the apostles repeatedly warned of the great falling away in the last days).

Zech 3.1 '*Then he showed me Joshua the high priest standing before the angel of the Lord...*' the angel of the Lord likely being, of course, Jesus.

Priestly language again - and aren't we as saints called to be a kingdom of priests who 'stand before the Lord'.

Zechariah 6.5 '*These are the four spirits of heaven, going out from standing in the presence of the Lord of the whole world*'

Revelation 11.4 similarly quotes the Old Testament about the two witnesses that they '*stand before the Lord of all the earth*' and fulfil their prophetic ministry (and martyrdom, note!)

So, if we are to be counted worthy of being priests in the promised kingdom of God, when the promise to Abraham is fulfilled, then we need to be counted worthy by living holy and faithful in a wicked and adulterous last days generation, which, as I've said before, fits the context of Jesus' teaching perfectly (Luke 21.34)

Not only that, but the apostles in the New Testament show the same pattern of teaching, particularly on the theme of the day of the Lord coming like a 'thief in the night'.

There's a subtle one in 1 Corinthians 15.58 - after talking about what is often called 'the rapture' (not as a separate event from the visible return of the Lord, note) Paul says 'Therefore' - i.e. because of the promised resurrection and new age - his readers should stand firm and let nothing move them, but give themselves fully to the Lord because their work is not in vain.

In 2 Thessalonians 2, after instructing them about what the church will endure under the anti-Christ, Pauls message in v15-17 is that they should stand firm and cling close to the apostle's teaching, and rely on God to give them grace and encouragement and strength in continuing to live righteously ('*in every good word and deed*')

But particularly look at the 'thief' passages in the epistles and Revelation.

Look at 1 Thessalonians 5.2-11: '*you know very well that the day of the Lord will come like a thief in the night. While people are saying, "Peace and safety," destruction will come on them suddenly, as labour pains on a pregnant woman, and they will not escape*'. Paul, as a good rabbi, similarly uses language to allude to Jesus' teaching. Notice the word 'escape' and how Paul uses it. How do we escape? Not by being zapped from the earth, but by living sober and righteous lives, just like Jesus taught in Luke 21.34-6 and parallels. We escape by doing - living righteous in the strength of Christ, practical steps - and think how much of the church now is falling away from righteous living and how prophetically relevant this teaching is today. V4 on instructs:

> *'But you, brothers and sisters, are not in darkness so that this day should surprise you like a thief. You are all children of the light and children of the day. We do not belong to the night or to the darkness. So then, let us not be like others, who are asleep, but let us be awake and sober. For those who sleep, sleep at night, and those who get drunk, get drunk at night. But since we belong to the day, let us be sober, putting on faith and love as a breastplate, and the hope of salvation as a helmet. For God did not appoint us to suffer wrath but to receive salvation through our Lord Jesus Christ. He died for us so that, whether we are awake or asleep, we may live together with him. Therefore encourage one another and build each other up, just as in fact you are doing'*

Out of the mouths of two or three witnesses. Let's look at the apostle Peter - apostle to the Jews as Paul was to the gentiles. In 2 Peter 2.10 he mentions the day of the Lord coming like a thief:

> *'But the day of the Lord will come like a thief. The heavens will disappear with a roar; the elements will be destroyed by fire, and the earth and everything done in it will be laid bare.'*

(Notice, this can't mean the rapture, because the whole universe is changed, as per Revelation 20-2, it's the visible return of the Lord that comes like a thief in the night)

But what is the practical response required to be ready for this day? It is to live righteously and not to abandon the law of God. V11 on:

> *Since everything will be destroyed in this way, what kind of people ought you to be? You ought to live holy and godly lives as you look forward to the day of God and speed its coming. That day will bring about the destruction of the heavens by fire, and the elements will melt in the heat. But in keeping with his promise we are looking forward to a new heaven and a new earth, where righteousness dwells.*
> *So then, dear friends, since you are looking forward to this, make every effort to be found spotless, blameless and at peace with him. Bear in mind that our Lord's patience means salvation....*

(and see what he means by this, he has talked about the Lord's patience earlier - it is patience to bring people to repentance - out of unrighteous living)

And so to the final warning and practical application in v17 : '...*Therefore, dear friends, since you have been forewarned, be on your guard so that you may not be carried away by the error of the lawless and fall from your secure position.*'

How and of what have they been forewarned? They have been forewarned, in keeping with Jesus' teaching about the last days, not to become lawless (disobedient to God's commands about honouring parents, loving not hating, keeping firm hold on the teaching of Jesus, and about the trial and tribulation coming for those who would stay faithful to the law and teaching of God). In other words, Peter, like Paul, simply applies and expounds Jesus warning and teaching about last days and the great falling away of faith.

A third and final witness that the early church and the apostles understood Jesus' teaching about his return and so on is the apostle John in Revelation. He links the theme of 'thief in the night' to righteous living twice: Revelation 3.1-6, especially v3. Most of the church in Sardis is not living righteously, and Jesus gives them a grave warning - they need to hold firm to the teaching and repent, but if they do not repent, THEN Jesus will come like a thief at a time they don't know. But for those who do walk in white, their reward is just what Jesus taught - their name will never be blotted from the book of life, and Jesus will acknowledge their name before the Father and the angels (implying that those who do not live worthy and faithful will not have this happen, again in accord with Jesus' teaching about those disciples who are ashamed of his teaching and the last day)

Finally Revelation 16.15 - in the middle of recounting the terrible judgements of the wrath of the last days on those murderers and rebels against God (see v5-6, 9-11) and the immediate run up to Armageddon (v12-4 and 16) Jesus suddenly warns his disciples :

> '*Look, I come like a thief! Blessed is the one who stays awake and remains clothed, so as not to go naked and be shamefully exposed.*'

In Revelation being clothed means righteous living, being naked and shamefully exposed means ungodly living (see the last passage 3.4-5, 17-18 and especially 19.8). In other words, the same message - 'live holy and faithful' - notice that the challenge is to REMAIN clothed - to keep on doing right in the wickedness of the last days.

Thus every single apostle clearly taught the understanding of Jesus teaching about the end times that I have given here. How blind the church is, thinking that 'escape' means escape from suffering when we are called, with our already suffering brothers and sisters, to be disciples of the suffering Saviour. Philippians 3.10-11 *'I want to know Christ—yes, to know the power of his resurrection and participation in his sufferings, becoming like him in his death, and so, somehow, attaining to the resurrection from the dead'* (i.e. the 'rapture' - the resurrection of the saints on the last day)

We must be faithful, because if we disown Jesus, he will disown us. Paul put it another way in 2 Timothy 2.11-13 and v19-21

> *Here is a trustworthy saying:*
> *If we died with him,*
> *we will also live with him;*
> *if we endure,*
> *we will also reign with him.*
> *If we disown him,*
> *he will also disown us;*
> *if we are faithless,*
> *he remains faithful,*
> *for he cannot disown himself*

and after warning about false teachers who have fallen away from the faith, he says *'Nevertheless, God's solid foundation stands firm, sealed with this inscription: "The Lord knows those who are his," and, "Everyone who confesses the name of the Lord must turn away from wickedness."*

In a large house there are articles not only of gold and silver, but also of wood and clay; some are for special purposes and some for common use. Those who cleanse themselves from the latter will be instruments for special purposes, made holy, useful to the Master and prepared to do any good work.'

This is the message and warning of Jesus about the last days - that we must be faithful and endure by living holy and not denying Jesus in the face of increasing wickedness and opposition to be *'counted worthy of standing before the Son of Man'* when he comes. What we escape from is the wrath of God that comes on those who live ungodly lives and rebel against the teaching of Jesus - not an escape by being zapped out of the way, but by living righteous and faithful to Christ.

OG

I agree that we Christians should expect to suffer at the hands of unbelievers; but, we are *"not appointed unto wrath"*. We will not have to endure *"all these things"* that

Jesus described in this chapter that shall come on all that live on the face of the earth.

Me

And once again you give basically no exegesis, and quote wildly out of context. You presume a pre-trib position to 'prove' a pre-trib position. '*not appointed to wrath*' is not a reference to escaping the tribulation, but to the wrath of God in the age to come - i.e. hell and judgement - it is what all Christians are 'not appointed to' because whether they live in peace or die in the tribulation, they belong to Christ - just look at each use of the phrase in 1 Thessalonians. Now look at Matthew 24 / Mark 13 / Luke 21. There Jesus warns that 'YOU' will be persecuted 'because of my name'. I challenge you to find any gap in which to put a rapture in Jesus' teaching here. He goes on to warn of the abomination of the desolation, and says when 'you' - i.e., those who are persecuted for Jesus' name - the church - see that, then you should run to the hills. '*Pray that YOUR flight will not be on the Sabbath. If THOSE days were not cut short.... but for the sake of the elect (see below) they are cut short. So if anyone says to YOU.... See I have told YOU ahead of time. So if anyone tells YOU 'He is in the inner place' (shades of secret rapture?) ... For the coming of the Son of Man will be like the lightening (or dawn light) rising from the east to the west - i.e. public and seen by all.... Immediately after the TRIBULATION of THOSE days...the rapture.*' In all these cases Jesus applies these things to 'YOU' who he has earlier identified as his disciples who are persecuted because of his name. The ONLY reference to a rapture-type event is after the 'tribulation of those days' when Jesus returns - only then are the elect gathered by angels from all the earth with the sound of a trumpet call. I challenge anyone who believes in the false teaching about a pre or mid tribulation rapture to find any reference to the rapture in Jesus' teaching of the last days, EXCEPT in the absolutely explicit '*After the TRIBULATION of those days...*' Jesus unequivocally and absolutely teaches a 'post-trib' rapture here. He leaves absolutely no room for any legitimate doubt....

Oh, and about 'wrath' as used in 1 Thessalonians. It is the Greek word 'orge'. There is another word 'thymos' used in many places, and interestingly, 'thymos' is the one used in much of Revelation for the judgements of God before Jesus' 2md coming, but 'orge' is used of the judgement at and after Jesus' return. See http://midnightwatcher.wordpress.com/2011/03/26/lost-in-translation-not-appointed-unto-wrath-what-scripture-is-really-saying/ for a useful summary

And Daniel 7 says that the elect will suffer defeat and persecution at the hands of the final 'boastful horn' right up until the point that he is overthrown, when judgement is made in favour of the elect and they possess the kingdom.

APPENDIX 4. 'NOT UNDER WRATH'?

OK, so I got into yet another debate on LinkedIn.

Someone put up a conversation topic that said 'I would like to challenge each Christian to make sure that everyone you work with is Rapture ready.' So of course I asked what exactly they meant by 'Rapture ready' and they quoted 1 Thessalonians 4. Other people chipped in, and then someone who I shall here call ELF (his initials) got involved and things sparked off.

He started off by saying he thought the rapture was part of the great commission (Matthew 28) and quoted Matthew 25.1-13, saying the shut door matched up with the one door in Noah's ark that God shut, and then took the *'not appointed to wrath'* line, ending up with

'IF you think he is not coming back "to save" and "rescue" you. so be it..' This is a line he seems to think is a killer argument, because he uses at the end of pretty much every post, as you shall see.

Me :

ELF.... I found your post a little confusing, but it looks like you are taking the line that there must be a pre-tribulation rapture because 'We will never suffer the wrath of God'. But all the passages referring to wrath use a Greek word that is used not of the wrath in the last days 'Tribulation' period, but the wrath of God as in final judgement and eternal hell - 1 Thessalonians 5.9-10 talks of receiving salvation, not of escaping suffering. After all, we follow a suffering Saviour, and Jesus, Paul and the apostles continually taught that we should suffer like Jesus, to obtain resurrection and reward with him. As to 1 Thessalonians 4.18, you are taking it badly out of context. The question Paul was addressing was not 'what will happen when at the return of Jesus', but 'what happens to those believers who have already died'. Paul, using Jewish methods of reference, is actually here clearly tying in the 'rapture' with the visible second coming of Jesus. He does this by using the same elements as Jesus used in teaching about his return in Matthew 24 - angels, a shout (of command), Jesus descending, the saints being gathered to meet him in the air. Check it out - the only other place that these all occur is in Matthew 24 (and parallels, to an extent). And Jesus was absolutely explicit that this was a *post* tribulation event – *'After the tribulation of those days'*. So, I do think Jesus is coming to save and rescue me - but not to stop the suffering or the enmity of man in the Tribulation period ever happening to me, but to rescue me from out of them at the end, if I still live and have been faithful to him. After all, when Daniel talked of the coming of the kingdom of the Son of Man, he talks of the saints being oppressed and having war made against them, and only then receiving the kingdom. And Jesus said *'Only those who endure to the end will be saved...'* In other words, Jesus never said to be rapture-ready, but he was emphatic about the need to be Tribulation ready....

ELF responded first by listing 14 passages in which the Greek word for 'wrath' 'orge' is used, citing them in the original Greek and three translations. The passages were Matthew 3:7, Mark 3:5, Luke 3:7, Romans 2:5, 5:9, and 9:22, Ephesians 2:3, 1 Thessalonians 1:10, 1 Timothy 2:8, Revelation 6:16 and 17, 14:10, 16:19 and 19:15.

ELF then continued 'IF you think he is not coming back "to save" and "rescue" you. so be it..

all the passages referring to wrath use a Greek word that is used not of the wrath in the last days ???

Nathanael...Looks like someone needs to brush up on there Greek.
and another thing... why would Paul write a letter to Gentile Believers use "Jewish methods of reference" ? nice try but... Paul's letters were to be clearly understood by all in the Gentile church at Thessalonica the capital of the Roman province of Macedonia.

1 Thessalonians 1:9-10 suggests that Paul subsequently spent some weeks ministering fruitfully to pagan Gentiles. However, rioters instigated by Jewish opponents dragged Jason (Paul's host) and some other Christians before the politarchs and charged them with sedition against Caesar (Acts 17:5-8), forcing the missionaries to leave Thessalonica prematurely (Acts 17:9-10). Paul was concerned for the new Christians, and therefore a few months later he sent Timothy back to Thessalonica (1 Thess. 3:1-2, 5; see note on Acts 17:15).

The most prominent theme in 1 Thessalonians is the second coming of Jesus. It is mentioned in every chapter of the book (1:10; 2:19-20; 3:13; 4:13-18; 5:1-11, 23-24).

At Jesus' future coming, the dead in Christ will rise and will be caught up along with the living to meet the Lord in the air (4:15-17).
same thing found in 1 Corinthians 15:52

Unbelievers will be subject to his wrath, but Christians will be delivered from this, inheriting salvation instead (1:10; 5:2-4, 9-10).

Those who are destined to participate as saints (lit., —holy ones‖) in the second coming must be holy and blameless (3:11-4:8; 5:23), and God, who is faithful, will produce holiness in the lives of those whom he calls (5:24).

So like I said....if you think he is not coming back "to save" and "rescue" you. so be it..'

Me :

ELF - I may well need to brush up on my Greek, but not, I think, in this instance. What I do need to brush up on is explaining myself clearly. :)

Actually, my answers to both your big posts involves Jewish approaches, so we may as well start by noting that all the authors of the New Testament, with the possible exception of Luke, were Jewish. This means that - just like Jesus - they would have lived and breathed Jewish ways of interpreting Scripture. Now, they may well have accommodated themselves to non-Jewish modes of thinking when addressing pagan audiences (as Paul did, for instance, at Athens in Acts 17), but remember that in many places - and Acts 17 is absolutely explicit that this was the case in Thessalonica - the first and most plentiful Gentile converts were those who were already 'God-fearers' and attended synagogue and worshipped the God of Israel. Someone needs to brush up on their social history of the New Testament... :) You don't need to be a scholar - it is explicitly stated in the very passage you quote! Thus these particular Gentiles were already significantly familiar with Jewish thinking and methods of interpretation, and even if some of them weren't, in a 'high context' society they would have quickly started to pick it up from those who did know it well. Thus Paul could expect most of his audience, though Gentile, to be quite familiar with Jewish methods of interpretation right from the moment of their conversion. And even if that hadn't been the case, Paul, like the other apostles, would have continued to spread the teaching of the church, not by saying 'This is Jewish', but because he, as a trained Pharisee and Torah Teacher would have lived and breathed it (in fulfilment, by the way, of Matthew 13.52 *'Therefore every teacher of the law who has become a disciple in the kingdom of heaven is like the owner of a house who brings out of his storeroom new treasures as well as **old')**. It would be woven through all the teaching of the new converts. We have a document called the Didache that is probably at least as old as most of the New Testament. It was the 12 apostles' church manual for specifically Gentile churches, and it was Jewish in teaching method and content through and through (and they explicitly taught the gentile converts a post-trib rapture, by the way - I challenge you to go read the final chapter, which is all about the last days and what Gentile Christians would have to endure along with their Jewish brethren).

Now, back to the issue of the Greek word for 'wrath' 'orge'. I didn't explain myself too well, so thank you for the chance to clarify. I should have said I was meaning instances where it refers to God's wrath (so Jesus in Mark 3 being angry and 1 Timothy 2 passages aren't applicable here).

So we are left with a number of other passages (I actually think you missed a couple) where it talks of 'wrath' in ways that are implicitly or explicitly eschatological. But again, Jewish idiom is important here. Matthew 3.7 and Luke 3.7 refer to the eternal wrath and judgement. This is because the qualification 'to come' is in effect a technical term referring to 'the age to come' where God's eternal justice will be seen. In other words, John the Baptist is not referring to a time of tribulation at the end of this age - although most Jews believed in that too - but to the eternal state after God's intervention and judgement to inaugurate the new age.

You actually missed a use of orge that on first glance might seem to support your position - Romans 1.18. But notice that this and Romans 2.5 both associate 'orge' with the term apokalupseus - 'revealing' or 'unveiling', again a term indicating the very final judgement. In Romans 1 Paul does go on to explain how this wrath is being seen in the present age - but remember that he held to a view that the age to come had already partly broken in. In 2.5 the context is that God is patient and tolerant, giving time for people to repent (2.4) but continued hardness will mean that wrath is stored up - not for later in one's life in this age, but in the age to come. This is made clear by v6-10 which talks of the righteousness being given eternal life at this time of judgement where the stored wrath is released on the wicked. In addition, 2.5 uses 'orge' twice, once in the term 'day of judgement', again a term typically used in Jewish thought for the very final judgement, not the troubles preceding the end of this age.

The same focus on the wrath of God as eternal judgement continues in two further uses of orge you missed - Romans 3.5 and 4.15. In chapter 5, Paul talks about the great hope Christians have due to being justified by faith (and interestingly, this is proved by sufferings, not by escaping tribulation - v 3-5). Jesus death on the cross means we are justified by his blood (v9a) and if that is so, then how much more will we be saved from God's wrath. In fact, the Greek simply says 'the wrath', and that also was a phrase denoting specifically the eternal wrath of God. If you examine 9.22, this also fits. God will show his wrath, but at this time he is showing the righteousness of his wrath by bearing patiently with unbelieving Jews - he is not yet in this life demonstrating wrath, but his patience will justify his wrath on the last day - those who continue in unbelief will have proven themselves fitting vessels for wrath and destruction. 12.19 also fits. We are not to take vengeance, because that usurps God's role as perfect judge, but we are to leave room for 'the wrath', when God will execute perfect justice and judgement at the end of the age. You also missed orge in Romans 13.4 and 13.5. v4 applies to human wrath and judgement by authorities (I believe here it means synagogue authorities, not secular authorities, but that's something for another day) and in v5 we are to submit to them, not just because of 'the wrath' but also conscience. Ephesians 2.3 easily fits into orge referring to permanent wrath in the age to come as well, although the context is not as explicit as to this meaning, but it is implied - after all many who are dead in trespass and sins (v1) don't experience great wrath now in this age. Similarly in 5.6 it uses the term 'coming wrath' to indicate that Paul means the wrath of the age to come. Colossians 3.6 also uses the same phrase - the 'coming wrath of God'. Is there a picture emerging here of the use of orge? I think there is. :)

So we come to 1 Thessalonians 1.10, which again uses 'coming wrath' to indicate it means not a time of end times tribulation, but the eternal wrath of the age to come. This is what Jesus rescues us from, not times of tribulation before his coming! Paul, the rabbi, teaching a Gentile audience who had mostly been synagogue attenders knew his audience would get the meaning of his Jewish idiom. And it was classic Jewish outlook - those who worship idols face the judgement of eternity. You missed another use of orge in 2.16, but again, it refers to 'the wrath' - these Jews who reject the Messiah promised in the scriptures are like the residents of the land from the time of Abraham to Joshua - they will continue to fill up their sins until the time of judgement - in this case eternal judgement - is at hand. And this context of the final judgement is what informs Paul's teaching about the coming of Jesus in chapters 4 and 5. In Jewish thought, judgement was not just a punishment of the guilty, but also a public vindication of the righteous. Thus, in chapter 4, the dead in Christ will be vindicated by resurrection to be like and with Jesus. The practical outworkings are found in chapter 5. The 'day of the Lord' (another Jewish term denoting the judgement of God, and supremely the final judgement at the start of the new age) comes as a thief in the night for those who are not living righteously. *'But you are not in darkness, that that day would surprise you like a thief'*. If they continue in righteous living, they will show that they are not 'appointed to wrath' - the wrath of eternity - but appointed to receive the salvation that comes to those who persist in righteousness (and if you don't believe that this is what the New Testament teaches, just take the 'Roman Road' to eternal life - look for each example of how Romans says you get it, particularly in chapter 2). Ultimate salvation comes at this time of judgement and apocalypse. Interestingly, although 2 Thessalonians doesn't use orge, chapter 1 is totally taken up with this theme of the vindication of the righteous and the destruction of the wicked, and makes it clear that it happens at the visible, physical return of Christ.

Now, in Revelation, there is another phrase sometimes used of the wrath of God, and this is the different word I was referring to that is used of God's wrath in the 'Tribulation', or troubles at the end of this age. There are also quite a few uses of orge in Revelation, as you have cited in your list. Here, we need to understand something else about Jewish interpretative methods and approaches. Especially in the Apocalyptic literature, of which Revelation is an example, Jewish writers would often return to the same event or point of interest again and again but view it from different angles. A good example is Daniel, where a number of different visions repeatedly cover the various world empires in relation to the coming kingdom of God, with different focuses and angles in each vision. This is a great key to understanding Revelation generally, and also the use of different words for God's wrath used in it. In Revelation, orge appears to be used exclusively for the moment of Jesus' return, but the other word 'thumou' or related terms, seems to be used of God's judgement poured out on the earth just before Jesus' return.

Revelation 6.16-17 use 'orge' because the events described here is the visible final return of Christ. Chapters 4-6 constitute one vision, with 4-5 focusing on the worship in heaven, and the introduction of the lamb who was slain and the sealed scroll. Chapter 6 outlines these seals, and as each is opened, time of tribulation comes on earth - war, conflict, death, economic trouble, famine - which matches what Jesus said in Matthew 24.4-8 (just the beginning of birth pangs). The fifth seal reveals the martyred saints and that they are still being martyred, just as Jesus said in Matthew 24.9-14. He then goes on to say his return will be visible and public, not secret (i.e. not a secret rapture event) in v22-27. Back to Revelation, the 6th seal matches up with Matthew 24.29 - which is straight after the tribulation, note - the stars fall, the sun and moon are darkened, and then in Matthew 24 the sign of the son of man appears in heaven, and Jesus returns for his saints. In Revelation 6, the focus is on unbelievers in that day of judgement. The language is explicit in Jewish terms - it is the 'great day of wrath' except here it is not 'coming', it has 'come'. This indicates this is the very end of the age, i.e. Jesus has come to rule. They mourn, terrified, just as Jesus said would happen in Matthew 24. Now, I know there's 12 more chapters until chapter 19, but here the focus shifts, in typical style. The same period is viewed from the point of view of the saints of God - they are sealed by God, and join in the worship of heaven, and are said in 7.14 to have 'come out of' the tribulation. This was a term that meant they had gone through it, and come out the other side faithful, whether they had lived or been martyred ('come out' was also a term for death or martyrdom), and the implication is that they have hungered and thirsted and been scorched in the tribulation.

Chapter 8 deals with the final seal, that happens straight after the 6th seal where we see the day of Jesus' return has come. Then come 7 trumpets, in which great judgement comes upon the earth. These parallel the 7 seals, with 6 in a row, and then a gap before the last. They are describing the same period, but with a different viewpoint. Chapter 10 says the 7th trumpet will not be delayed, and with it, the great mystery of God will be accomplished, as prophesied (and remember, the resurrection of the saints is described in 1 Corinthians 15 as a 'great mystery' too). There is in chapter 11 the final period of Tribulation, with the focus on the Temple and Jerusalem for three and a half years. Then the 7th trumpet is blown and the words of the elders and angels again make it quite clear that here is the visible return to rule of the Messiah and the time of final judgement. Just like happened with the 7th seal, there are peals of thunder, rumblings, lightning and an earthquake - in other words, it describes the same event! And once again, here Revelation uses 'orge' right at the point when Jesus comes in final judgement. (Also, in Jewish thought, the 7th and final trumpet was always the trumpet of final judgement and resurrection).

Chapter 12 starts again to view the same period, but this time it talks in terms of a cosmic battle, and in it the same pattern emerges - persecution of those who are Christians (v10-17). Chapter 13 covers the same ground, but in terms of 'beasts', political powers or leaders who are given power to persecute and crush the believers (shades of Daniel 7 - check it out). It goes on to detail how these powers enforce their false worship in practical economic terms. Chapter 14 switches the focus somewhat to these persecuted saints, but still also their oppressors. Here is where the language of 'wrath' gets interesting. Those who make allegiance with the beast who oppresses the saints are made to drink the wine of God's fury (thumuou), which has been poured full strength into the cup of his wrath (orge). In other words, here is something more temporary, but is mixed in with the permanent (cup) of eternal judgement. These people have so hardened, that the fury in this age is the start of the eternal wrath in the age to come. The passage makes it quite clear that this is the case, as it refers to their torment being forever and ever. (And it is significant for those who believe the lie that we escape the rapture, that the lesson drawn in v12 is that those who are faithful to Jesus need patient endurance). The last half, interestingly enough, match the first half of the chapter. First it describes the harvest (and in the first half the saints are called 'first fruits', a harvest term), and then the grapes are harvested because they are ripe - and these are harvested into the great winepress of God's fury (thumou). It is clear from the final verse 20 that this 'thumou' is physical punishment in which blood is shed, not eternal judgement per se.

Chapter 15 has 7 plagues which will complete the fury (thumos) of God. 15.7 uses the same word for anger, and the song of praise in the middle makes it clear that as a result of these plagues, God's righteousness and vindication will be revealed, and all nations will worship him. 16.1 also uses this word Thumou, and it is clear that all the plagues involve physical judgement lining up pretty well with the 7 trumpets. The final climactic bowl is again associated with thunder, rumblings and a huge hailstorm and great earthquake, just like the final trumpet. In v19 it again uses both words - Thumou and orge. In other words, here is the moment when the tribulation wrath that could have, but hasn't, brought repentance from the unrighteous, turns into the eternal wrath of God. This is the moment of final judgement again - i.e. Jesus returns. In Chapter 17, the vision changes to focus on the nature of 'Babylon the Great' on whom God pours out this final fury of judgement. Just like before, it is clear (v6) that Christians have gone through the tribulation and suffered greatly at the hands of those enemies who suffer God's judgement. Chapter 18 similarly talks about her, but about her economic power and wickedness, and calls God's people (Christians) to come out of her. Like Lot, they must leave before the judgement of God comes down. V24 again indicates that God's saints have been around to be slaughtered by her, but also that she has slaughtered many others around the earth. Once the full nature of her evil has been revealed, chapter 19 goes on to speak in full detail about the return of Jesus and the long anticipated final judgement. Once again, in v15, as it describes Jesus physical return and physical war on his enemies, it uses both words to describe God's wrath, the point where the physical fury of the last days judgements turns into the eternal judgement - the battle lines have been drawn finally, and both physical and eternal judgement join as one in the final battle against the ungodly (v19-21). The final judgement and age are described in chapter 20, and chapters 21-2 describe the final union of Christ and his bride in various symbolic terms.

Thus we can see that 'orge' is NEVER used of the tribulation of the last days, and is ALWAYS used of the actual physical and visible return of Christ and the associated eternal judgement. I stand by my claim unequivocally. And as we have seen, all the way through, it has been explicit that we, the church, go through the great tribulation, but are rescued from the final eternal wrath of God.

So once again, I do think Jesus is coming to rescue and save me, but I believe the words of this same Jesus, and his apostles, when they all explicitly taught in the New Testament, and in the other document we have of their teaching, Didache, that all the saints alive at that time would go through the great tribulation before the return of Jesus. I note that you never even tried to refute the fact that Jesus explicitly stated the rapture would be post-tribulation in Matthew 24. A telling silence, that!

And I guess I'll say it again. Jesus and the New Testament NEVER talk in terms of needing to be 'rapture-ready', but over and over again in terms of needing to be 'tribulation ready'. This is why the pre-trib left-behind rapture concept is such a dangerous satanic lie and must be vigorously exposed and refuted. In the 50's, most of the Chinese evangelical church, which had been fed this lie that they wouldn't undergo great persecution but would escape in the rapture, apostasized and fell away from the faith. The evangelical church in the west will have an even greater falling away and apostasy, the one prophesied by Jesus in Matthew 24 and Paul in 2 Thessalonians, unless it repents of this false doctrine, among others.

———

I'm glad I copied and pasted this for this appendix, because things got nasty after that and the moderators moved in. ELF dismissed this by saying he 'hadn't got time' or had 'no need' to read all this, or something similar and ended up 'IF you think he is not coming back "to save" and "rescue" you. so be it..' I replied that I hadn't copied and pasted this but had taken the time to answer thoughtfully his specific objections, and maybe he should read it and learn something. I then made the mistake of adding that to keep using the 'If you think he is not coming back to save' line without engaging the arguments offered was annoying and puerile. He took offence and started quoting the dictionary definitions and asked if I was saying he was 'childish'. Someone else was offended because I had said the rapture was a 'satanic delusion', and in came the moderators. But this does show something I have found again and again, which is that often those who sincerely believe and are committed to a position (often a lie) can turn vicious when they can't actually offer cogent counter-arguments to evidence that exposes the lie for what it is.

APPENDIX 5 : THE GRACE SPACE

A Gap in Daniel's 70 weeks?

Whenever you get a prolonged discussion of 'the end times', you will find that Daniel's prophecy in Daniel 9 about '70 weeks' nearly always crops up. This fascination is not just a modern phenomenon. Both Jesus and Paul clearly allude to this passage when they talk about the troubled end times, and many of the early church 'fathers' also touched on it. It reads as follows (I include an earlier passage for context as well)

> In the first year of Darius the son of Ahasuerus, of the lineage of the Medes, who was made king over the realm of the Chaldeans— in the first year of his reign I, Daniel, understood by the books the number of the years specified by the word of the Lord through Jeremiah the prophet, that He would accomplish seventy years in the desolations of Jerusalem..... (here Daniel prays and fasts to God, and then an angel appears to explain 'the vision' as follows)

> Seventy weeks are determined

For your people and for your holy city,
To finish the transgression,
To make an end of sins,
To make reconciliation for iniquity,
To bring in everlasting righteousness,
To seal up vision and prophecy,
And to anoint the Most Holy.

Know therefore and understand,
That from the going forth of the command
To restore and build Jerusalem
Until Messiah the Prince,
There shall be seven weeks and sixty-two weeks;
The street shall be built again, and the wall,
Even in troublesome times.

And after the sixty-two weeks
Messiah shall be cut off, but not for Himself;
And the people of the prince who is to come
Shall destroy the city and the sanctuary.
The end of it shall be with a flood,
And till the end of the war desolations are determined.

Then he shall confirm a covenant with many for one week;
But in the middle of the week
He shall bring an end to sacrifice and offering.
And on the wing of abominations shall be one who makes desolate,
Even until the consummation, which is determined,
Is poured out on the desolate. (Daniel 9.1-2, 24-7, New King James Version)

One reason that this passage is so fascinating, both then and now, is that it is almost certainly the *only* Old Testament prophecy of the Messiah that gives an explicit chronological setting for his coming. Whatever the specific interpretation of the details, the timing had to have been early to mid 1st Century AD, and it is quite possible that the expectation of a coming Messiah was part of the motivation behind the Jewish revolt against Rome in the late 60's. The Jewish Babylonian Talmud quotes several leading rabbi's as having said that the appointed time had already come and gone, and condemning those who said that the promised redemption would never come. Their way of dealing with the issue was to say that the calculated periods were fulfilled, but now the Jews had to wait and all that was left was for the doing of good deeds and repentance, to pave the way for the Messiah.

For Christians, things are much easier because Jesus came at just about the right time to fulfil these prophecies. In fact, some conservative scholars follow Sir Robert Anderson to claim that, for instance, Jesus triumphal entry into Jerusalem is 483 years (i.e. 69 'weeks' of years - there is widespread agreement amongst commentators ancient and modern that the 'weeks' refer to sets of 7 years) to the day after the decree to rebuild Jerusalem. There are a number of variations in details, but Jesus certainly came in the right ball-park period. In Luke 19.41-5, on the day he made his triumphal entry, weeping, Jesus said the following:

> *'If you, even you, had only known on this day what would bring you peace- but now it is hidden from your eyes. The days will come upon you when your enemies will build an embankment against you and encircle you and hem you in on every side. They will dash you to the ground, you and the children within your walls. They will not leave one stone on another, because you did not recognize the time of God's coming to you.'*

That would certainly lend credence, at the least, to the view that Jesus was referring to this time prophecy, and probably that his triumphal entry happened at the right time, down to the very day.

Where interpretations have widely differed amongst Christian scholars is on how to understand the 70th week. Does it follow on immediately after the end of the 69th week and thus ended in the mid 1st century, or is there a gap and is it yet to be fulfilled? Those who take the first option tend to see the final verse as referring to Jesus. They usually argue that the 70th week started when Jesus was baptised, and that the ending of sacrifices was accomplished through his death on the cross, three and a half years later - in other words in the middle of the final 'week'. They would argue that, even though the temple sacrifices continued for another four decades or so, they were no longer acceptable to God because Jesus' greater sacrifice had happened. Interestingly, the Jewish Talmuds (authoritative religious writings) record that several features of Temple life, particularly to do with the day of atonement for sin, suddenly stopped working as they had before, 40 years before it's destruction in 70AD. However, this does not necessarily mean that this interpretation of Daniels 70th week is correct, because the significant changes in AD30 could fit any particular Christian interpretation of the 70th week - it signifies something about Jesus death, regardless of where we fit it into Daniels prophecy. (You can read more details about these mysterious happenings at this webpage -
http://www3.telus.net/public/kstam/en/temple/details/evidence.htm)

Now, some of you might be wondering, if Jesus' death is in the middle of the 70th 'week', what do people who take this position do with the final half of that 'week'? There are at least two or three approaches that I have seen. One is to say that for about 3 ½ years after Jesus' death and resurrection, the apostles and the church preached the gospel about Jesus exclusively to the Jews, but that after that they also started to preach it to the Gentiles. For these people, the destruction associated with the abomination and desolation in the final verse is the destruction of the Temple and Jerusalem in AD 70, and is the after effects of the Jewish religious leaders' rejection of the gospel a generation before. Others introduce a gap, and say that there was the length of a generation given for Israel to repent and come to Messiah, and that after that, the actual last half of the 'week' was fulfilled at the AD70 destruction. I think I have also seen at least one person arguing for an interpretation that is a hybrid of this understanding and the one discussed below by claiming that the first half of the 70th week ended at Jesus' death, and that the final half is yet to be fulfilled in the years leading up to Jesus future return. I have also seen at least one interpretation arguing that there are two gaps - one gap between Jesus' death at the end of the 69th week and the start of the 70th week in AD 66.5, and then another gap in the middle of the final 'week' from AD70 up until a future restart of the 'prophetic clock'.

The other main view is that Jesus' death occurs at the end of the 69th week, and that there is then a long gap (in which we now live) before the final week occurs in the 7 years leading up to Jesus' second coming. They believe that the 'He' who makes a covenant with many (understood to be Israel) is someone different to 'Messiah the prince (Jesus)' mentioned earlier, but is in fact the 'prince who is to come' whose people had earlier destroyed the temple, and that he will be what later Christian tradition names as the 'anti-Christ'. This position is held by just about every single dispensationalist, and can almost be said to be a clear signal that a person is a dispensationalist. Almost, but not quite, as we shall see. Those who take the first variation of the opposing position - that the 70th 'week' ends 3 ½ years after Jesus death often attack dispensationalists on the basis that there are no grounds for seeing any kind of gap in the 70 weeks (although you will notice that even they have a gap of a different sort - between the end of the 70th week and the desolation and destruction mentioned in the rest of the description of the 70th week). This has prompted many dispensationalist scholars to respond with rebuttals. I am not going to go into all the details of this debate, but I will say that despite being very anti-dispensationalist, on this point I thoroughly agree with most of the arguments dispensationalists use on this point - and I know I am far from being the only non-dispensationalist to take this 'gap' view. One of the reasons why there is such room for debate is because there is no immediately clear answer as to how the different phrases in this passage work together - the structure, in other words. Structure is often very important in interpreting Hebrew passages, because phrases can be understood as following on in chronological sequence, or - and it is not clear if and when this happens in this passage - some can be understood as employing a fairly common Hebrew literary habit of going over the same ground but from a different angle. It is also highly likely that in addition there is a structural pattern often used in Hebrew writing called 'chiasm', which is where elements lead up to a central key climax phrase, and following that there are mirror elements coming back down from it, usually expressed by scholars like this: A - B - C - D - C - B - A, although sometimes it can be more complex with multiple overlapping chiasms in the same passage. Some chiasms are obvious, but on some there can be a considerable degree of subjectivity as to whether they really exist, or are just something an over-stretching scholar has forced on the text. So, I'm not going to go into the intricate details, but I do want to cover the basics.

The first way is to simply argue that there is a gap between the last two 'weeks'. Let's remind ourselves again of the relevant passage:

> *And after the sixty-two weeks*
> *Messiah shall be cut off, but not for Himself;*
> *And the people of the prince who is to come*
> *Shall destroy the city and the sanctuary.*
> *The end of it shall be with a flood,*
> *And till the end of the war desolations are determined.*
>
> *Then he shall confirm a covenant with many for one week;*
> *But in the middle of the week*
> *He shall bring an end to sacrifice and offering.*
> *And on the wing of abominations shall be one who makes desolate,*
> *Even until the consummation, which is determined,*
> *Is poured out on the desolate.*

Firstly notice that the Messiah shall be cut off (a Hebrew phrase usually meaning to be killed, although possibly in some circumstances also meaning ostracised or expelled) *after* the 62 weeks (which came after 7 'weeks' so we are talking about after the 69th week here). Then it refers to the destruction of the Temple and Jerusalem by the 'people of the prince who is to come', and implies some period of conflict. The above translation uses the word 'then' which isn't explicitly there in the Hebrew. However, it probably gives the correct sense. Who does the 'He' refer to? The simplest explanation is that it is referring back to the 'prince who is to come' whose people had earlier destroyed the Temple and the holy city. (This may not necessarily refer to the Romans. The Romans did command the armies that besieged Jerusalem, but those armies were largely made up of Arabs and Syrians, some of whom set fire to and destroyed the Temple, apparently in direct defiance of the Roman commanders order to preserve the Temple).

But why can't the 'prince who is to come' refer to the 'Messiah, the Prince' mentioned in earlier verses? After all, when this prophecy was written down, the Messiah was still 'to come'. They can't be one and the same because how can the prince be a Jewish Messiah and be of the people who destroy the Jewish holy place and capital city? Not once in history has a Jewish army destroyed the temple and Jerusalem, they have only fought over Jerusalem and the Temple to protect and / or restore them. I have only seen one attempt to get round this fact, and it wasn't very convincing (as I recall, it argued that although the Romans and their armies actually destroyed Jerusalem, the real cause of the destruction was some of the Jewish zealots within the besieged city, who desecrated the temple by killing people within it, and caused the destruction of the people of Jerusalem by starving them and destroying rivals food stores). There is no Jewish tradition or understanding that I am aware of that says that the Messiah would destroy the city of Jerusalem and the Temple; all the Messianic prophecies refer to rescue, restoration and exaltation of the Temple and Jerusalem.

Anyway, this sequence - death of the Messiah *after* the 69th week, a tale of destruction by the people of 'the prince to come', a period of conflict, and then mention of the final 'week' - at the very least, is entirely consistent with a gap between the last two 'weeks' of the prophecy, and arguably actually *requires* there to be such a gap.

This position is strengthened further when we consider the wider context of this prophecy. You'll notice that the phrase 'desolation' or similar crops up several times. At the start of the chapter Daniel starts to fast and pray because he has read the prophecy of Jeremiah that the desolation of Jerusalem (and indeed the desolation of all the surrounding nations) would end when Babylon and its king were defeated at the end of a 70 year period. The prophecy can be found in Jeremiah 25.1-14, and is also referred to in 29.10. Daniel in 9.1 is praying in the first year of the reign of the king who conquered Babylon. In other words, the prophesied 70 years are up, and yet Jerusalem was still desolate and abandoned. Daniel assumed that the promised desolation of Babylon for their guilt must mean the restoration of Jerusalem, but it seemed like this restoration had not been fulfilled when it should, so Daniel set himself to fast and pray to God over the issue, confessing the deep sin of Israel and asking for Jerusalem's restoration. In reply, God sends the angel Gabriel to give Daniel 'understanding' through the prophecy of '70 weeks', (and additionally, it was probably in that very year that the new rulers issued a decree allowing Jews back to their homeland, and other conquered peoples back to their homelands also).

Daniel had been desperately concerned that prophecy had not been fulfilled, Jerusalem had not been restored, and (it seems implied in his prayer) he is concerned that the sin of Israel had been so great that it was blocking the fulfilment of Jeremiah's prophecy. The vision of the 'weeks' is stated by Gabriel to cover these areas – the 70 'weeks' period is to deal with sin, transgression and wickedness, bring in everlasting righteousness, restoration of the Holiest place and to fulfil or seal vision and prophecy. In other words, here is the reason why the prophecy does not appear to be immediately fulfilled - it will be a further process - encompassing not just the 70 years, but a further 70 'weeks' of years. Jeremiah's prophecy had started in the first year of King Nebuchadnezzar, who later destroyed the temple and Jerusalem; this was the start of the 70 years. Jeremiah's prophecy had been explicit that the 70 years desolation under Babylon was because Israel had rejected the prophets call to repentance and obedience to the law, and in particular their condemnation of idolatry (see 25.7 *'you have aroused my anger with what your hands have made'*). In the prophecy of 70 weeks, one of the purposes of these 'weeks' is to accomplish the end of transgression, sin and wickedness. The evil is not yet atoned for, and the city must endure much more - and the promised Messiah or Prince must be killed as part of that process of redemption. None of this implies any need for gaps, but there is one other passage in the bible that refers to Jeremiah's prophecy of 70 years, and that is 2 Chronicles 36.21 which adds another element into the mix. After describing how the Babylonians ransacked and destroyed Jerusalem, it reads :

'The land enjoyed its sabbath rests; all the time of its desolation it rested, until the seventy years were completed in fulfilment of the word of the Lord spoken by Jeremiah'

Sabbath means 'seven'. The seventh day of the week was a Sabbath, when everyone had to rest, according to the 10 commandments and the law of Moses. However, the law of Moses also referred to another kind of 'Sabbath' or 'seven', that of a period of 7 years. On every seventh year, the people of Israel were to give the land a 'rest' by not doing any kind of agricultural work. They were to let the land go fallow, and were to only eat what the land naturally provided. (In fact, as I write, religiously observant farmers in Israel are preparing to obey this command, as the Sabbath year is about to start.) It also had social implications in the care of the poor too (and nearly all the prophets had strong words to say about Israel's mistreatment of the poor). If you want to read them, these Sabbath year laws are found in Exodus 23.10-11 and Leviticus 25.1-7. The clear implication of the 2 Chronicles passage is that part of the purpose of Jeremiah's prophesied 70 year desolation was to make up for all the Sabbath years that had not been observed during the time leading up to the Babylonian period. Now, if the land was having 70 consecutive Sabbath rests to catch up, that means that we are talking about a period of 70 times 7 years in total where the law of Sabbath years were not observed – 490 years, a period that exactly matches the 70 'weeks' or 490 years of Daniel 9. Now, nowhere in the bible explicitly tells us when this period of 490 years where the Sabbath years laws were not obeyed falls, but it is pretty much impossible for it to be an uninterrupted period of 490 years. The bible does recount long periods of disobedience to the Law on the part of the Israelites, but it also records times when righteous leaders or kings called the nation back to faithful obedience to the Law. We can reasonably assume that under the rule of these righteous leaders, the Sabbath laws were obeyed. Now, from the time that the Israelites entered the land of Canaan up until the start of the 70 year 'desolation' period under the Babylonians, there were at most something like 8 to 9 centuries (some say more like 6). In all this period there was never a 490 year continuous period in which there were no righteous reforming leaders. Thus the 490 period of non Sabbath year observances cannot have been one continuous period without gaps. Since the 490 year period before the 70 year 'desolation' had gaps, then it is highly likely that the 490 year period after the 70 year desolation may also contain a gap or gaps somewhere, to keep any semblance of symmetry, and some sort of symmetry does seem to be required by the internal logic implied here.

So far so good; this is fairly standard dispensationalist argument. They, of course, say that the gap between the 69th and 70th week is their 'church dispensation' that interrupts the 'Mosaic' or 'Israelite' dispensation, and ends with the alleged rapture of the church before the prophetic 'clock' starts ticking again with the 70th week, but that is nowhere implied in the text of Daniel; rather it is read into it by the dispensationalists. As I have already argued elsewhere, the relation of Israel and the church as described in Romans 11 strongly militates against the kind of 'chop-shop' approach of dispensationalists and suggests a rather more organic and integrated approach. What I want to do here is add one other factor which supports the idea of a gap between the 69th and 70th week. I came upon this when recently reading a book called 'The Real Kosher Jesus', by the Messianic Jew Michael Brown. In it, he discusses several early rabbinic beliefs about the Messiah that are relevant or interesting. The interesting, but not directly relevant, one is the belief that the world would last about 6000 years and that the messianic age would start about 4000 years after creation. They taught that there would be 2000 years of 'desolation' (from Adam to Abraham), 2000 years of Torah or Law (Abraham on) and then 2000 years of the Messianic age. If we accept the chronology of the Hebrew bible, creation would be about 4004 BC, and if we accept the date most scholars teach for Jesus' birth – 4 BC, Jesus was born exactly 4000 years after the creation of the world. The rabbinic teachers thought the true date of creation was about 3750 BC, but clearly even by that date, the predicted start of the Messianic age had passed by the time of the Talmud, and so they gave several different reasons as to why this was so. More relevant to our purposes is the belief of these Talmudic teachers that the Messiah could come in one of two ways, depending on whether or not Israel was ready for the Messiah. If Israel was ready for the Messiah, he would come to Jerusalem in clouds of glory, but if Israel was not ready for the Messiah, he would come to Jerusalem riding on a donkey. This sheds new light on Jesus' 'triumphal' entry into Jerusalem. The crowds might have acclaimed him, but he was coming on a donkey because, as we saw in the Luke 19 passage we referred to above, he knew that Jerusalem was not ready for him – they did not know 'on this day' what would bring them peace. Instead, Jesus predicted, it would be destroyed and its children killed, just as Daniel had predicted would happen after the Messiah was killed. The real triumphal entry is yet to come, when Israel becomes ready for her Messiah, during the final 'week' of Daniel, amidst much desolation and disruption. Yes, in the gap between these two 'weeks' that we are currently living in, what we now know as the 'church' has arisen, but it is not because there is some sudden 'church dispensation' separate from the 'Israel dispensation'. Instead, as Paul argues in Romans 11, this gap is God's great 'grace space' when he uses the disobedience and hardness of Israel to enable non-Jews, the Gentiles, to be grafted in to God's people; as the prophets foretold, Gentiles will worship the God of Israel, as Gentiles, and this is a sign of the Messianic age. Ultimately, Israel as a whole will come to recognize this, and will turn to the Messiah, resulting in, as Paul says 'life from the dead', even amidst the desecrations of the final opposing 'prince who is to come'. They will be 'grafted back in' (Romans 11.23) and now that they are ready, the Messiah will come again in great glory to Jerusalem to rule forever. As Paul goes on to say in v30-2:

'Just as you who were at one time disobedient to God have now received mercy as a result of their disobedience, so they too have now become disobedient in order that they too may now receive mercy as a result of God's mercy to you. For God has bound everyone over to disobedience so that he may have mercy on them all'

This is the purpose of the gap between weeks 69 and 70 – not for some so called 'church dispensation', but rather a space where God in his mercy and wisdom renders Jew and Gentile equally disobedient, and equally objects of mercy so that together they can be made ready for their one shared (not separate) destiny in God.

As is so often the case, dispensationalists' admirably close reading of the text gets them so close to a true understanding, and makes them seem truly 'biblical', but their adherence to the rigid dispensationalist schema means that they go just a little bit astray, but dangerously so – like being pipped at the post in a race and being denied the winners prize. The gap between the last two weeks is not the place for a distinct church dispensation, but rather a grace space which will end with church and Israel *together* being made ready for their one, shared Messiah to return. May He come soon. Amen.

USEFUL SOURCES OF ADDITIONAL INFORMATION

Just as I was finishing the book, I found a lot of excellent material broadly supporting my position on the following website sub-section, http://www.answersinrevelation.org/Rapture.html and while I might not agree with everything on the website as a whole (the author has apparently – according to some at least – more recently been involved in some dodgy 'date-setting' along with some other controversial teaching since about 2011), I very much recommend these pages, and I give brief(ish) summaries below. Perhaps most strikingly of all for the rapture debate, he notes how dispensationalism's core ideology – the splitting of God's people into two bodies (the church and Israel) with separate destinies – is almost identical to a view that the first disciples of the apostles openly called out and out heresy, and it's proponents blasphemers (see the last few articles)!

(I've also found the following three pages on a website that I often disagree with profoundly, but here the authors argue that Darby, probably the main originator of Dispensationalism, repeatedly uses theosophist words – theosophism being an occult movement, a kind of precursor of the modern New Age movement – in his teachings on dispensationalism and the bible. There is just sufficient evidence in them for me to be intrigued at the idea, but not totally convinced. I include them here for anyone who is interested :
http://libertytothecaptives.net/darby_writings_occult.html
http://libertytothecaptives.net/darby_pretrib_immediacy.html and
http://libertytothecaptives.net/darby_doctrinal_changes.html)

Anyway, back to the original website :

http://www.answersinrevelation.org/0000.pdf A brief survey of the issue, showing clearly why both pre-tribulation positions and 'pan-tribulation' apathy (it will all 'pan out' in the end) are dangerous. He also shows the necessity of understanding Jesus' and the apostles' teachings from the Jewish standpoint, from what they would have then known and understood, and then understand what was new and more detailed in Jesus' teachings. He also shows how pre-tribulationists – despite their claims to 'literalness' or proper 'grammatical-historical' exegesis – routinely have to resort to allegory and non-literal interpretations to support their position. It also shows why it is absolutely impossible that the unanimous post-tribulationist teachings of the earliest church writers could be in substantial variance to the teaching of the apostles.

http://www.answersinrevelation.org/000.pdf On Jesus' parable of the wheat and tares, and how Jesus introduced his disciples to the concept that he would have two comings; it also covers the Jewish background understanding of the Kingdom of

Heaven. Jesus used this parable both to teach a period before a second coming and to warn of false teachings and movements within his church and how God will deal with them decisively - but only at the end of the age. The parable preaches a separation and binding of these wicked ones, reserved for burning. Then angels gather the righteous into the Kingdom.

http://www.answersinrevelation.org/002.pdf On Matthew 24 and the apostles reliance on it in their teaching Christians - both Jew and Gentile - about the end times. It usefully notes the differences between Luke 21 and Matthew 24 / Mark 13, as well as the link between the Great Commission in Matthew 28 and Jesus' words about the gospel in Matthew 24, showing that Jesus meant the teaching in Matthew 24 to be about the church, not some separate group of 'saints'.

http://www.answersinrevelation.org/003.pdf A discussion of John 14.1-3 arguing that the disciples understanding would be of Jesus second coming and the Messianic kingdom. It exposes the double standard of pre-tribulationists who try and claim Matthew 24 etc is just for the Jews, not the church. He makes pretty much the same basic arguments that I do on this passage - and perhaps a little more clearly than I in some regards. He also neatly skewers a common pre-tribulation contention that Jesus refers to his ascension in Chapter 16, noting that Jesus prediction of sorrowful disciples is directly contradicted by the accounts in Luke 24 / Acts 1 of the disciples being supremely joyful after the ascension. 'Jesus is not building Christian condo's in heaven!' He also makes strong additional arguments for Temple imagery - that Jesus was saying he would prepare places for them in the future Temple, including the fact that there were apartments for priests in the Temple complex the disciples were familiar with. Jesus had just prior to this warned the current priestly inhabitants of these 'many rooms' that they were unfit for service and would be judged and thrown out.

http://www.answersinrevelation.org/004.pdf and
http://www.answersinrevelation.org/005.pdf Show how Peter's first two sermons in Acts 3 and especially 2 allude to Jesus' end time teaching in Matthew 24

http://www.answersinrevelation.org/006.pdf Shows how Peter's two letters demonstrate a post-tribulation position and preclude a pre-tribulation one, and also that the delay is God's patience with the church, to allow them to complete the Great Commission.

http://www.answersinrevelation.org/007.pdf Discusses 1 Corinthians 15, noting that for a Jew like Paul, the kingdom of God which required incorruptible flesh was not heaven, but the future Messianic rule on earth.

http://www.answersinrevelation.org/008.pdf Discusses 1 Thessalonians 4 - broadly using my arguments, but teaching that the order of the resurrection was a new teaching of Paul rather than rooted in the teaching of Jesus. However, his approach is useful in noticing that Paul was teaching details to a new church that knew the basics, but was sketchy and concerned about some particular details of the Second Coming.

http://www.answersinrevelation.org/009.pdf Discusses 1 Thessalonians 5, noting that Paul says the rapture happens during 'the day of the Lord' - i.e. the inauguration of the kingdom, a.k.a. the second coming, when the enemies of Israel would, according to Old Testament prophecies, be destroyed. These prophecies said the sun and moon would be darkened after the Tribulation, as did Jesus, who said that *after* this *post*-tribulation event, he would return. The day of the Lord as described in Isaiah 2 says that in that day only God will be exalted, and all the proud laid low, precluding a pre-tribulation interpretation in which the rapture is the start of the Day of the Lord before the boastful and blasphemous anti-Christ's rise to power. Paul simply followed Jesus teaching in Matthew 24 about the timing of the rapture, and made it crystal clear he was doing so. In a good use of a table of comparison - unlike LaHaye's - he shows how clearly the language of 1 Thessalonians 4-5 matches Jesus' teaching and language about his return. He also neatly shows how Paul's warning that escape from destruction is impossible for those who rely on 'peace and security' precludes the pre-tribulation position which teaches that many left behind can still escape final destruction by believing.

http://www.answersinrevelation.org/010.pdf Discusses 2 Thessalonians 1, noting that it is in response to Thessalonian saints undergoing severe persecution and who thought that the end of the tribulation and Jesus' return was near, and shows how Paul's language makes it clear that the church will go through the Tribulation and only find rest when Jesus *appears* with the angelic hosts.

http://www.answersinrevelation.org/011.pdf on 2 Thessalonians 2. In v1, the Greek makes it clear Paul links the coming of Jesus and the 'gathering' as one event, and isn't distinguishing between them. The gathering together is a rare word and is the word Jesus used for the post-tribulational rapture in Matthew 24. Paul is narrowing down to the main point - the timing of the rapture. In v2 Paul is refuting a belief that the tribulation is nearly over and Jesus is about to return (and in a practical note in Chapter 3 reminds them of his personal signature style so they will not again be taken in by a fraudulent letter in his name). It appears the Thessalonians had come to believe that something had happened that meant the return of Jesus was suddenly about to come upon them. In v3, Paul responds by saying that there has to be a falling away and the revealing of the anti-Christ first, and he echoes Jesus' warnings that no-one deceive them about his second coming. The anti-Christ is revealed by his usurpation at the Temple in Matthew 24. In fact, here Paul echoes Matthew 24 by referring to 5 themes - the gathering of the saints, the coming of Jesus in glory, apostasy, the 'man of sin' or anti-Christ, and a warning about deception. V4 covers the two negative signs – one general and perhaps difficult to identify – the great apostasy, and one very specific – the abomination of desolation that the anti-Christ sets up in the Temple, according to Daniel, this will happen 3.5 years before the end of the age.

http://www.answersinrevelation.org/012.pdf on Titus 2.13, including a detailed discussion of the relevant Granville-Sharp rules, and then goes on to show that 'glorious appearing' has to be the 'coming in Glory' after the tribulation spoken of by Jesus in Matthew 24 etc.

http://www.answersinrevelation.org/013.pdf On Revelation, showing how a) it assumes continuity between the seven churches it was written to and the return of Jesus and b) that Revelation describes the rapture as happening at the same time as in Armageddon, in 14.14-20, a similar perspective to Jesus' teaching in Luke 17.24-37, and to the prophecy in Joel 3.12-16 (and shows how, like Daniel, Revelation must have some level of recapitulation – portraying the same period in several different ways).

http://www.answersinrevelation.org/014.pdf On the 'first resurrection' in Revelation 20, noting first that the verb tense used and context shows these dead had already been resurrected before they were given positions of authority, and were people who had gone through the tribulation, because they were slain by the anti-Christ, and that there is no other resurrection event of any kind preceding it in Revelation. It also compares the teaching of Paul in 1 Corinthians 15 and Jesus in John 6.39-44 and v54 and 11.24 that **all** those who belong to Christ are raised 'at the last day' / 'at His coming'. In addition, the Greek in Revelation 20 shows that some of those so resurrected and reigning were those souls slain in the Tribulation – the 'souls' under the altar in Revelation 6.9-11.

http://www.answersinrevelation.org/015.pdf A discussion of how the technical terms and usages of modern pre-tribulationist evangelicals are at odds with the technical terms of the New Testament and the apostles teaching, specifically on 'tribulation'. By itself, this doesn't mean 'THE tribulation'. However, technical terms in the New Testament were such things as 'Day of the Lord / God / Jesus' were terms referring to a specific event, and these were used both of the 'rapture' and Jesus' visible second coming. He then goes on to discuss how 'rapture' is a technical term for pre-tribulation rapture today, but the Greek word used for being 'caught up' in 1 Thessalonians 4.17 was emphatically not a technical term and was used in many different contexts, despite pre-tribulationist claims it was a technical tem. Similarly the 'Revealing' or 'Revelation' of Jesus, which many pre-tribulationists think is exclusively used for Jesus visible appearing at Armageddon, is also used for the Christian's hope of being with Jesus, so can't be a technical term to distinguish Jesus' visible return from a pre-trib rapture. All three technical terms about Jesus return (coming, appearing, revealing) are used in the New Testament of both the Christian hope and a post-tribulation event. He also discusses the misuse of the word church by dispensationalists (and hence pre-tribbers) – it is not a technical term for an age or period, or for only those who are saved between Pentecost and the Tribulation, but is used in the New Testament to refer to Old Testament Jews as well, on occasion.

http://www.answersinrevelation.org/016.pdf

'Double talk : How Many Second Comings'. The author does a similar but shorter deconstruction of a very similar chart of 13 oppositional 'proofs' that the rapture and Jesus return are separate, also from one of LaHaye's close pre-trib colleagues. He notes the low-bar these teachers set themselves for satisfactory levels of 'proof' of their position, and notes – as I have, although not so much in this book – that they repeatedly have to have two of everything – two 'last trumpets', two 'first resurrections', and sometimes even two occasions when the sun and moon darken. He also notes the use of very weak 'arguments from silence' and forced or false claims of 'mutual exclusivity' in much the same way I do, and how the same type of argument could 'prove' that there were two different Jesus's based on the difference between John and the synoptic Gospels, etc. He also shows how such arguments from silence could be applied to Matthew 24 and Revelation 19 to 'prove' they refer to different events when all involved in the debate accept without question that they are talking of the same event – Jesus' visible return to earth. Similarly it could be used to 'prove' that 1 Corinthians 15 and 1 Thessalonians 4 refer to different events even though all agree they describe a 'rapture'. Going through the 13 'proofs' he shows how they are all based on an ineffective 'argument from silence' approach and usually assume what they try to prove, the very same basic arguments I use. He also comments usefully on the use of 'mystery' in Paul and the gospels, and on some claimed 'problems' in a post-tribulation position to do with the church, and turns the arguments on their head, proving that the pre-tribulation position in effect has Jesus committing 'adultery' with the church for 7 years before his return and violating all contemporary Jewish marriage customs to boot!

http://www.answersinrevelation.org/017.pdf A detailed examination of the concept of 'Immanence' which is foundational to the pre-tribulation position, immanence here being taken to mean 'absolutely no signs needed before Jesus comes again'. He shows such a view of immanence is basically a fabrication of modern pre-tribulation teachers, and not a New Testament teaching (as I also show in several of my points). Using an ingenious argument, he shows how the pre-tribulation view itself fails the 'immanence' test, since Paul's letters were all written before Peter died, and Jesus had said Peter would be old and martyred before he came again! Paul in his early letters, of which 1 Thessalonians is one – assuming he knew Jesus' comments about Peter, which is virtually certain since Paul spent time staying with the apostles and learning from them – would have known that Jesus couldn't return for some time yet, so could not have taught 'immanence'. In addition, Jesus' Great Commission scotches this concept of immanence, as indeed does his actual teaching in Matthew 24, which both speak of the gospel being preached to all the tribes and tongues, something which was no-where near complete then (and, I should add, is only nearing completion now). He then notes, as I do, that Paul in 1 Thessalonians 5 contradicts 'immanence' by saying the wicked will be taken by surprise by Jesus' return, but not the righteous. Similarly in 2 Thessalonians 2, where he notes v1 - according to the Granville-Sharp rule (see the Titus 2 article) - clearly says the rapture is part of the second coming. The rest of the passage deals with necessary signs before this rapture-second coming event. James 5 contradicts immanency, where Jesus' brother says that our attitude to Jesus' return should be that of a farmer waiting patiently for the harvest - which happens at an expected season, and after visible things happen - i.e. the crops rising out of the ground and developing, and in this specific case, the two rainy seasons that must come in the Holy Land before the harvest. Jesus and the apostles continually linked 'watching and praying' for the second coming with teaching about the signs that had to precede his coming, which totally contradicts the pre-tribulation 'immanence' doctrine. In fact, Jesus conceived (if you'll pardon the pun) his teaching on the end times around the notion of labour and of birth pains preceding his return. A mother may have to endure the travails of labour but longs and waits for what it will bring - which neatly skewers the 'Jesus wouldn't let his church suffer' lie of the pre-tribulation teachers (as is the fact that Paul's letters to Thessalonians were written precisely to a church already suffering great tribulation, unlike the comfortable ease of the Western pre-trib teachers). In Matthew 24 Jesus gave his definition of 'immanence' - the parable of the fig tree. When you saw the leaves emerging, you know summer is near. So when you see the signs Jesus listed, you knew his coming was near.

http://www.answersinrevelation.org/019.pdf covers the 'Not appointed to wrath' argument of pre-tribbers, starting with 1 Thessalonians 5.9, showing it refers to the destruction of the wicked after the Tribulation, at the second coming. When Paul further explains in 1.4-10 of his next letter, he makes it clear that the saints find rest from Tribulation only at his visible second coming. He notes that the Tribulation period actually involves the wrath of man and Satan against God's people at least as much as it involves God's wrath against the wicked, and that the bible teaches that overcomers will come through and out of the Tribulation period. He also notes that several passages refer to God's wrath in AD 70 and the destruction of the Temple and asks if there can be no divine wrath in the church age, why wasn't the church raptured then? When Luke 21.36 talks of 'escaping these things' it uses an active verb meaning to 'flee' (i.e. active choice, not a passive being snatched away in some pre-trib rapture). Just as the Jerusalem church fled Jerusalem at the signs predicted here, so must the church in the last days flee to the mountains / wilderness to escape. He also notes, as I do, that all views have some sort of saints on earth in Revelation, and Revelation clearly shows them to be followers of Jesus, in which case, every pre-trib argument about believers being unable to be on earth during 'wrath' are falsified, even in their own belief system! He also gives a number of examples where God preserves the righteous through judgement in the Old Testament, and never zaps them out of it (the Flood, the Passover in Egypt, Lot in Sodom and Gomorrah, Ezekiel 9 etc).

http://www.answersinrevelation.org/pretrib_history.pdf This covers the history and pre-history of the pre-tribulation views, showing it only ever emerged in the UK in the early to mid 19th Century, and was unknown before (with the exception of a theoretical school exercise by a later famous preacher who did not believe it himself – and even then it was 'mid-tribulation'). It seems to have stemmed originally from the visions of a Scottish girl in a weird Charismatic group, but then was taken up by someone who founded what is – ironically – a notoriously anti-Charismatic group, the Plymouth Brethren. It includes texts of many of the original documents showing the rise of the belief.

http://www.answersinrevelation.org/wedding.pdf A fuller version of the article on Jewish wedding customs and the rapture / return of Christ.

http://www.answersinrevelation.org/24elders.pdf This deals with pre-trib claims that the 24 elders represent the church and therefore the church must be in heaven during the Tribulation . It shows that a) even if the 24 elders somehow represent the church, they cannot *be* the church and b) they must be angelic beings. In addition, they aren't confined to the Tribulation but do their representing role continually. 'Elder' seems to indicate a high rank of heavenly being / angel.

http://www.answersinrevelation.org/Heaven.html This set is not directly relevant to us, but it was so good, I thought I'd include it anyway. They are against a-millenialists, who say that heaven is our ultimate destiny, not an earthly millennial kingdom, and against dispensationalists, who argue that the Holy Land on earth is for Jews, and heaven is for Christians.

http://www.answersinrevelation.org/Abraham.pdf Argues that in the case of Abraham, Isaac and Jacob, each patriarch was given a permanent promise of the land for eternity, both to them personally, **and** to their 'seed' or descendants, but the Patriarchs never received the promised inheritance – and that the only way they could inherit it eternally, personally, in any case was at the time of the resurrection. The New Testament, both in Acts 7 and Hebrews 11 takes this view of the patriarchs and the promise of the land, and in the latter passage, that the promise is only fulfilled together with the church. The 'faith of Abraham' was the permanent promise of the land, as well as descendants (and Abraham is the Father of the faith' in the New Testament). Contrary to the Dispensationalists, Galatians 3 shows that the inheritance was for Abraham's seed - specifically Christ - and all who are baptized into him (and this is referring to the land because all 'to your seed' passages in Genesis only occur with the promise of the Land).

http://www.answersinrevelation.org/Prophets.pdf He argues that Joshua's invasion of the land wasn't a fulfilment of the permanent promise of the Land, but rather a fulfilment of a temporary letting of the land by God under the Mosaic covenant, which was dependant on the nation of Israel's obedience to the Law. In dedicating the Temple, Solomon made it explicit that when he saw God fulfilling the promise of rest to his people, it was the promise through Moses. He then argues that there is a greater fulfilment to come of the permanent promise of the Land - one that is fulfilled by Jesus, as the promised son of David, to whom God had promised lands as a lasting inheritance (Psalm 2 and 16, the latter being quoted as referring to Christ by Peter in Acts 2). Psalm 37 says that the meek and righteous will inherit the land, and will do so 'when the wicked are cut off'. Jesus quoted this psalm and applied it to his disciples, the church - but in a future tense. Prophecies about a return to the land such as Isaiah 9 cannot refer to the return from Babylon, as they explicitly refer to God drawing the people back to the land a second time - and shows how Isaiah 9 clearly alludes to Psalm 2. Isaiah 61 talks also of inheriting the land for a second time. Isaiah 60 talks of all God's people being righteous and inheriting the land permanently in the future when God is the sun and moon for his people. Isaiah 65 talks of inheriting God's holy mountain at a time of new heavens and new earth / land (from where 2 Peter 3 gets the new heavens and land / earth promise), but says that this will be done by the seed (singular) that comes from Jacob and Judah - so cannot mean the nation of Israel - but by all his servants and chosen ones (that's us according to Galatians 3). Ezekiel 37 talks of a restoration to the Land, but at a time when the dead will be resurrected from their graves, and God's Spirit shall be upon them, and in 39 talks of bringing Israel back to the land and never turning away again, which can't have been the return from Babylon, because there was another exile in AD70. (It is why Joseph wanted his bones moved to the Land, so he could be resurrected there). Daniel similarly talks of an eternal kingdom and dominion, and tells Daniel in 12.13 that it will happen at the resurrection - then he will receive his inheritance. Hebrews 4 states that Joshua did not give the people the 'rest' that was promised - it is yet to come, because the promises fulfilled under Joshua were those to Moses, not the patriarchs. This is what Paul is arguing for in Galatians 3 - the promises under the Mosaic law could not annul the earlier covenant that promised the Land in perpetuity.

http://www.answersinrevelation.org/Jesus.pdf When Jesus spoke of the Kingdom of Heaven / God this was a reference to Daniel 2.44 when the God of heaven sets up a kingdom on earth, which was promised to the 'Son of Man' and his saints in Daniel 7. So when Jesus tells his disciples that those who are poor in spirit will inherit the kingdom of heaven, he was referring to God's kingdom on earth in the last age (even if that kingdom is partially inaugurated now) - and the poor in spirit here is a reference to Isaiah 66 in which the poor in Spirit rejoice with and in a restored Jerusalem, who had previously mourned for her – this was the context of Jesus' blessing about those who mourn being comforted too. Jesus said 'great is your reward in heaven' in Matthew 5.12, but this didn't mean they would go to heaven – they were aware of Isaiah 40 and 62 where God brings his reward with him – see also Jesus in Revelation 22.12 saying the same of himself. Jesus parables were nearly all about the end and the kingdom of heaven, and most of them made it clear the kingdom of heaven was earthly in scope. Matthew 24 ends up on the dispensationalists chopping block as they try and dissect Israel and the earthly kingdom and the church in heaven, and they end up negating the commands of Christ and contradicting him. Jesus says 'What I say to you, I say to all 'Watch!'' – the 'all' being those who obeyed and followed the apostles teaching. John 14.1-3 refers to the apostles being with Jesus in rooms in the Temple, and in Luke 22 at the same event Jesus teaches that they apostles will rule with him in the Kingdom of God, alluding to Psalm 2. Jesus also alludes to Psalm 2 and earthly rule when he makes promises in Revelation 2 to those who are victorious, and in 3.12 refers to the victorious being pillars in God's Temple. In Matthew 21, Jesus warned that the current priesthood would have their rule taken, but in John 14 tells his disciples they will be priests in the New Temple, after Jesus has made atonement and set up the new Priesthood, outside the law of Moses, whose shepherds had failed. In Revelation 20.5-6, all Christians will be priests and kings – and like the Old Testament temple priests will rotate in and out of the temple for service, and will rule elsewhere the rest of the time.

http://www.answersinrevelation.org/Apostles.pdf The apostles heard all of Jesus' teaching about the Kingdom of God, including Jesus' teaching for 40 days after his resurrection, and their question was not about going to heaven, but the restoration of the physical kingdom. In Acts 2, Peter preached not on heaven, but the fulfilment of Psalm 16 which talks both of inheriting the Land and resurrection. Acts 3.19-21 speaks of the fulfilment of prophecies about a time of refreshing and restoration (Isaiah 35 is one example). In Romans 8, Paul links resurrection with the restoration of creation, not an escape to heaven. Paul also generally framed his message in terms of the fulfilment of the Abrahamic promise of the Land (associated with the resurrection of the dead, so that the Patriarchs would finally receive their promised inheritance) as seen in Acts 26.6-8, and in Galatians 3 he deals in detail with how most Jews failed to inherit the permanent promise because they clung to the temporary promise under the law as a way of inheriting it, rather than the way of Christ, the 'seed' of Abraham, and faith in him. Hebrews 6 also refers to this promise as 'the hope set before us' and 'an anchor for our soul', and urges readers not to be slack in seeking to obtain the promised inheritance

http://www.answersinrevelation.org/man_of_sin.pdf Showing that the 'man of sin' in 2 Thessalonians 2 must be an individual, not a general system of false doctrine or the like. In particular 'son of perdition' is only ever used of an individual – for instance of Judas, in John 17 - so the anti-Christ will be an individual end-times Judas, a betrayer. It includes detailed grammatical considerations of why 'lawless' is best translated as 'the lawless one / man' and why the passage has to be speaking of the anti-Christ in future terms. He shows that the 'mystery of lawlessness' cannot be the same as the 'man of sin' and claims that the term must refer to the new Gnostic doctrine, and thus the anti-Christ will be the leader of a Gnostic cult. Finally 2 Thessalonians 2.8 quotes Isaiah 11, clearly connecting the coming of the kingdom of God in fullness with the slaying of the anti-Christ. Isaiah 11 talks of consuming the wicked one with the breath of his lips.

http://www.answersinrevelation.org/Gnosticism_Unveiled.pdf An article showing that Gnostic theology has crept into the theology of the church, chiefly through mistranslations / misunderstandings of the words 'spiritual' and 'heavenly'. It deals with the latter, showing it does not mean 'heaven' or 'heavenly realms' but rather 'heavenly dominion' here on earth - places where heaven and Christ's rule already is, or will be according to prophecy, and shows how passages such as Ephesians 1, 2, and 6, 1 Corinthians 15 and Hebrews 11 and 12 that use the word 'heavenly' make so much more sense when viewed that way. He also believes it transforms how we should view 'spiritual warfare' in Ephesians 6, with the primary battleground being the church or Christian family, not wider society at large.

http://www.answersinrevelation.org/hebrews_hope.pdf A detailed study of Hebrews to show that the 'sure hope' of 6.17-20 used to motivate the readers to persevere in faith was the promise of the Land in the final fulfilment at the end of the age - the promise to Abraham. He notes that Hebrews uses Rabbinic teaching methods - citing a passage but having the whole context in view, yet nearly always using the Greek Septuagint translation of the Old Testament. Hebrews 1 quotes Psalms and prophecies that were about the future Davidic kingdom, or from Deuteronomy 32 that would be taken as a prophecy of the Messianic kingdom when the enemies of God are punished, his people purged and vindicated, and finally Psalm 102, taken as referring to a transformed nature in the renewal at the end of the age and the eternal security of Israel. In Hebrews 2.5 the literal translation of 'world to come' is actually 'land' or 'inhabited land to come', but before humans - the saints - can rule with Christ as intended, they must be brought to glory through the suffering and death of Christ their captain, citing Psalm 22 at the very point that it turns from speaking of the suffering of Christ to the triumph of the King of Israel, when the Kingdom is the Lord's. Similarly he quotes Isaiah 8.16-7 when it prophecies about Jesus' first coming and the disciples he takes - who must persevere to be the ones that Christ will honour in the assembly at his kingdom rule. Hebrews 3 and 4 are an exposition of one passage from Psalm 95, a passage warning Israel about the dangers of disobeying God and not entering into the promised 'rest' - the Land of Israel. In chapter 4, the writer takes it to mean that there is another promise of future rest in the Land still to come - something described as entering into God's rest - the full promise to

Abraham, which he also called 'A Sabbath rest'. In Hebrews, Christ's priestly role is now, but his kingly role is future. Chapter 6 warns of the need to persevere in faith to enter the rest, and talks of the sure hope that God promised to Abraham - the promise of a great nation, and the land from the River of Egypt to the Euphrates, a promise never fully fulfilled and never permanently fulfilled even in part. After Abraham endured by offering his promised son Isaac as a sacrifice (Genesis 22), God confirmed the promise with an oath, because Abraham had persevered in faith and not drawn back - Abraham attained the promise, not in actuality, but with a solemn and binding oath by God. This promise was made to show the surety of the promise to Abraham's descendants, Israel. This was the hope of these Jewish Christians, who have, he argues been driven away from their homeland by persecution - the promise of return in the final age. Hebrews 7 then turns to Melchisedec (here I think the author oversteps the bounds in believing Hebrews portrays Melchisedec as Christ pre-incarnation and that John 8.54-9 refers to this incident) and shows how, using Psalm 110, it presents Jesus as the promised eternal Priest-King who will come and rule the nations - the promise to Abraham will come about through this promised Priest-King. He goes on to show that this tying in of the Abrahamic covenant promise of the Land and the Davidic covenant was not unique to Hebrews - John the Baptist's father (himself a priest) made the same point in Luke 1.67-79, especially v 69 and 71-4. Hebrews 8 deals with the promised new covenant of Jeremiah, showing how it supersedes the Mosaic covenant, and has already come (I would just suggest that it is noteworthy that it is only in regards to the Priesthood that Hebrews seems to apply the supersession of the Mosaic covenant). However, although the New Covenant has come, not all of it has been fulfilled, as not all of Israel - yet - believes and follows Jesus; there is still a future fulfilment to look forward to with hope. In Chapter 9, the writer continues this theme, focusing on the eternal (and current) priesthood of Christ in heaven (in the terms of Psalm 110, reigning as priest until God's promise to make his enemies a footstool is fulfilled) in anticipation of when he comes a second time to bring salvation fully - i.e. resurrection and reigning with Christ. Chapter 10 warns of the huge danger of falling away from and not persevering in the New Covenant (eternal damnation), but exhorts readers to indeed persevere so they could obtain the promise to Abraham (the Land inheritance) at the Resurrection. The promised 'Sabbath Rest' is only for those who persevere in the New Covenant. Hebrews 11 shows the kind of persevering faith that was needed, as exemplified in the Old Covenant saints - the famous v6 is actually a quote of / allusion to Psalm 9.10 where God never forsakes those who diligently seek him - they will be rewarded in the promised Kingdom - see the context of Psalm 9. When it talks of Abraham, Isaac and Jacob, it emphasizes that though they lived in the land it was 'as if in a foreign country' - the fulfilment to them was in the future, not a celestial hope *in* heaven, but the fulfilment *from* heaven of the full promise. This was expressed in terms of Psalm 48 - the city of the Great King that was to come. The patriarchs lived in the land that was their promised inheritance - the land of Israel. Abraham had seen the city promised - and met it's king, Melchizedek. V 13 should be translated 'strangers and pilgrims on the (promised) land' not strangers on earth passing through as pilgrims on the way to heaven. The patriarchs stayed in the land in tents because they waited for the day when it would become - as promised by heaven - their homeland. They saw it as better than the prosperous Ur from which they had come. The writer ends the chapter by saying all these never received the promise (to Abraham) but would receive it with the church in the future. Chapter 12 again urges perseverance, and not to be like Esau who forfeited his share in the promise and the inheritance for mere food and current physical advantage and need, even though he bitterly regretted and sought to get it back with tears. It goes on to contrast the awesomeness of the giving of the law to Moses and the even greater and better day when Jesus comes to rule in Jerusalem, filled with the messengers who had proclaimed the good news (see Isaiah 66.19, but often translated angels rather than the more generic 'messengers') and saints and the righteous ones made perfect, again an allusion to Psalm 48. It is heavenly Jerusalem because it is built by God, not man, but it is not in heaven. It is the city referred to in chapter 11 'whose builder and maker is God', the Jerusalem of perfect harmony with Jew and Gentile, predator and prey promised in Isaiah 65 and 66 (the author of Hebrews is alluding to this passage when he refers to the 'general assembly' - 66.10). The reference to 'the firstborn ones' refers to Israel (see Exodus 4.22). The chapter ends with another exhortation to persevere, because after a great shaking of the heavens and the earth, what is left, the promise of an earthly kingdom, will remain steadfast and sure - this after God cleans the earth with his own nature, a consuming fire, something also predicted in Isaiah 66.15-6 and 24. The writer also quotes Haggai about the great shaking, from Haggai 2 which in context talks of the day when all the nations bring tribute to the Jerusalem temple restored and surpassingly glorious, and when God overthrows kings and nations - i.e. it is the time of the promised kingdom.

http://www.answersinrevelation.org/1_2_resurrections.pdf It deals with the idea that there is only one resurrection of all the dead, and that the 'first resurrection' in Revelation 20 is allegorical and not a resurrection of the body. Jesus in John 12 spoke of the resurrection of Jesus on 'the last day' and that he was the source of Resurrection. He often talked of the present age and the age to come, and 'the last day' likely means the last day of this present age. In Luke 14 Jesus talks of a specific 'resurrection of the just' and in John 5 talks of the resurrection of life and the resurrection of condemnation, although he doesn't specify whether they happen at the same time or not. In Matthew 25 Jesus speaks of a simultaneous judgement of good and evil, but mentions no resurrection - it is just judgement of those alive at the time. Daniel 12.1-3 similarly implies separate resurrections of the righteous and the wicked, with the righteous coming to life at the end of a period of great trouble. Paul in 1 Corinthians 15.22-6 speaks of multiple resurrections - that of Christ, then of Christians and only then comes the end when Jesus rules over all his enemies, and eventually destroys death, the final enemy. The language used is that of ranks or military movements each moving at particular times, and in actual fact there is a progressive conquering of death – Jesus conquered death for himself as first fruits, then he conquered death for all those saints resurrected at his return, and finally death is destroyed at the end of the Millennium (as per Revelation 20) for all of mankind who was not resurrected at Jesus' return. A close examination of how Paul and Hebrews (this writer believes Paul to be the author of that work too) use Psalm 110 shows that Paul probably isn't quoting Psalm 110 here. Jesus reigns as prince and Saviour in heaven seated at God's right hand until God makes Christ's enemies a footstool, but here *Christ himself* puts all enemies under his feet. Acts 4.1-2, properly translated, shows a partial resurrection too – the good news the apostles preached was that in Jesus there is a '*resurrection out from among the dead*', not the resurrection of all. Acts 26.23 similarly has Paul preaching that Christ is '*first to rise from out of the dead ones*'. Paul says the same in Romans 1.3-4, and in Philippians 3.10-1 he talks of attaining to the (literally) '*out from the dead resurrection, the out from the dead ones*' – i.e. the resurrection of the righteous. He was aiming for the specific resurrection of those raised at Christ's coming.

http://www.answersinrevelation.org/Revelation_date.pdf A discussion of the date when Revelation was written, mainly aimed at 'preterist' interpretations, showing lots of evidence from both ancient Christian and ancient secular historians, that exile to Patmos was under Domitian and therefore after the fall of Jerusalem. It also destroys an alleged argument from internal evidence that Revelation had to have been written before AD 70 because of the Temple language (and I should add that I believe that the author of all the Johannine books in the bible, including Revelation, was not John who was one of the twelve, but another John who was actually a priest himself, and so would have been personally very familiar with the inner workings of the Temple anyway, long after it was destroyed). John's vision of the Temple is very similar to Ezekiel (another priest) who had a vision about restoration of the Temple 14 years after the original Temple was destroyed, and the implication is that John is here similarly predicting the future rebuilding of the Temple.

http://www.answersinrevelation.org/amill_003.pdf deals with Amillennialism and Revelation 20 specifically, since this is the only place in the bible that mentions 1000 years; is the 1000 years literal, or allegorical in some way? It covers the difference between allegory (a fictional tale meant to illustrate a point) and metaphor (a single non-literal phrase or word used in an otherwise factual context). Revelation 20 is clearly not an allegory, but key and chain are metaphors. It debunks various arguments which claim, for instance, that the devil being bound so he can deceive the nations no longer cannot be a reference to the spread of the gospel in this age. It deals with the inherent contradictions involved in claiming that the 'first resurrection' in Revelation 20 is a metaphor for salvation, and notes that the word 'the resurrection' is NEVER used as a metaphor for salvation in the New Testament. He argues that amillennialism largely stems from the ancient heresy of Gnosticism, and that if taken to its ultimate logical conclusion must result in the heresy of full preterism (the idea that Jesus' second coming was an invisible coming in judgement at the AD 70 destruction of Jerusalem, and that ever since then we have been living in the promised New Heavens and New Earth). Revelation 20.6 speaks of a future reward – blessed are those who have a share in the first resurrection... they **will** reign as priests and reign as kings for 1000 years, not *are* reigning.

http://www.answersinrevelation.org/New_Jerusalem.pdf The New Jerusalem is not heaven or some celestial city hovering above the earth, but the New Testament passages that describe the New Jerusalem (Revelation 21-2, Galatians 4) clearly cite Old Testament prophecies that talk of a restored earthly Jerusalem under divine rule (Isaiah 54, 60, 62, 65-6, Ezekiel 43, 47-8). Hebrews 13.10-6 talks of Jesus suffering outside the gate of Jerusalem, but that Jewish Christians have no permanent city here, but look for one to come. Any reference to a New Heavens and earth is a reference to Isaiah's promise about the Messianic kingdom (Isaiah 65.17-19). The writer goes on to answer four common objections or questions, firstly as to why if this is the same earth restored, there are no seas. In actual fact Revelation only says 'the sea is no longer', which is a reference to passages like Isaiah 11.15-16 and 51.10-11 that prophecy that God will eliminate the Red Sea, creating a great land bridge between Africa and the holy land to ease travel for worship in Jerusalem. Secondly, John sees no Temple in Jerusalem, while Ezekiel describes a Temple in great detail. However Greek has two words for temple, one for the whole building and a second, which John here uses, which just refers to the inner sanctum, the holy of holies, where the ark of the covenant was and entry was forbidden. Instead, God and the lamb are this inner sanctum, says John. Ezekiel 43.6-7 and Jeremiah 3.16-7 both describe a Temple with no ark of the covenant, but instead the Temple and Jerusalem will be called 'the Throne of the Lord', consistent with Revelation. Thirdly, it examines the claim that the Temple dimensions in Ezekiel are smaller than those in Revelation, and shows that this is false. Finally, in Revelation, the New Jerusalem descends from heaven, which means, it is claimed, that it cannot be earthly Jerusalem restored. However, Revelation 21.10-2 exactly parallels Ezekiel 40.2-3 - both the prophets are placed on a high mountain to see the 'New Jerusalem' and the Ezekiel passage can be read as referring to him seeing a city suspended in the air and descending. To answer why this might be so, we need to look at how Jerusalem is described in the Old Testament - it is both the city and the inhabitants, viewed together as a unit. Isaiah 54.5-8 refers to Jerusalem as a widow, forsaken woman and the wife of the Lord - divorced, but whom God would re-marry. Hence, in Revelation, Jerusalem is called 'the Lamb's wife' (21.9-10). In Galatians 4.26 Paul says the elevated Jerusalem is 'the mother of us all' and quotes the Isaiah passage to prove it. A Jerusalem from heaven could never be described as desolate or forlorn, which the passages Revelation refers back to do. But if we understand that this 'New Jerusalem' is the dwelling place of God and man together it makes sense. Jesus descends from heaven, the redeemed rise to meet him in the rapture, and together they form the 'New Jerusalem' descending to earth at Jerusalem to renew it to what it should be.

http://www.answersinrevelation.org/on_end_time.pdf and
http://www.answersinrevelation.org/on_antichrist.pdf Two articles covering the views
of multiple early church writers on the end times, all clearly indicating the belief that
the church would go through suffering and the Tribulation under the anti-Christ.

http://www.answersinrevelation.org/Martyrs.pdf This deals with several very early
church writers from the mid 2nd Century, Irenaeus and Justin Martyr, who were
absolutely explicit that the kingdom of God was the inheritance of Land promised to
Abraham – they even framed the Lord's supper in that context and emphasized that
this was an earthly and not a celestial kingdom and promise. They never split off the
church from Israel but rather saw the church as the joining of Gentiles to Israel in
the fulfilment of the promise to Abraham of the Land as inheritance and eternal
possession. In fact, one of them explicitly says that anyone calling themselves a
Christian who says that there is no bodily resurrection, but that souls go to heaven is
really in fact no Christian at all, and blasphemes against the God of Abraham, Isaac
and Jacob!

http://www.answersinrevelation.org/Jeffrey.pdf Exposes one teacher's deliberate and
systematic manipulation of those early church writers to claim they were 'pre-trib'

http://www.answersinrevelation.org/Paganism.pdf This covers how the teaching of
the church regarding the promised inheritance changed from fulfilment of the
promise of Land to an ascent to dwell in heaven. The answer is that after the first
apologists, like those mentioned above, died (usually martyred), new teachers who
were converted Greek philosophers came to intellectual leadership in the church in
the late 2nd Century. This new breed of teachers wanted to make Christianity
acceptable to the dominant philosophy of the time, which by that time saw material
matter and the body as traps for souls that needed to return to heaven from where
they originally came. To avoid the teaching about resurrection and the promise of the
land, they treated such passages as allegory, as symbolizing something else, usually the
system of the philosopher Plato, who believed in heavenly spheres (planets) which the
soul ascended through by gaining wisdom and eventually thus could reach God. The
chief culprits were Clement of Alexandria, and his pupil Origen, who placed Greek
philosophy almost on a par with the Old Testament, believing it was divinely
ordained to prepare Greeks for the gospel of Jesus as the Old Testament was meant to
prepare the Jews for the same. This view grew in dominance, and when the Empire
became Christian the question had to be settled, and the emperor Constantine openly
declared to the church council convened over this and other issues that the Platonic
view that souls go to heaven was the correct one, and many bishops rushed to obey,
perhaps to gain power and influence and to avoid being labelled 'heretic' or
'schismatic' and their property seized and worship under their leadership forbidden.
This, the author of this article believes, was the start of the Roman Catholic church.

The Protestants just adapted this way of thinking to what we now call a-millennialism, while the later dispensationalists simply agreed with the Pharisees that the land was for the Jews, regardless of whether they adhered to Christ, whilst assuming that the church continues to have the Platonic 'heavenly hope' - in other words, that the church's destiny is heaven, not earth.

http://www.answersinrevelation.org/gnostic_roots.pdf of Amillennialism and Dispensationalism. This is a more or less a more detailed version of the above article. Plato's views, and the later Gnostic heresy that caused both Paul and, especially, John as well as the later church so many problems, can be traced back to a common pagan belief about the soul's ascent to heaven, a type of belief found in Egyptian religion, and which was quite probably started at the Tower of Babel; a similar approach is also found in the pagan king (and possibly Satan by extension) who in Isaiah 14.12-15 boasts that he will ascend to heaven and be seated in the clouds. This was very different to the Jewish-Christian hope which was for a resurrection and restoration in the Land, utterly alien to the pagan Greek / Gnostic belief that the body and physical matter was evil and had to be escaped from. 1 Corinthians 15 is one of the first clashes with Greek philosophy when Paul has to defend the resurrection of Jesus. The Gnostics believed that the Christ-spirit descended on Jesus the man at his baptism and left just before the crucifixion, which is why John in his letters defined the anti-Christ spirit as denying that Christ had come in physical flesh. Later on, in the 2nd Century, Justin Martyr noted that many were beginning to cave in and deny the promise of the physical kingdom - these he called out and out heretics who blasphemed the God of Abraham, Isaac and Jacob. However, there was another group whom he regarded as truly Christian, but as being in error, a group that was influenced by Greek philosophy in a more subtle way. They believed that the New Jerusalem was a heavenly city come down to earth, not the restoration of the current physical city (which had been destroyed in AD 70 - and even more recently had been a centre of a brutal revolt that the Romans had managed to put down at great cost in AD 135). The early apologists who defended the belief in the Resurrection and earthly kingdom were priests and pastors of churches, in direct line from the apostles. However the newer theologians who were converted Greek philosophers set up Christian philosophical schools separate from the local church, and began to gain influence. This coincided with a rising hatred of all things Jewish, due to mainstream Judaism's rejection of Jesus, and the fulfilment of Jesus' prophecy against Jerusalem (and I suspect, partly because the AD 135 revolt had cost the Roman Empire so dearly - it is likely that whole legions were decimated). Jewish community religious leaders were frantically trying to stop the flow of Jews converting to Christianity and re-interpret the prophecies that were so effective in telling about Christ - to the point that Justin Martyr accused them of actually changing and corrupting the text of some Old Testament copies. Some Christians started to revile the Sabbath and Jewish festivals, and many started to distance themselves from belief in an earthly kingdom as it was very Jewish (and I would guess anathema to the Romans who aimed to crush any sign of belief in an earthly Jewish kingdom which could ferment another revolt). Clement of Alexandria, the head of the main philosophical Christian school, managed to do the opposite of what Paul commanded Timothy – he abandoned apostolic doctrine, and embraced Greek modes of knowledge or 'wisdom'. His interpretation of John 14.1-3 (many mansions meaning 'in heaven') contrary to the original context (actually Temple language promising a priestly role in the Kingdom Temple) shows how far he had strayed from the apostles' worldview. The school developed allegorical interpretations of Scripture to fit their philosophy and deny the plain sense of scripture. They believed the resurrection was spiritual, not physical, but considered themselves orthodox because they still believed in the 'resurrection'. Origen, Clement's successor developed doctrines even further away from biblical truth, believing that the dead ascended by gaining knowledge to eventually reach God (a very Gnostic-style view). He even denied that Jesus retained a physical resurrected body in heaven and created a mystical other world to which he claimed the scriptures were actually referring, rather than actual physical places on earth when it talks of Jerusalem, etc. The school put out a huge amount of disciples and literature, but many in the church despised them and their doctrine, including the bishop of Alexandria, where the school was based; he denounced Origen just before he suffered martyrdom. Origen counter-attacked by mocking his opponents' belief in 6000 years of this age, and then the final 1000 year millennium or 'Sabbath'. When the Emperor Constantine became a Christian, he wanted unity in his empire above all things, and the controversy over the nature of Christ was a major threat to that unity, so he called a council, but also used his opening address to 'settle' the issue about the nature of God's promised kingdom by openly siding with the Plato-based opinion, and ordering that any who held to the 'deluded perversions' of belief in the physical kingdom would have their houses of worship seized, and their assemblies banned until they came to the 'truth'. However, the writings of earlier more traditional authors were still popular, so the bishop Eusebius, a cheer-leader for Constantine, wrote a very revisionist history of the church that charged these faithful followers of the apostles with heresy – and often the earlier works were edited of unacceptable content. In fact, Revelation itself was accused of being written not by John, but by the heretic Cerinthus whom John opposed, and a man to whom, as a Gnostic, the idea of a physical kingdom and resurrection was anathema! In addition, the bishop and theologian Augustine rose to high influence, and he 'perfected' the new views into a form that has dominated church thinking ever since – he too, being heavily influenced by his former philosophical upbringing. It was foundational for the new Christian Roman state's justification and for Roman Catholic doctrines in which the Roman Empire was the Kingdom of God on earth and the pope would declare the Emperor God's representative ruler (the initial Protestants took over this view, except that for them, *they* were the Kingdom of God on earth and the papacy was the beast of Revelation). The very earliest of the post-apostolic fathers, Clement of Rome, whom Paul describes as his fellow worker, was a believer in the physical kingdom in the Promised Land, and used this promise as a motivation for righteous living.

Ignatius and Polycarp, disciples of John, had the same belief. Another early disciple of the apostles, Papias, wrote lengthy works which have been destroyed precisely because they held to a physical kingdom in the final age. Eusebius said he was a man of 'limited understanding' because he failed to 'realize' that Jesus and the apostles only spoke mystically and allegorically on these matters. These days, some claim that the Millennial views of the early church fathers came from the Jews, but the Jews never had a belief in a specific 1000 year kingdom or period during that time, although some of them did adopt it several hundred years **after** Christ. Modern day dispensationalism was originally developed by men who were amillennialists and believed that the beast of Revelation was the papacy through its centuries of existence. They realized that Scripture didn't really support such a view, and the prophecies of Revelation etc were yet to be fulfilled in the future, yet they didn't want to - or didn't see the need to - abandon their amillennial based belief in a heavenly hope, so they devised a scheme where God had a heavenly people (the church) and an earthly people (the Jews), the latter group being the ones who would attain the promise of an earthly Kingdom. It entailed a strict division between the two 'peoples of God', a division which, ironically enough, was the foundation of one of the earliest heresies in the church, Marcionism, which held pretty much the same thing, except it went further and held there were two Gods, a sort of inadequate or evil God of Israel who made the physical promise, and the Father of Jesus, who promised a heavenly, spiritual homeland for the church. The article finishes by saying that there are two streams in church history, one the original apostolic belief in the earthly kingdom, and the other a false teaching about a 'heavenly hope' that has given rise to both a-millennialism and dispensationalism. The former is the Virgin bride of Christ, the latter the Whore of Revelation, it concludes.

BUT... WHAT ABOUT ME?

This book has been aimed mainly at Christians. However, if you are reading this and are not a Christian, then you may be wondering about how this all affects you. This is an in-house debate among some Christians.

However, one thing that will have come across clearly is that Jesus, arguably the most seminal and influential person in human history, was clear in his teachings that he would return, and that before he returns, things will get really, really bad, and not just for Christians. The final book of the bible, Revelation, talks about not only forces persecuting Christians, but also some form of world-wide tyranny that will demand allegiance at the pain of death, and will enforce that by utter economic control - no one will be able to buy or sell without what Revelation calls 'the mark of the Beast', the infamous 666, whatever that may turn out to be (see Revelation 13 about that).

The bible also talks about deception and great signs and wonders that will cause 'all those who do not love the truth' to fall into a delusion at this time.

This same Jesus who prophesied great trouble before his return also accurately predicted the fall of Jerusalem to the Roman Armies and the destruction of the Jewish Temple, which was fulfilled about 40 years after his death. He also seems to imply that the temple would be rebuilt before his return, an event which would not go down well in today's Middle East, that's for sure.

International political ramifications aside, Jesus and the book of Revelation also make it clear that by the time of the end there will be no middle ground - you will either be for Jesus, and be a true disciple of his, or you will be at emnity with him and allied to the forces arrayed against him and his people, Israel and the church. Those who stay faithful to him and continue to do good will enter into the joy of his kingdom when he comes again. Those who fall away from the faith and do evil, who make common cause with the enemies of Jesus and all that is good, will face eternal judgement.

Thus, it is important to deal now with the issue of where you stand with Jesus. It will not be enough to have 'prayed a prayer' or been baptised or dedicated as an infant, or to go to church. The message Jesus preached was good news, but good news against a background of bad news. The bad news is that all of humanity has rebelled against the worship of God and the commands of God and thus deserve punishment for this - an offence against an infinite, good and just Creator God is an infinite offence. However, God has chosen to provide a way to escape, to be restored to true relationship and obedience to him. He did this by the way of supreme sacrifice. He sent his Son, Jesus into the world, a man who lived a perfect life and never abandoned God, even when faced with the most painful and degrading death of all, public crucifixion, and worst of all, separation for a time from God his Father, the source of all life, goodness, love and satisfaction. God vindicated him by raising him from the dead, and giving him a new, supernatural - although physical - resurrection body. The bible teaches that this is a kind of downpayment, or 'firstfruits harvest', and anyone who believes in him and follows him faithfully - even through persecution and death - will be like him when he returns - they too will gain resurrection bodies at the moment of the 'rapture' when he returns to bring judgement on all evildoers and persistent, unrepentant enemies of God. They will share in his rule and reign.

This is possible because Jesus deserved the reward of the perfectly righteous, but willingly took on the punishment due for sin, so that we who are sinners against God and yet who trust in him and are faithful to him and do the good works that he commands can gain the reward for perfect righteousness that he earned. We will be united with him in receiving that reward, because he united with sinful humanity by taking on our punishment.

This book has only touched on one small, but important area of the teaching of Jesus and his appointed apostles, but he taught a way of life that the Christian church - however imperfectly (sometimes **very** imperfectly) - has carried out and brought about much good in the world; hospitals, charities, helping the poor, and doing all kinds of good. Without his teaching this world would be very much a worse place. However, what matters most to Jesus is something that should last forever - your soul, your very being and personality. He has made a way, but you have to make the choice. Jesus gave it all up for you, and he requires all in return - fidelity to him - not perfect obedience, because no-one can do that, even after receiving God's help, but fidelity to him and allegiance to his teaching and his code of conduct, his Way, if you will, that he taught.

The entry point into this Way, that leads to salvation in the day when Jesus comes again, is to repent and believe in the work that Jesus has done on the cross for you. It is to acknowledge that you have been sinfully living apart from God and relationship with him, and with Jesus, and that this is wrong and you want to change, but cannot in your own power. It is to acknowledge that your own ways are ineffective, but the way that God has provided - the death and resurrection of Jesus to pay for your sins - is effective, and ask for it to be effective in your own life.

This is a matter of the heart first, and then of public allegiance to Jesus through baptism. There is no set formula, because God looks on the true intent of the heart, but a prayer like this is generally a good guide :

Dear God, I acknowledge that I have lived a sinful life - not just in the wrong things I have done, but in living life apart from You and Jesus whom you sent. I want to change and I cannot do it without your help. I believe that Jesus died for my sins and was raised from the dead, and is the legitimate Lord of all. I accept all he has done for me by shedding his blood and dying on the cross to take the punishment my sins deserve and to make a way for me to be restored back to You. I ask you to come, by your Holy Spirit, into my heart and start your work of transformation in me, to make me more and more like Jesus, as I should be. I thank you for all you have done and receive you into my heart. In Jesus name. Amen.

If you have prayed that prayer sincerely, then you are on the start of a journey towards full salvation. There are a number of things you will need to do - to make a habit of - to help you grow in your walk with God.

One is to pray - to relate to and talk to God. Another is to read his word, the Bible, and ask God to teach you, to change you, to help you overcome sin and addiction and shame in your life. Another is to find a good church and become part of it. God didn't call us to be lone wolves. No church is perfect, but a good church is one that will hold to the teachings of Jesus as found in the bible, that will help you in your walk with God and to obey his commands without being controlling.

You may well have issues over some of the main stumbling blocks to believing the bible in our age of unbelief. There are a number of good resources out there on the internet. I thoroughly recommend www.creation.com as a good starting place.

In any case, this is a journey of transformation of mind and heart that you have to keep choosing to walk down. Remember, this is no spiritual insurance policy you can keep filed away in a corner. Jesus said *'Only those who endure to the end will be saved'* and about his return *'The one who acknowledges me before men, I will acknowledge before my Father in heaven, but the one who denies me before men, I will deny before my Father in heaven.'*

Lightning Source UK Ltd.
Milton Keynes UK
UKOW03f0501140914

238516UK00001B/3/P